T0294122

THESE SEATS ARE
RESERVED

THESE SEATS ARE
RESERVED

Caste, Quotas and the Constitution *of* India

ABHINAV
CHANDRACHUD

PENGUIN
VIKING
An imprint of Penguin Random House

VIKING

USA | Canada | UK | Ireland | Australia
New Zealand | India | South Africa | China

Viking is part of the Penguin Random House group of companies
whose addresses can be found at global.penguinrandomhouse.com

Published by Penguin Random House India Pvt. Ltd
4th Floor, Capital Tower 1, MG Road,
Gurugram 122 002, Haryana, India

First published in Viking by Penguin Random House India 2023

ISBN 9780670094752

Typeset in Adobe Garamond Pro by Manipal Technologies Limited, Manipal
Printed at Thomson Press India Ltd, New Delhi

www.penguin.co.in

To Radha,
For reminding me that 'love is not love
which alters when it alteration finds'

Contents

Introduction

In January 2019, a few months prior to the general elections held that year, India's Parliament amended the Constitution for the 103rd time to bring about a 10 per cent quota in government jobs and higher educational institutions for 'economically weaker sections' (EWS) of Indian society.[1] Until then, usually[2] the rule was that you would be eligible to receive reservations in those positions if your caste was 'socially' (and in some cases also 'educationally') backward.[3] This was the first time in India's history that the Constitution enabled quotas in government jobs and colleges for the upper-caste poor.[4] Decades ago, in a case decided in 1985, Justice Chinnappa Reddy of the Supreme Court had once opined that giving reserved seats to poor Brahmins was 'too grotesque even to be considered'.[5] Now, seats were reserved even for those who were not Scheduled Castes (SCs), Scheduled Tribes (STs), or Other Backward Classes (OBCs). However, until this amendment, the general principle also was that reservations would not exceed 50 per cent of the total available seats, barring exceptional circumstances. The 103rd amendment raised this to 60 per cent.[6]

A young student who applies for admission to the Indian Institute of Technology (IIT) Bombay or Indian Institute of Management (IIM) Ahmedabad may therefore feel that the number of seats on offer is fewer than expected. Seats there are reserved—27 per cent for 'non-creamy layer' Other Backward Classes, 15 per cent for Scheduled Castes, 7.5 per cent for Scheduled Tribes, and 10 per cent for 'EWS' candidates.[7] In other words, a student who does not belong to any of these categories competes for around 40 per cent of the total available seats. Even that figure is somewhat misleading. The 40 per cent general seats can be taken up by anyone—even those who are eligible for reservations but get in on their own merit (students called 'meritorious reserved candidates', or MRCs). Those seats are also subject to 5 per cent reservations for persons with disabilities,[8] or 'horizontal' reservations.

All this may seem to be quite puzzling for the student who is not eligible for any reserved seats. She might ask: Why should doctors and engineers not be picked purely on the basis of merit? I have worked so hard my whole life: why are there so few seats available for me? Why am I being penalized for the wrongs that my ancestors might have committed—I have never discriminated against anyone on the basis of caste. Why am I worse off because of mine?[9] Why are seats being given to politically powerful communities under the garb of Other Backward Class reservations? Is this not vote bank politics of the worst kind?

On the other hand, a reserved category student might have some questions of her own for the general candidate: How do you define 'merit'? Do you really feel that your privileged environment (your family's ability to pay for coaching classes, their 'social capital'[10] or network of connections, your 'cultural capital'[11]—being brought up by English-educated parents in an environment conducive to learning) had nothing to do with your success in the entrance exam? Do you feel it's fair that the overwhelming majority of the population of India should settle for only 50 per cent of the available seats? For instance, 'Other Backward Classes' constitute 52 per cent of India's population—is it not unfair for them to get a quota for only 27 per cent of the positions on offer? The preamble to India's Constitution says that we are a socialist state—isn't reserving seats like redistributing wealth: taking from those who have too much and giving to those who have almost nothing?[12] If India ignores her hopeless masses, isn't there a possibility that they might take up arms to violently overthrow the government?

According to the 2011 census, there were 201.3 million Scheduled Castes (16.6 per cent of India's population) and 104.5 million Scheduled Tribes (8.6 per cent of India's population) in India[13]—more than the estimated population of the United Kingdom, France, Germany and Spain combined.[14] As Winston Churchill said in the House of Commons in 1946, 'When one speaks of a community as large as [this], the word 'minority' loses much of its significance.'[15] The 'Other Backward Classes' are considered to be even more numerous.[16] Unlike 'affirmative action' in the US, which is primarily for racial minorities, quotas in India are theoretically meant to protect the political majority from the alleged tyranny of a powerful elite minority.[17]

The question of how to identify and define Other Backward Classes has been one of the most contentious issues to come up before the Supreme Court. Even today, Other Backward Class reservations remain highly controversial.[18] Nobody really knows how many Other Backward Classes there are in the country—the Mandal Commission used estimates from the 1931 census to guess that 52 per cent of Indians were Other Backward Classes.[19] More recently, the National Sample Survey estimates that Other Backward Classes constitute around 36 to 42 per cent of India's population.[20] Unlike Scheduled Castes and Scheduled Tribes, it is very difficult to come up with precise criteria to define membership of the Other Backward Class community. Governments are often accused of conferring Other Backward Class reservations on politically powerful groups, like the Maratha community in Maharashtra.[21] Though Other Backward Classes obtained reservations in some Indian provinces even in the colonial period, the Central government introduced Other Backward Class reservations in public services and educational institutions in 1990 and 2006, respectively.[22] Unlike Scheduled

Castes and Scheduled Tribes, Other Backward Classes cannot get reservations in promotions. In 2020, none of the 80 seats that were on offer at the National Law School in Bangalore were reserved for Other Backward Classes.[23]

Reservations continue to be deeply relevant for every new generation that seeks admission into colleges or enters the workforce. In 2020 alone, the Uttarakhand government scrapped reservations in promotions,[24] while the Karnataka High Court struck down the government's decision to introduce 25 per cent reservations for local students (in addition to the pre-existing reservations for Scheduled Castes and Scheduled Tribes) at the National Law School in Bangalore.[25] Scheduled Castes are communities that were traditionally considered to be 'untouchable' in India. Though formally repudiated by the Constitution, untouchability continues to be practised in insidious forms.[26] In urban India, empirical evidence suggests that companies discriminate between potential employees on the basis of caste and religion. In response to newspaper advertisements, job applicants who had Hindu upper-caste names were more likely to get called for interviews than those with backward caste or Muslim names.[27] Employers are not merely interested in the 'merit' of interviewees—they often ask about the 'family background' of job applicants in employment interviews.[28] A study found that landlords in Delhi were more willing to give their homes on rent to tenants with upper-caste Hindu names, rather than those who had Dalit or Muslim names.[29] Scheduled Tribes generally are much worse off than Scheduled Castes. They are not as literate and have lesser access to doctors.[30] They have never had a leader of the stature of Ambedkar, nor has any Scheduled Tribe person held the position of Vice President or Chief Justice of India or a major cabinet portfolio.[31] Yet, one of the best books written on the law and history of caste-based reservations in India is now decades old.[32]

* * *

By examining the history and evolution of some of the equality provisions of India's Constitution, this book seeks to shed light on the emotionally charged, decades-old[33] debate concerning caste-based reservations in India.[34] Its objective is to introduce the reader to the law and history of quotas in the country. The book traces how groups eligible for reservations were identified and defined: how the terms 'depressed classes' and 'backward classes' were used in British India and how they evolved into the constitutional concepts of 'Scheduled Castes', 'Scheduled Tribes', and 'Other Backward Classes'. It looks at how the Supreme Court invented tests to impose limits on quotas in the country—the rule that no more than 50 per cent of the available seats or positions can be reserved, the principle that the 'creamy layer' must not receive the benefit of quotas, and the requirement that governments must have 'quantifiable data' before providing certain kinds of reservations.

This book examines the intellectual debates that have taken place on these questions over the course of India's history in the Constituent Assembly, the Supreme Court, and Parliament. For instance: Are reservations an exception to the principle of equality of opportunity? Do quotas in government service, especially in promotions, undermine efficiency? Can 'merit' really be defined neutrally, and do marks in board exams or entrance exams really demonstrate a student's intelligence? Like reservations in Parliament and state legislatures, should seats in colleges and government jobs be reserved in proportion to the population of backward classes? Can caste be made the primary criterion for reservations? What happens when a person from a backward caste migrates to another state, converts to another religion or marries a person of another caste— does she become ineligible for a reserved seat? Is there a fundamental right to reservation—can an Indian citizen compel a government to reserve seats even if it doesn't want to do so?

This book also seeks to demystify and unclutter complex concepts like vertical and horizontal (or 'interlocking') reservations, the carry-forward rule, the catch-up rule, consequential seniority, the

'L'-shaped 13-point roster and the 200-point roster in government employment. Readers who go through this book should be able to tell the difference between seemingly confusing terms like 'Backward Class', 'Other Backward Class', 'Socially and Educationally Backward Class' (SEBC), 'Most Backward Class' (MBC), 'Depressed Class', 'Scheduled Caste', 'Scheduled Tribe', 'Meritorious Reserved Candidate' (MRC) and 'Economically Weaker Sections' (EWS).

* * *

Chapter 1 traces the evolution of the term 'depressed classes'. A label popularized by Christian priests and missionaries, 'depressed classes' was initially a phrase used in ordinary English to generally describe people who were desperately poor and downtrodden. However, after 1918, the term started being used in India only for the members of those Hindu castes who suffered from the stigma of untouchability. The word 'class' was really a euphemism for caste. This chapter also investigates Ambedkar's thought processes towards reservations in the colonial era, before he donned the mantle of chairman of the committee to draft India's Constitution. In the Simon Commission, Ambedkar mounted an impressive attack on the now-familiar argument that reservations in government jobs would harm the 'efficiency' of the services. In the round table conferences in London, he tried to ask for universal adult franchise, so that all depressed class voters would get the right to vote. In the Poona Pact, Ambedkar failed to secure separate electorates and proportional representation for the depressed classes in legislative bodies.

Chapter 2 looks at how the phrase 'backward classes' (used in Article 16(4) of the Constitution of independent India) evolved against the backdrop of non-Brahmin movements that were taking place in early 20th-century peninsular India. The term 'backward classes' was used in 19th-century England to describe middling people. The Starte Committee in Bombay (of which Ambedkar was a member) decided to use the term 'backward classes' to describe three specific groups: depressed classes, backward tribes, and 'other backward classes'—which is broadly how the term 'backward classes' is now understood under the Constitution. Once again, the word 'class' in 'backward class' and 'other backward class' was really a euphemism for caste. The Bombay government's definition of OBCs (i.e., that Other Backward Classes must suffer a level of backwardness that is comparable to the depressed classes and backward tribes) would also go on to hold the field for many years in independent India. In this chapter, we will see how Lokmanya Tilak's newspaper invoked 'merit' in an argument with the King of Kolhapur about reservations, how the Miller Committee in the princely state of Mysore evoked the idea of 'adequate' (not proportional) representation for the backward classes (Article 16(4) of our Constitution speaks of 'adequate' representation), and how the depressed classes came to be called 'Scheduled Castes'.

Chapter 3 sets out some of the striking features of the provisions of the Constitution concerning reservations and examines key debates that took place on quotas in the Constituent Assembly and its sub-committees. The Constitution only provided for reservations in the lower house of legislative bodies and government jobs—not in the judiciary, cabinets, or the Rajya Sabha, the upper house of Parliament. In a crucial speech made in the Constituent Assembly, Ambedkar said that reservations in government jobs constituted an exception to the principle of equality of opportunity and that quotas there should be confined only to a 'minority of seats'. These words formed the basis of the 50 per cent rule, which was later developed by the Supreme Court. The Constitution adopted the formula of 'proportional representation' for reservations in legislative bodies but 'adequate representation' for quotas in government jobs. Courts were not given the power to reject reservations on the grounds that the communities for whom seats were being reserved were sufficiently represented in the services. Article 16(4) of the Constitution used the words 'backward classes' instead of Scheduled Castes and Scheduled

Tribes, thereby opening up reservations in government jobs for Other Backward Classes as well, but without specifying who exactly the Other Backward Classes were. Since Ambedkar had become a part of the government, in the Constituent Assembly, it was H.J. Khandekar who made the most impressive arguments against those who opposed reservations on the grounds of merit and efficiency.

Chapter 4 sheds light on how India grappled with some issues concerning reservations in the early years of the republic. We will see that the Supreme Court's decisions in 1951 barring caste-based quotas in educational institutions gave rise to the first constitutional amendment. The Kaka Kalelkar Committee attempted to define who the Other Backward Classes were, but its recommendations were incredibly vague and imprecise. Even superstitious people were deemed by it to be backward, which would perhaps have included President Rajendra Prasad, who once asked Nehru to pick a more astrologically auspicious date for India's first Republic Day. We will see that though Prime Minister Nehru was genuinely interested in improving the condition of the backward classes, he was against reservations, believing that quotas harmed efficiency and merit. We will also see how the government adopted a strange norm on religious conversions: Scheduled Castes who converted out of Hinduism lost their caste, but Scheduled Tribes who converted to Hinduism (or to any other religion) retained their tribal status. The goal appeared to be to keep Hindu Scheduled Castes within the fold and to encourage Scheduled Tribes to convert to Hinduism.

Against the backdrop of the Mandal Commission and the Indra Sawhney case, Chapter 5 discusses how the 50 per cent rule and the creamy layer concept emerged in India. Over the years, there were three views on whether there should be a cap on quotas: Ambedkar took the conservative position and said that only a minority of seats could be reserved; Justice Gajendragadkar took a centrist view and wrote that reservations could not exceed 50 per cent; Justice Chinnappa Reddy adopted a liberal stance and held that reservations could go much beyond 50 per cent. In the Indra Sawhney judgement,

the Supreme Court balanced these different viewpoints by holding
that quotas could exceed 50 per cent of the available seats, but only
in very rare and exceptional cases. At a time when Other Backward
Classes were becoming politically powerful, the court accepted the
Mandal Commission's heavy reliance on caste to identify Other
Backward Classes, but with one caveat—that the 'creamy layer' of
affluent and well-off families must not get the benefit of quotas.

In Chapter 6, we will see how Parliament enacted a series of
constitutional amendments after the Indra Sawhney case to essentially
overrule the Supreme Court on several issues concerning quotas.
Amendments were passed to breach the 50 per cent rule, to enable
Scheduled Caste/Scheduled Tribe (but not Other Backward Class)
reservation in promotions, and to extend reservations beyond their
traditional domain, into private colleges (provided they were not
minority institutions) and for economically weaker communities.
The Supreme Court usually responded by accepting the amendment
but reiterating its rules of the game: the 50 per cent cap on quotas, the
creamy layer principle, and a new 'quantifiable data' requirement. We
will examine debates that took place in the Supreme Court between
judges like Justice Sujata Manohar and Justice B. Sudershan Reddy
on the meaning of merit and whether reservations harm efficiency.
We will also see how the Supreme Court said that reservation is not a
fundamental right, despite also having held that it is part and parcel
of the principle of equality of opportunity—a contradiction in terms.

In order to get a reserved seat in India, you first have to establish
that you belong to a Scheduled Caste, Scheduled Tribe, or Other
Backward Class community. Chapter 7 looks at what happens to a
person's caste or tribe status when she marries a man of another caste,
converts to another religion, reconverts to Hinduism, or migrates
to another state. A complicated jurisprudence has been developed
by the Supreme Court in such cases, with outcomes that are not
always intuitive. For instance, a Scheduled Caste person from Tamil
Nadu can apply for a reserved job with the Central government in
Bihar but not with the state government there—migration results

in loss of caste status for the state government but not the Central government. A Scheduled Tribe person who converts to Christianity must show that she still follows the customs and traditions of her tribe, even though a Scheduled Tribe person who has not converted remains a Scheduled Tribe member despite having abandoned her tribe altogether. For a long time, the law presumed that all Scheduled Castes were as backward as one another, which was not true—there was nothing to prevent a relatively better off Scheduled Caste community from capturing most of the reserved seats.

1

The Depressed Classes

This chapter examines the origin and evolution of the term 'depressed classes' in British India. A nomenclature often used by Christian missionaries, 'depressed classes' was how the poor and downtrodden sections of society were loosely referred to in the beginning. A wide array of untouchable castes, aboriginal tribes, and other backward communities were all lumped together under that label. However, by 1918, the term 'depressed classes' began to be used for only low-caste Hindus who suffered from the stigma of untouchability. The word 'class' in 'depressed class' was really a synonym for caste. As we will see in the next chapter, it was the 'depressed classes' who were eventually called 'Scheduled Classes' and then 'Scheduled Castes' under the Government of India Act, 1935. This chapter then examines Ambedkar's trenchant criticisms of the 'efficiency' argument—the argument that reservations in government jobs would harm the efficiency of government departments. It also looks at Ambedkar's frustrations with the Poona Pact—an agreement that formed an important backdrop to the reservation provisions of the Indian Constitution.

A Loosely Used Label

The British initially referred to a whole host of backward communities in India, castes or tribes that were poor, illiterate or untouchable, as the 'depressed classes'. This was not a term unique or peculiar to India and was used in ordinary English to describe the poorest and most downtrodden section of any society. For instance, in 1837, an American author wrote that in certain parts of Germany, there was a 'degree of intellectual culture' among 'the most depressed classes', which was 'not generally supposed to consist with their lot'.[1] In 1849, an American politician wrote of the 'depressed classes in Great Britain and Ireland.'[2] A book published in New York in 1866 described how the mortality rates at hospitals in Paris that treated 'the poorer and most depressed classes' were high.[3]

The label 'depressed classes' was often used by Christian priests and missionaries. For example, in 1868, an Irish preacher wrote about how Christianity 'establishes a link between the different orders of men, the richer and the poorer' or the 'favored classes' and the 'weaker and depressed classes'.[4] In 1894, an American priest explained that 'the depressed classes' were much more amenable to being converted to Christianity than 'the higher classes'.[5]

Predictably, Christian priests or their relatives in India frequently used the term 'depressed classes'. In 1885, a British official in the education department of the Bombay government, William Lee-Warner, whose father was a member of the clergy in England,[6] referred to the 'depressed classes' in Bombay in a letter to the Chief Secretary.[7] In 1894, an American missionary explained that over the years, though 'converts had been coming to us from various castes, and from both Hindu and Mohammedan camps . . . the vast majority . . . had come from the lower castes, now widely known as "the depressed classes".'[8] The following year an American missionary wrote about 'the great depressed classes' of India, the 'forty millions that will lie down in India tonight hungry upon a mud floor', people 'depressed and degraded because of their false religious systems'.[9]

By 1909, leaders like Gopal Krishna Gokhale[10] and Annie Besant[11] referred to low caste or marginalized communities in India as the 'depressed classes'. Besant compared the 'depressed classes' in India to the 'submerged tenth' in England, i.e., unskilled labourers, scavengers, sweepers, casual dock labourers, etc., constituting 10 per cent of the population of that country.[12]

There was no precise definition of who the 'depressed classes' were. In 1914, a report on the progress of education in India prepared by the colonial government referred to the 'depressed classes' as not merely the 'untouchable castes'[13] but also 'criminal tribes'.[14] In 1916, the Secretary to the Government of India noted that the term 'depressed classes' was being used to denote 'criminal and wandering tribes', 'aboriginal tribes', and 'untouchables'.[15] The following year, Sir Henry Sharp, Educational Commissioner with the Government of India, prepared a list of depressed classes, which were not merely those that suffered from untouchability but also those communities which were 'backward and educationally poor', including some classes of Muslims.[16]

Gandhi probably used the term 'depressed classes' for the first time in 1917.[17] He later coined the word 'Harijan' in the 1930s, using it instead of 'depressed classes'. He renamed Sabarmati Ashram and called it 'Harijan Ashram'.[18] In 1933, he even changed the name of his newspaper 'Young India' to 'Harijan'. However, 'Harijan' was considered to be a pejorative term by the depressed classes and did not catch on,[19] though it was used by leaders like Nehru several years after Independence. In 1931, Census Commissioner J.H. Hutton tried to replace 'depressed classes', which he considered an 'unfortunate and depressing label', with 'exterior castes',[20] though this did not stick either.

In short, the term 'depressed classes' was used in ordinary English to describe the poor and downtrodden sections of any society. It was originally applied by Christian missionaries or their relatives in India and became more widely used, as a label for backward communities, but not necessarily only those who suffered from the stigma of untouchability.

The Congress Switches Gears

Over the years, the meaning of the term 'depressed classes' in India started changing. Originally used for any desperately poor, illiterate or untouchable communities,[21] it soon started being applied exclusively to castes that were considered untouchable. This phenomenon occurred just as the 'depressed classes' started being given political representation in the legislative councils in India. So though the census reports of 1901 and 1911 in India referred to backward communities generally as 'depressed castes' or 'depressed classes',[22] in 1918, Charles Roberts, an MP, made a speech in the House of Commons in which he referred to the estimated 60 million 'depressed classes' in India as 'untouchables' and 'unapproachables'.[23] This was perhaps one of the first instances when untouchability was considered a prerequisite for membership of the depressed classes.

That year, the Montagu–Chelmsford constitutional reforms in India, named after Secretary of State for India Edwin Montagu and Viceroy Chelmsford, announced, for the first time, that the 'depressed classes' in India would be given representation in the legislative councils through nomination. In other words, the colonial government's plan was that since depressed class candidates would be unable to get themselves elected to office, governors would nominate some representatives of the depressed classes to the legislative councils in the provinces to ensure that the voices of the community were heard. 'We intend to make the best arrangements that we can for their representation', said the government, 'in order that they too may ultimately learn the lesson of self-protection'.[24]

Before the Montagu–Chelmsford reforms came on the horizon, the Indian National Congress had not taken a formal position on improving the condition of the depressed classes in India. Untouchability was considered by the Congress to be a social, not a political problem, and was addressed in social forums rather than in the political platform of the Congress. However, just as it became clear that the depressed classes would gain political representation in

India, the Congress passed a resolution in its Calcutta session in 1917 calling for the removal of all the 'vexatious and oppressive' customary disabilities suffered by the 'depressed classes' in India.[25]

Dr B.R. Ambedkar later pointed out that this was obviously done by the Congress to garner support from the depressed class community, which was soon going to become politically important. He wrote that Annie Besant was the president of the Congress the year that this resolution was passed, and Besant had dubious views on the depressed class community. For instance, in 1909, Besant had argued against allowing the children of the depressed classes to sit in the same schools as those of the higher castes. The bodies of children of the depressed classes, she wrote, 'are ill-odorous and foul with . . . liquor and strong-smelling food'. 'A man in England who proposed that ragged school-children should be admitted to Eton and Harrow would not be argued with, but laughed at', she had added.[26]

Since the depressed classes in India were going to be given political representation for the first time, it became necessary for the colonial government to identify and define who exactly they were and how many such communities were in existence. With this in mind, various statutory committees soon took the view that the depressed classes were only those communities that suffered from untouchability.[27] Thereafter, in 1921, the census (which was conducted every ten years) said that it had become 'usual in recent years to speak of a certain section of the community as the "depressed classes"', though 'the term has no final definition nor is it certain exactly whom it covers.'[28] Estimating that there were some 55–60 million of them in India, the census report identified only 'impure' or untouchable communities as depressed classes.[29]

After the Montagu–Chelmsford constitutional reforms were brought about, representatives of the depressed classes were nominated by the colonial government to the various legislatures in India.[30] However, even thereafter, the precise meaning of the term 'depressed classes' was unclear. In 1925, for instance, the Under-Secretary of State for India, Earl Winterton, said in the House of

Commons that the label 'depressed classes' was still 'susceptible of varying definition'.[31]

Hutton's Census

It was only in 1931, when the next census was conducted, that it became a clear official principle that the 'depressed classes' were only those communities in India, within the Hindu fold, who suffered from the stigma of untouchability. In the instructions that he gave to his team for collecting data, Census Commissioner J.H. Hutton explained that the 'depressed castes' were those castes 'contact with whom entails purification on the part of high caste Hindus'. These were communities, he added, which suffered social disabilities such as being 'denied access to temples', having to use 'separate wells', and not being 'allowed to sit inside a school house'.[32] Access to these three things—temples, wells, and schools[33]—was almost definitive in determining whether a community was a depressed class or not.[34]

For instance, in 1900, B.R. Ambedkar, later the chairman of the drafting committee of the Indian Constitution, attended an English school in Satara where he had to sit separately from the other students, because he belonged to the Mahar caste, considered untouchable in Bombay province.[35] As an undergraduate student at Elphinstone College in Bombay, he was barred from studying Sanskrit on account of his caste and had to learn Persian instead.[36]

The social disabilities faced by the depressed classes varied throughout India but were more severe in the south. For example, in December 1930, the Kallar community in Ramnad (now Ramanathapuram, located about 540 kilometres south of Chennai, in the state of Tamil Nadu) had imposed some very severe restrictions on members of the depressed classes. Men were prohibited from wearing coats, shirts, sandals, or clothes below the knees and above the hips. Women were barred from covering the upper portion of their bodies, wearing gold or silver ornaments, or even using flowers or saffron paste.[37] In Assam, on the other hand, the number of depressed classes was so high that the disabilities suffered by them were comparatively fewer.[38] While a list of such depressed classes could be prepared for an area, it could not be prepared for 'India as a whole'. In Hutton's words, 'It certainly is not the case that a caste which is depressed in one part of India is depressed everywhere.'[39]

If members of a caste were prohibited from giving water to high-caste Hindus, being served by 'clean Brahmans', or being attended to by the barbers, water-carriers, tailors, etc., who served high-caste Hindus, then this was indicative of untouchability.[40] Those who were considered to have 'polluted' a high-caste Hindu 'by contact or by proximity' were also thought of as part of the depressed classes.[41] However, prejudices were sometimes just as strongly harboured between different sections of the depressed classes. For instance, the Mahars in Bombay refused to share lawyers with the Chamars, and both the Mahars and Chamars 'unanimously spurned the Bhangi caste'.[42]

The census report recorded that while several movements had recently taken place to rid the depressed classes of these disabilities, many such attempts to achieve social equality had been unsuccessful. For instance, in November 1931, when Baroda State unified schools for the high and low castes, some high-caste Hindus withdrew their children from the schools, while others destroyed the crops of the depressed classes or poured kerosene oil into their wells.[43] Roughly around that time, Gandhi advised members of the depressed classes not to use satyagraha to gain entry into temples, which were forbidden to them, arguing that 'God resided in their breasts'.[44] A movement by the depressed classes to gain access to the Kala Ram temple at Nasik in March 1930 met with violence.[45] In some cases, high-caste Hindus shunned temples that had opened to the depressed classes.[46] However, though they were barred from entering Hindu temples, the depressed classes were still considered Hindus.[47] This was because they sometimes worshipped the same deities and were often allowed up to a certain point at temples to offer their prayers.[48]

Similarly, in 1935, when the depressed classes of Kavitha village near Ahmedabad asked that their children be allowed to attend the village school, high-caste Hindus took 'an oath before the image of God that they would enforce [a] strict boycott of the Harijans'.[49] Sardar Patel resolved the dispute by leaving this question 'to the good sense of both the communities'.[50] Often, the law was stacked against the depressed classes. For instance, in 1946, a depressed class man in Madras was sentenced to six months' rigorous imprisonment for 'cremat[ing] the dead body of his son in a public municipal crematorium'.[51]

Several incidents of violence against depressed classes were reported even in 1947.[52] For instance, in Punjab, high-caste Hindus 'severely thrashed' chamars who refused to sell them shoes for 3 rupees.[53] That year, some buses and hotels in Vadodara refused entry to depressed classes. Patel felt that the government ought to cancel their licenses. 'We should be impatient to eradicate untouchability', he said to students in a speech there.[54]

The term 'depressed classes' was not synonymous with backwardness. Census officials in 1931 were instructed that if a caste was 'merely depressed on account of its own ignorance, illiteracy or poverty', and but for these would not suffer any social disability, then it was not to be counted as a 'depressed class'.[55] Untouchability was often associated with occupations considered to be unhygienic or taboo, for example, grave-digging or handling dead cattle.[56] However, even those who left such occupations but were still considered untouchable and 'outside the pale of decent society' were regarded as part of the 'depressed classes'.[57]

At the same time, in addition to untouchability, backwardness was essential for being a part of the depressed classes. Some untouchable castes that had 'strong caste organizations', like the Iruvans from Cochin[58] and the Shahas, Telis and Mahishyas of Bengal and Assam, were considered not to be a part of the 'depressed classes'. This was because many of them had been educated and had 'built up for themselves a strong position which obviates the need of any special measures for their social, political or religious protection'.[59]

Muslims and Christians were to be excluded from the depressed classes,[60] even though the conversion by an untouchable person to Islam or Christianity did not immediately wipe out the stigma of untouchability. For instance, often, south Indian Christians provided different seating arrangements in their churches, based on the castes of converts.[61] It took three generations for Christian converts from untouchable castes in the south to be seen as the equals of converts from other castes.[62] Mazhbi Sikhs, converted to Sikhism from a lower caste in Hinduism, were looked down upon by non-Mazhbi Sikhs.[63] However, the 1931 census did not include these communities in the 'depressed classes'.

The census report set out a list of depressed classes in each province after applying these criteria, and this report found that there were about 50.1 million depressed classes in India, amounting to 21 per cent of the Hindu population, and 14 per cent of the total Indian population.[64] Only 1.9 per cent of them were literate.[65] Their numbers went down in the 1941 census to 48.8 million (or 12.6 per cent of the population),[66] probably because of political efforts to have their numbers reduced.[67] The population figures in the 1941 census were often looked upon with suspicion thereafter.

Adopting the rule that only untouchable communities could be part of the depressed classes, the Simon Commission in 1930 reported that 'the great body of the untouchables, as yet, accept their destiny as natural and inevitable.' 'Their state is indeed pitiable', it added, 'inside the Hindu fold and yet not of it—living on the edge of starvation, and unaware of any hope of improving their lot.'[68] Likewise, in a report published in 1932, the Indian Franchise Committee took the view that the term 'depressed classes' would only apply to untouchables. It would not include 'primitive or aboriginal tribes' nor 'those Hindus who are only economically poor and in other ways backward but are not regarded as untouchables.'[69] This definition, making untouchability a necessary condition for membership of the depressed classes, was accepted by Ambedkar around 1932.[70] Speaking in the House of Lords in 1935, Viscount

Fitzalan of Derwent reminded his listeners that the term 'depressed classes' was 'only a more refined way of calling them "Untouchables", for that is what they are.'[71]

Ambedkar and the 'Efficiency' Argument

We have seen that after the Montagu–Chelmsford constitutional reforms in 1919, some representatives of the depressed classes were nominated to the legislative councils.[72] However, unlike Muslims, the depressed classes did not have 'separate electorates'.[73] Since 1909, Muslims in India had been given separate electorates—their representatives were voted to office by an electorate consisting exclusively of Muslims. In the system of separate electorates, voters were segregated on the basis of their religion. Only Muslim voters could vote for Muslim candidates. This regime was almost single-handedly responsible for the polarization of the country and the creation of Pakistan. Since Muslim politicians did not have to worry about what Hindu voters thought of their policies, they could demand the partition of the country without political consequence. In the 1930s, the colonial government seriously contemplated extending separate electorates to the depressed classes as well. Gandhi and the Congress were opposed to this because it would divide the Hindu community and splinter the country even further.

In 1927, a commission was set up by the British government to consider constitutional reforms in India. Under the joint chairmanship of liberal lawyer Sir John Simon and a future Prime Minister, Clement Attlee, the 'Simon Commission', as it came to be called, was boycotted by Indian leaders because it had no Indian members.[74] However, Ambedkar participated in the deliberations of the Simon Commission.[75] He submitted a report to the Bombay Legislative Council in which he argued that government jobs ought to be reserved for backward class communities. In his report, he wrote that it was 'notorious that the public services of the country' were 'a close preserve for the Brahmins and allied castes.'[76] Those who opposed reservations in public services contended that they would harm efficiency. Ambedkar provided several reasons why efficiency would not suffer if seats in government jobs were reserved.

Firstly, Ambedkar suggested that 'educational merit' could not be the 'only test' to guarantee efficiency. He wrote that though the upper-caste argument—that competitive exams alone ensured efficiency—had 'no doubt the appearance of fairness', it presupposed certain conditions which did not exist in India. If educational facilities in the country were freely and equally accessible to all communities, then reservations would not be required. However, since this was not so in India, telling the backward classes that they could only get government jobs through competitive exams was like '[practising] a delusion upon them'.[77]

Secondly, Ambedkar wrote that the 'welfare of large classes of people' could not be left in the hands of administrators drawn from a community that was 'opposed to the rest of the population in its motives and interests'.[78] In his characteristically sharp style, Ambedkar wrote that government officers from particular castes could 'easily prostitute their offices to the aggrandizement of their community and to the detriment of the general public.'[79]

Thirdly, he argued that an efficient government was not necessarily a good government. Ambedkar wrote that the disadvantages that were being faced by the backward classes far outweighed the efficiency of government departments in previous years. In other words, it was better to have an inefficient but just government, rather than an efficient unjust one. He therefore suggested that a certain number of vacancies in government positions be reserved[80] for depressed classes, Muslims, and non-Brahmins,[81] ensuring a 'proper admixture of the different communities in the public service.'[82]

The Poona Pact

Since the Simon Commission was criticized for not including Indians in the decision-making process, the colonial administration

organized a series of round table conferences in London between
1930 and 1932.[83] This was done in order to involve Indians in the
process of determining India's constitutional future.[84]

The first such conference (1930–31) was boycotted by the
Congress. However, Ambedkar attended it and essentially made two
demands. Firstly, he asked for separate electorates for the depressed
classes. He believed that since the depressed classes represented
only around 14 per cent of the population, they would be unable
to get their true representatives elected into the legislative councils.
There were too few depressed class voters who were eligible to vote.
Depressed class candidates who stood for elections needed the support
of high-caste Hindus to get elected. For this reason, through separate
electorates, Ambedkar wanted to see to it that only depressed class
voters would be able to vote for depressed class electoral candidates,
thereby ensuring that their elected politicians would not have to
pander to the sentiments of high-caste Hindus.

In his memorandum to the minorities committee at the
conference,[85] Ambedkar proposed that separate electorates could
be abolished after ten years, but only if this was 'accompanied by
adult suffrage'.[86] In other words, Ambedkar was open to having
the proposed system of separate electorates for the depressed classes
abolished after ten years, upon which all depressed class candidates
would be elected by a general electorate consisting of voters from all
religions and communities. However, this should only be done, he
said, if all adults had the right to vote in the elections. At the time,
mainly those who owned property had the right to vote,[87] which
disenfranchised many depressed class voters.

Secondly, Ambedkar also asked that depressed class candidates
be appointed to jobs in the colonial government. He complained
that 'high caste officers' had 'monopolized the Public Services'
and hoped that the colonial government would 'secure due and
adequate representation of all communities' in public jobs, subject to
maintaining the efficiency of the services.[88] In his memorandum, he
also asked for depressed class representation in the cabinet.[89] There

was no reservation for backward communities in the Indian Civil Service at that time.[90]

Interestingly, in his memorandum to the committee, Ambedkar used the word 'adequate' instead of 'proportional' in describing the extent of reservation which he wanted for the depressed classes. In other words, he did not say that the depressed classes should get seats in legislatures and government jobs in proportion to their numbers in the population. Instead, he asked only for 'adequate' representation for the depressed classes. This one word—'adequate' instead of 'proportional'—would play an important role in the evolution of the 50 per cent rule that the Supreme Court of independent India would develop in the years to come.

In 1931, Gandhi attended the second round table conference in London as the Congress representative. It was there that he realized, for the first time, that Ambedkar represented the backward classes. As he recalled later on, until then, he 'thought [Ambedkar] was some Brahman who took [a] deep interest in Harijans and therefore talked intemperately.'[91]

At the second round table conference, the various delegates were unable to arrive at an agreement on whether separate electorates would be granted to the depressed classes. In order to break the deadlock, many delegates, including Gandhi, then signed a document asking Britain's Prime Minister, Ramsay Macdonald, to decide this dispute as an arbitrator.[92] In other words, Macdonald was given the power to determine whether the depressed classes would be given separate electorates or not. Accordingly, on 17 August 1932, Macdonald announced his 'communal award' (the decision of an arbitrator is usually called an 'award'), in which he agreed that the depressed classes would get separate electorates.[93]

Then something unexpected happened. On 18 August, Gandhi wrote to Prime Minister Macdonald from Yeravda Central Prison (where he was being held after his return to India) and said that he would resist the communal award with his life. 'The only way I can do so', he added, 'is by declaring a perpetual fast unto death from food of any kind save water with or without salt and soda.'[94] In other words, though he never undertook a fast to secure the right of depressed classes to enter Hindu temples, Gandhi was prepared to give up his life to ensure that the depressed classes did not get separate electorates. On 20 September, Gandhi commenced his 'fast unto death' to oppose the communal award.[95] Macdonald refused to withdraw his award. However, he said that his plan could be replaced by a settlement arrived at between Ambedkar and the Congress. Gandhi's son, Devadas, visited Ambedkar in tears and pleaded for his father's life.[96]

Four days later, on 24 September, Ambedkar relented and signed an agreement with Gandhi called the Poona Pact.[97] The agreement provided that though the depressed classes would not get separate electorates like Muslims, seats would be reserved for their candidates in the legislative councils.[98] Some 148 seats were to be reserved for the depressed classes in the provincial legislative councils, which was much higher than the 78 seats they would have received under the communal award[99]—an incentive offered to them for giving up separate electorates.[100] The system of reservations for depressed classes would continue until everyone agreed that it should stop.[101]

Further, though there was no separate electorate for depressed classes, the candidates who stood for elections in constituencies reserved for the depressed classes were to be selected in a primary system—somewhat similar to the Democratic and Republican primaries held in the US—in which only depressed class voters would vote.[102] If more than four depressed class candidates stood for elections in a constituency, four of them would first have to be selected in a primary in which only depressed class voters could vote.[103] These four successful candidates would then contest elections in a general electorate in which all voters (i.e., depressed class and others) would vote. The pact provided that '[e]very endeavour' would be made 'to secure fair representation of the Depressed Classes' in government jobs.[104] It also said that in every province, a sum would be set apart for educating students of the depressed classes.[105]

Ambedkar was subsequently very critical of Gandhi for forcing him into signing the Poona Pact. In the elections that were held in 1937, the Congress obtained 78 of the 151 seats that were reserved for Scheduled Caste (i.e., depressed class) candidates.[106] Ambedkar's Independent Labour Party put up a decent show, winning 11 out of 15 reserved seats,[107] apart from 3 general seats, in the Bombay Legislative Assembly.[108] Though the Congress was not very popular in many reserved constituencies, its strategy often was to put up an independent candidate and then induct him into the party after the elections.[109] For instance, in a letter written in January 1946, Sardar Vallabhbhai Patel instructed his party machinery that a depressed class candidate in Bombay 'should be allowed to contest as an independent candidate, but after election he will sign the Congress pledge and join the party.' This was because 'a large majority of voters are not likely to support him if he takes the Congress ticket'.[110]

After the Montagu–Chelmsford reforms, only 3 per cent of the population of British India had the right to vote.[111] Once the Government of India Act, 1935, came into being, this figure increased to around 14 per cent (or 27 per cent of the adult population).[112] However, only 10 per cent of the depressed class population could vote.[113] Typically, those who had property or educational qualifications got the right to vote.[114] This worked to the disadvantage of the depressed classes (called 'Scheduled Castes' under the Government of India Act, 1935), of whom very few were literate or owned property. Only a few provinces relaxed the qualifications necessary for Scheduled Castes to be able to vote.[115] The result was that very few Scheduled Caste candidates could get elected without substantial support from high-caste Hindu voters. For instance, out of some 87,000 voters in the reserved 'Belgaum North' constituency in Bombay province, only 17,000 voters were Scheduled Castes,[116] and no candidate could therefore be elected without the support of the general electorate. This often meant that among the four Scheduled Caste candidates who had won the primaries, the candidate who placed fourth in the primary won the general election, while the candidate who had placed first in the primary lost the election.[117]

Ambedkar's grievance was that this meant that the 'true representatives' of the Scheduled Castes were not being elected to office.[118] He therefore argued that though the Congress had won more reserved seats than his party in the 1946 elections,[119] the Congress was not the real representative of the Scheduled Castes, a claim which was heavily contested by the Congress.

Under the Government of India Act, 1935, no seats were reserved for Scheduled Caste candidates in cabinet ministries in the executive government. So, in July 1937, while deciding whom to select for the cabinet in the Central Provinces and Berar, Sardar Patel thought that it was better 'to select men from point of view of ability rather than from point of placating groups.'[120] However, the provincial governments of Assam, Bihar and Madras considered it necessary to appoint Scheduled Caste ministers.[121]

In the 1937 elections, reserved seats were often contested in 'multi-member' constituencies.[122] In other words, more than one candidate could be elected from the same constituency (for example, one general candidate and one reserved candidate), with voters having as many votes as there were seats. For instance, in February 1937, Sardar Patel asked voters in the E, F, and G wards' constituencies in Bombay to 'give one of their votes to the Congress Harijan candidate as a matter of duty',[123] regardless of whom the other votes were given to. The primary elections for selecting Scheduled Caste candidates would only be held when more than four such candidates sought election in the same constituency, which was not a very frequent occurrence.[124]

Backward Tribes

Backward tribes got political reservations for the first time under the Government of India Act, 1935. In the early years, when the term 'depressed classes' was used loosely, as we have seen above, backward tribes were considered to be a part of the 'depressed classes'. For instance, in 1916, the central legislative council in India said that the term 'depressed classes' must include not merely untouchable communities but also 'criminal and wandering tribes' and 'aboriginal tribes'.[125] '[O]ther backward and economically poor classes' were also considered to be part of the 'depressed classes'.[126] However, this changed once the meaning of 'depressed classes' was narrowed down only to the untouchable castes as we have previously seen.

Thus, the 1931 census report said that 'hill and forest tribes' that had not become Hindu were not to be considered part of the 'depressed classes'.[127] Census officials found that there were 25 million primitive tribes in India at this time,[128] of whom 8.2 million adhered to tribal religions.[129] The remainder were mostly Hindu but, in some cases, Christians, Buddhists, or Muslims.[130] Primitive tribes that were Hindu and suffered from untouchability would be considered part of the 'depressed classes'[131] but not others.

However, the 1931 census report indicated that many tribals in India were being taken advantage of and needed protection. For instance, moneylenders were charging them usurious rates of interest.[132] Some of their customs were in conflict with the laws of British India.[133] For instance, Assamese tribals employed by the government were being forced to enter the names of their wives as nominees in their general provident fund accounts, instead of their brothers or brothers' sons, which would have been customary under their laws of succession.[134] Some were perishing from diseases to which they had not developed immunity. For example, tribes in the Andaman were nearing extinction because of diseases brought there by convicts in the penal settlement.[135] The census report suggested that primitive tribes in India needed a way of 'making themselves heard'.[136]

Similarly, in 1932, while recommending that the primitive tribes of India should not be included in the 'depressed classes',[137] the Indian Franchise Committee took the view that they needed some protection. It found that it was 'of the greatest importance that the interests of these people, who live a life entirely apart from the rest of the population of India, should be protected by effective representation in the councils, or, if this is not possible, by some other arrangement in the new constitution'.[138] Though he did not ask for reservations for backward tribes, at the second round table conference in 1931, Ambedkar said that it was the colonial government's duty to bring the 'jungle tribes . . . within the pale of civilisation'.[139]

Under the Government of India Act, 1935, backward tribes got 24 reserved seats in the provincial legislative councils, amounting to only 1.5 per cent of the total number of seats on offer.[140] In rules brought about subsequently, the colonial government published a list of 'backward tribes' entitled to contest these elections.[141]

During the period of British colonial rule in India, there had been several tribal uprisings, for example the Santal rebellion in 1855.[142] The British pursued a policy of isolating various regions where they lived[143]—referring to them, over time, as 'scheduled districts',[144] 'backward tracts',[145] or 'excluded' and 'partially excluded areas',[146] which later became centrally administered 'scheduled areas'[147] under the Constitution of independent India.[148] While Christian missionaries were allowed to go to some of these regions, Indians were not.[149] The result was that the freedom movement did not really reach some of these areas.[150]

2

The Other Backward Class of Colonial Bombay

As we shall shortly see in the coming chapters, Articles 15(4) and 16(4) of India's Constitution enable the government to reserve seats in educational institutions and government jobs in favour of a 'class' instead of 'caste'. For instance, Article 16(4) of the Constitution allows the government to introduce quotas for 'any backward class of citizens'. Over the years, the use of the word 'class' instead of 'caste' in the Constitution gave rise to a heated debate in the Supreme Court on the question of whether caste could be made the basis of reservations and whether 'Other Backward Classes' could be identified on the basis of caste alone. Through the lens of legal history, this chapter explains how the word 'class' was understood in colonial India to mean 'caste' or 'tribe'. The terms 'backward classes' and 'depressed classes' were not invented in India. They came to British India from 19th-century England, which was a class-based society. However, these terms underwent a transformation upon being imported to India and the word 'class' in 'backward class' was understood here to mean 'caste' or 'tribe'.

This chapter looks at how the early 20th-century non-Brahmin movements in peninsular India, in places like Kolhapur, Mysore,

Madras, and Bombay, gave rise to the emergence of categories like 'backward classes' and 'Other Backward Classes'. It was a committee in colonial Bombay—a committee in which Ambedkar was a member—which used the term 'backward classes' to denote three distinct groups: untouchable castes, backward tribes, and 'Other Backward Classes'. This is primarily how the term 'backward classes' is now understood under the Indian Constitution. The Bombay government's definition of Other Backward Classes—communities that were as backward as depressed classes (though they were not considered 'untouchable')—held the field for many years in independent India. It was also in colonial Bombay that the 'depressed classes' started being referred to as the 'scheduled classes'—a precursor to 'Scheduled Castes' under the Constitution.

Phule's Anti-Aryanism

The term 'backward classes' emerged in 19th-century England and was often used to describe the middling or lower classes of English society. For instance, in 1870, a British writer explained how two-thirds of the undergraduates at Oxford University came largely from the 'most backward classes in the country—the sons of squires, clergymen, and capitalists', in other words, middling people, as opposed to the sons of aristocrats and gentlemen. This writer believed that backward class students at Oxford were not very interested in their studies and were 'content with a pass-degree'.[1] A magazine published in London in 1877 wrote of how '[e]very highly developed society includes backward classes' and how 'the great society of mankind includes backward races'.[2]

The label 'backward classes' had been in vogue in colonial India since the late 19th century. For example, in 1885, the Madras government referred to the 'poor and backward classes' while discussing the level of education in its province.[3] That same year, the Bombay government decided to reserve half of its scholarships for students who were Muslims or 'backward' Hindus.[4] In a report on the progress of education in India prepared by the colonial government in 1914, the term 'backward classes' was used to describe 'aboriginals and hill and forest tribes', 'depressed classes' (including 'untouchable' castes and 'criminal tribes'), and 'communities who, though not necessarily either backward or depressed, present problems of education different from the ordinary'.[5]

However, the term 'backward classes' gained currency against the backdrop of non-Brahmin movements that were gaining momentum in places like Kolhapur, Madras, Mysore, and Bombay. These movements were premised on the idea that unlike the four-fold varna[6] division of castes in north India, peninsular Indian society was divided into three groups: Brahmins, non-Brahmins, and outcastes.[7] Around 1930, the Bombay government, for instance, divided society into three categories: advanced (e.g. Brahmins), intermediate (Marathas and allied castes), and backward.[8]

The non-Brahmin movement in western India really began with the work of Jyotirao Phule (1827–1890) in Poona.[9] Phule's movement was, in some sense, pro-British and anti-Brahmin.[10] He felt that the 1857 revolt was a Brahmin movement led by high-caste leaders like Tantya Tope.[11] In fact, many non-Brahmins believed that the freedom struggle at that time was an elite Brahmin movement, which sought to restore the country to the days of the Peshwa regime,[12] which was oppressive towards the lower castes. In various polemical tracts that he published over the years, he argued that all the castes beneath the Brahmins in western India—Marathas, Kunbis, Malis, Mahars, Mangs, etc.—really belonged to the Kshatriya caste. In that sense, he tried to unite all the lower castes into one caste grouping, to give them all one collective identity.[13] He hardly ever used the term 'Hindu' in his written work.[14] In a break from tradition, he allowed untouchable castes to use his well,[15] though he himself belonged to a non-Brahmin caste which was considered respectable.[16]

Adopting the Aryan race theory in his tracts, Phule suggested that Brahmins were alien invaders who had subjugated the original inhabitants, the lower castes. He even reasoned that the various avatars of Vishnu in Hindu philosophy were evidence of successive Brahmin-Aryan invasions into India. For instance, he said that the first two avatars of Vishnu, a fish and a tortoise respectively, were indicative of a sea-borne Brahmin attack on India.[17] Developed by German philologists and popularized by Max Muller, the Aryan invasion theory was accepted by Brahmin leaders like Tilak and Ranade, who thereby identified themselves as being members of the same race as their colonial superiors.[18] Turning this argument around, Phule wrote that the Brahmin elite were foreigners.

In his various writings, Phule also appealed to the British colonial government to increase the number of non-Brahmins in the colonial administration.[19] For instance, in one tract, he asked the administration to appoint more non-Brahmin teachers. Brahmin school-teachers, he felt, withheld education from lower-caste students by, among other things, inflicting harsher punishments on them for getting answers wrong.[20] In 1873, he founded the Satyashodhak Samaj or Truth-Seeking Society, which, among other things, encouraged religious ceremonies to be performed without Brahmins.[21] Besides prescribing adherence to the theory that there is only one God, the society asked its members to subscribe to a declaration that said 'I shall always be loyal to the British Government.'[22]

At the time, the caste label 'Maratha' really applied to a small number of aristocratic landholding families believed to have descended from the Rajputs, while the 'Kunbi' caste consisted of the more numerous peasant cultivators of the region whose varna was considered to be 'Shudra'.[23] In his non-Brahmin movement, Phule hoped that he could unite the Marathas, Kunbis, and even untouchable castes into one grouping as Kshatriyas. However, he failed in this endeavour.[24] More and more non-Brahmin groups gained upward mobility into the Maratha category,[25] with the result that the distinction between the Marathas and Kunbis soon faded away.[26] Eventually, non-Brahmins like the Maratha–Kunbi group considered themselves to be high-caste Hindus, above the lower castes.[27] Local non-Brahmin deities like Khandoba were 'Sanskritized'[28] and incorporated into the Brahmanical pantheon.[29] The Maratha–Kunbi adopted high-caste Hindu customs like prohibiting widow remarriage.[30] Eventually, non-Brahmins formed a substantial proportion of the elite in Maharashtra.[31]

The Vedic Rites of the Kolhapur King

Reservations for backward classes began in Kolhapur, a moderately sized princely state of 3,200 square miles in western India.[32] Despite its relatively modest size, Kolhapur was politically important because the dynasty that ruled over it was directly descended from the 17th-century king Shivaji,[33] still an icon of Marathi pride in Maharashtra politics. In 1884, Maharaja Shivaji V of Kolhapur, who had no heir, decided to adopt the eldest son of one of his feudatories.[34] Around ten years later, the adopted son, Shahu Chhatrapati Maharaj, assumed office as the prince of Kolhapur at the age of 20.[35] At the time, out of 71 officers in the state's administration, 60 were Brahmins,[36] most of them Chitpavan Brahmins.[37] Though they constituted only 4 per cent of the state's population, Brahmins were the most literate community in Kolhapur.[38]

Shahu, a Maratha by caste, started his reign by establishing, supporting, or inaugurating hostels for the students of other communities in the state—Marathas, Jains, Veerashivas (Lingayats), and untouchable groups.[39] Three of Kolhapur's feudatories (Vishalgad, Bavda, and Ichalkaranji) were run by Brahmin families. Shahu petitioned the colonial government to regain his kingdom's powers over these regions.[40] He tried to increase the number of Marathas employed by the government and hired a non-Brahmin as a senior advisor.[41] These measures stirred the cauldron of inter-caste tensions in the state. Lokamanya Tilak's English newspaper, the *Mahratta*, criticized Shahu's decision to fund communal hostels, arguing that a 'ruler of a state should be practically above caste or sectarian prejudices'.[42] The 17th-century king Shivaji, wrote the

Mahratta, 'encouraged merit wherever it was found'[43]—perhaps one of the earliest invocations of 'merit' in a debate of this kind.

However, an incident occurred in 1901, called the Vedokta controversy,[44] which changed things forever. In August 1901, a Brahmin priest in Kolhapur called Narayan Bhat Sevekari performed a thread ceremony called the 'Shravani' for Shahu's family according to Vedic rites.[45] The Brahmin panchayat of Kolhapur, the Brahmavrinda, excommunicated Sevekari for doing so.[46] They believed that the family from which Shahu had been adopted was not really Kshatriya by caste and that Vedic rituals could therefore not be performed for Shahu or any members of his family.[47] The Vedokta ritual could only be performed for Brahmins, Kshatriyas, and Vaishyas, while the Puranokta ritual was for others.[48]

In turn, in October 1901, Shahu issued an order saying that all palace ceremonies had to be performed in accordance with the Vedokta forms of worship.[49] When the royal priest or Rajopadhye refused to do so, in May 1902, Shahu withdrew his *inam* lands[50] and confiscated the properties of some other Brahmin families in Kolhapur. This drew sharp reactions from the *Mahratta*, which wrote that Shahu had acted out of a sense of 'personal vindictiveness and rancorous hatred of Brahmans'.[51]

Strictly speaking, the Vedokta controversy was not unprecedented in the socio-political context of the region. When the British defeated the Brahmin Peshwa regime of Bajirao II in western India in 1818, they installed a Maratha king in Satara, Pratapsinh Bhosale. As a descendant of Shivaji, Pratapsinh claimed Kshatriya origins and asked Brahmins to perform Vedic rituals for his family. The Chitpavan Brahmins in Satara, on the other hand, rejected the idea that Marathas like Pratapsinh were Kshatriyas. They argued that there was no intermediate caste between the Brahmins and Shudras in the region and that all the Kshatriyas had been killed by Parshuram.[52] The controversy, partly instigated by British colonial officials, was eventually decided against the Brahmins in 1830.[53]

Interestingly, at around the time of the Vedokta controversy in Kolhapur, Tilak and Shahu were on opposite sides of the highly contested Tai Maharaj adoption case.[54] In 1897, a wealthy man called Baba Maharaj died, leaving considerable property to his widow, Tai Maharaj. In his will, Baba Maharaj asked his widow to adopt a son, but she needed the approval of the executors of the will to do so. Tilak, one of the executors,[55] wanted the widow to adopt a boy from Aurangabad, while Shahu wanted her to adopt one from Kolhapur.[56] Tilak spent Rs 60,000 on the case and eventually won it on appeal in the Privy Council in London[57], only shortly before his death.[58] The British Governor of Bombay, Sir Henry Stafford Northcote, thought that the Vedokta controversy might have been instigated by Tilak as payback for the Tai Maharaj case.[59]

Soon after passing his order against the Rajopadhye, Shahu left for England.[60] While he was there, on 26 July 1902, he issued a unique and unprecedented resolution. In it, he said that 50 per cent of all vacancies in his administration would be 'filled with recruits from among the backward classes'.[61] By 'backward classes', he meant 'all castes other than Brahmins, Prabhus, Shenvis, Parsees and other advanced classes'.[62] This was meant to be an incentive to try and get backward classes in his state to educate themselves.[63] The Brahmin community in Kolhapur was obviously unhappy about this. A Brahmin-owned Kolhapur weekly, the *Samarth*, wrote: 'A whole community, we mean the Brahman, is put under ban . . . All possible offices are given to Marathas under the guise of encouraging the backward classes.'[64] The *Mahratta* wrote that Shahu's decision put caste above merit.[65]

This was not the only step Shahu took against Brahmins in his state. For instance, he supported the creation of a non-Brahmin priesthood[66] and arrested a Brahmin professor at Rajaram college on charges of sedition.[67] Later, Ambedkar was able to resume his MSc. at the London School of Economics and get called to the bar in London thanks to financial assistance provided by Shahu.[68] Shahu had hoped that Ambedkar would espouse the non-Brahmin cause in London.[69]

All this had the tacit consent of the colonial government in Bombay.[70] In the 19th century, British officials in Bombay looked at Brahmins with suspicion,[71] and as far back as in 1881, the government unsuccessfully attempted to dilute Brahmin dominance in the administration by seeking 'a due admixture of the various races and castes' in government jobs.[72] At the turn of the century, Brahmins like Tilak and Gokhale were leaders of the nationalist movement, and British officials saw Shahu's actions against the Brahmins as being in their interests.[73] In 1906, Tilak's English newspaper, the *Mahratta*, referred to the British Resident in Kolhapur, Colonel Ferris, as the 'selected Angel sent by God to the wretched Brahmin-ridden State to assist the Maharaja in his holy work of regenerating the backward classes'.[74] In 1910, the Bombay government once again suggested that the number of Brahmins in their administration ought to be reduced.[75] A wider non-Brahmin movement was also taking place at this time in Bombay province[76] and in other parts of peninsular India more generally.

In fact, there is evidence that the British might have provoked Shahu to take strong actions against the Brahmins in Kolhapur as part of their age-old divide and rule policy. Writing to the Secretary of State in England after the Vedokta controversy, Governor Northcote took credit for Shahu's actions against the Brahmins. Shahu had visited British officials in Mahabaleshwar before his decision against the Rajopadhye and, wrote Northcote, 'we quietly instilled a little pluck into him'.[77] Northcote felt that Shahu would otherwise have given in to the Brahmins on the matter. Further, during his trip to England in 1902, Shahu visited Secretary of State George Hamilton, who advised him that he 'ought to stand up to the Brahmins'.[78] The 1902 resolution reserving 50 per cent seats for non-Brahmins might therefore have been inspired by Hamilton.

At around this time, Poona Brahmins like Tilak were organizing political festivals celebrating Ganpati or commemorating Shivaji, and propagating the idea that the interests of Brahmins and Marathas were similar and that Brahmins were recognized leaders.[79] Secretary of State Hamilton therefore felt that Shahu was an important ally for the colonial administration. '[W]e are subject to a common danger from the preponderance of Brahmins in the public services both of the British government and of the Native Princes', he wrote.[80] However, colonial officials did not think very highly of Shahu. 'I only wish we had a more resolute ally than this timid prince', wrote Hamilton.[81] Governor Northcote called him an 'arrant coward'.[82]

Over a century later, in 2014, when the Maharashtra government introduced a law to grant reservations to the Marathas, they relied on the 1902 resolution passed by Shahu Maharaj in Kolhapur after the Vedokta controversy.[83]

The Justice Party's Communal G.O.s

Despite constituting a minority of the population, Brahmins in south India were overrepresented in government jobs. For instance, in 1912 in Madras, though male Brahmins constituted 3.2 per cent of the population, they held 83.3 per cent of all positions as sub-judges in the province, while male non-Brahmins, who were 85.6 per cent of the population, held only 16.7 per cent of these posts.[84] This caused much resentment. In 1916, a new political party called the South Indian Liberal Federation was formed. Known as the 'Justice Party' after a newspaper it ran,[85] its aim was to look after the interests of non-Brahmins in Madras.

The Justice Party submitted a memorandum to Secretary of State Montagu when he arrived in Madras in 1917 and asked that non-Brahmins be adequately represented in the legislature and all branches of the government.[86] Their demand was that, like Muslims, non-Brahmins too should get separate electorates.[87] Eventually, the government agreed to reserve 28 out of 65 general seats in the Madras legislature for non-Brahmins[88]—possibly the first caste-based reservation in a legislature in British India. Further, in Bombay, 7 out of 46 general seats were reserved for Marathas and allied castes.[89] These were on the basis of a joint electorate, not separate electorates.[90]

The 1920 elections were boycotted by the Congress, and the Justice Party won the election in Madras,[91] with non-Brahmins securing much more than their reserved quota of seats.[92]

After coming to power in Madras, the Justice Party took steps to reduce the representation of Brahmins in government services. The Madras government thereafter issued a series of orders called 'Communal G.O.s', which essentially said that government positions in Madras should be distributed among the various communities like Brahmins, non-Brahmins, Indian Christians, Muslims, and others.[93]

Mysore Brahmins Aren't Backward

As all of this was taking place in Madras, in 1918, a deputation of non-Brahmin leaders met the Maharaja of Mysore and asked him to ensure that non-Brahmins would be adequately represented in government jobs there.[94] The Maharaja swiftly appointed a committee headed by Sir Leslie Miller, chief judge of the court there,[95] to look into this question.[96]

In its report submitted to the Maharaja a year later,[97] the Miller Committee said a few interesting things. Firstly, it opined that 'adequate' representation for non-Brahmins in government jobs did not mean proportional representation.[98] In other words, it was not necessary that non-Brahmins should occupy as many government jobs as the strength of their population. It said that the government's goal was to reduce the number of Brahmin government servants to 50 per cent of the higher services and to 33 per cent of the lower services. Secondly, it also felt that reservations in government jobs would not hurt the efficiency of the department, because that was 'not to be measured . . . by academic qualifications'. The committee recognized that government servants required 'other qualities such as sympathy, honesty of purpose, energy and common sense', which were as important as academic brilliance.[99] Thirdly, it added that having non-Brahmin officers in the government would ensure that the non-Brahmin population of Mysore would not be neglected by government officers.[100]

However, the Miller Committee came up with an odd definition of 'backwardness'. All communities that had a literacy in English of less than 5 per cent were considered to be backward.[101] This essentially meant that only Brahmins were not backward in Mysore, while all the other communities (barring a few) were backward there.[102] Accordingly, in 1921, the Mysore government defined 'backward communities' as all communities excluding Brahmins that were inadequately represented in the services.[103] The Maharaja implemented the Miller Committee's recommendations in a watered-down form.[104]

The 'Other Backward Classes' in Bombay

In 1928,[105] the Bombay government appointed a committee[106] headed by a member of the Indian Civil Service, O.H.B. Starte, to inquire into the educational, economic, and social condition of the depressed classes and aboriginal tribes. Included in this committee was a relatively young Bombay legislator, Dr B.R. Ambedkar.[107] In July 1930, the Starte Committee submitted its report to the government in which it recommended that the term 'backward classes' be used to denote three kinds of communities: (i) depressed classes (i.e., 'untouchable' castes); (ii) aboriginal and hill tribes (i.e., tribes that were residing in forests, or those that had been doing so in the recent past); and (iii) 'other Backward Classes'.[108] The committee did not prescribe any fixed or certain criteria for determining who the 'Other Backward Classes' were. It only opined that the term would include 'wandering tribes' who may not be forest-dwellers or aboriginals but who may still be in need of special care.[109] It suggested that a 'backward class board' be set up to ensure that communities that had ceased to be backward were no longer on the list. It recommended three conditions for removing a caste from the list of backward classes: (i) the caste should no longer be untouchable (if it was untouchable to begin with); (ii) it should have reached a satisfactory level of literacy; and (iii) it should acquire an economic status such that it no longer requires special assistance.[110]

In 1931, census officials in Bombay decided to categorize Hindus on the basis of their education and economic condition. No attempt had been made thus far, they said, to group people 'by literacy and economic status'. They acknowledged that 'the average level of education of a social group' was very closely linked with 'the general economic position of the group'. They classified Hindus into five clusters: 'advanced', 'intermediate', 'other backward', 'primitive', and 'depressed'. This division, they said, was based on 'the standard of comfort and culture attained by the groups', where 'comfort' and 'culture' were euphemisms for money and education, respectively.[111]

In May 1933, the Bombay government passed a resolution accepting the recommendations of the Starte Committee, with one modification. The government noted that the committee had 'laid down no definite criterion' for determining who the 'Other Backward Classes' were. There was a great demand for inclusion in the list of Other Backward Classes, which would have made the list unwieldy. So, the Bombay government decided to adopt the 'rough working' principle that the 'Other Backward Classes' would 'comprise classes which are approximately at the same stage of social and educational advancement as' the depressed classes (i.e., untouchable castes) and aboriginal and hill tribes, and 'are so backward as to need special help from the Backward Class Officer'.[112]

By 1945–46, Bombay province conferred the following benefits on members of the 'backward classes'.[113] Firstly, some backward class students would receive scholarships, grants, and fee-waivers. Secondly, 15 per cent of the seats in teacher training colleges were reserved for male backward class teachers. Thirdly, in government services, between 10 and 20 per cent of posts, like clerks, revenue officers called 'talathis', and bailiffs in courts, were reserved for the backward classes.[114] Finally, the government provided housing to depressed class families at nominal rates.[115]

From Depressed Classes to Scheduled Castes

The Bombay government prepared three schedules to its 1933 resolution accepting the Starte Committee recommendations. Schedule I contained a list of 47 'depressed classes'. Schedule II had 29 aboriginal and hill tribes. Schedule III was the longest list—it consisted of 125 'Other Backward Classes'.[116] Though the word 'class' was used in 'backward class' and 'Other Backward Class', it was really a euphemism for caste or tribe—all the communities in the schedules were castes or tribes. However, the term was not restricted to Hindus. Included among the Other Backward Classes was the 'Miana' tribe[117] of Muslims. The following year, in October 1934, the backward class officer appointed by the Bombay government prepared an annual report on the working of his department. In it, he referred to the depressed classes that had been set out in Schedule I as the 'scheduled classes'. This was perhaps one of the earliest references to the depressed classes as the 'scheduled classes'.[118]

The Government of India Act, 1935, referred to the 'depressed classes' as 'Scheduled Castes', like the backward class officer in Bombay had done a year before. This was because the first and fifth appendices or 'schedules' to the 1935 Act provided that some seats in the central and provincial legislative councils would be reserved for certain castes. The term 'Scheduled Castes' was applied because these castes were spoken about in the schedules. However, the law made it clear that the 'Scheduled Castes' were none other than those who had previously been known as the 'depressed classes'.[119] In other words, it was only untouchable castes that would be considered as 'Scheduled Castes'. As Viscount Templewood later observed in the House of Lords, the Scheduled Castes were 'those millions of Indians who at one time we called "Untouchables" at another time "Depressed Classes" and whom now, in the Government of India Act, we call "Scheduled Castes".'[120]

Under the 1935 Act, a total of 151 seats (three more in number than the Poona Pact) were reserved for the Scheduled Castes in the provincial legislative councils.[121] However, since there were 1,585 seats in total in these councils, only about 9.5 per cent of the seats were reserved for Scheduled Castes, which was much less than their proportion of the population.[122] Similarly, in the central legislature, only 25 out of 400 seats (i.e., 6.25 per cent) were reserved for the Scheduled Castes, substantially lower than their numbers in the population.[123] However, looked at from another angle, Scheduled Castes got 18 per cent of the 'general' seats,[124] i.e., the seats that were not reserved for religious minorities, special interest groups (e.g., landholders, representatives of industry, or labour), or women. In rules that were subsequently issued under the statute, the colonial government provided a list of Scheduled Castes who were entitled to reservations.[125]

The Government of India Act, 1935, also provided that the colonial government had a 'special responsibility' of ensuring that the 'legitimate interests of minorities' would be safeguarded (in public employment).[126] In the meantime, the government decided to nominate duly qualified members of the depressed classes to public services, in order to ensure their 'fair representation' in government jobs. Though 25 per cent of the seats in government jobs were reserved for Muslims, a fixed percentage of seats was initially not reserved for depressed class candidates because the general level of education of the depressed classes was not considered to be very high.[127] However, in 1943, a fixed quota of reservations was introduced for Scheduled Castes in government services.[128] Even so, it was difficult to find suitable Scheduled Caste candidates to fill reserved seats. In 1947, for instance, out of 529 candidates who got 45 marks or more in the qualifying examination, only two belonged to the Scheduled Castes.[129] '[T]hey were so low down in the list', said Sardar Patel, 'that we had to make an exception in order to take them in.'[130]

3

Ambedkar Produces a Formula

This chapter outlines some of the key themes concerning reservations that were discussed in the Constituent Assembly and its subcommittees. There were an estimated 60 million[1] Scheduled Castes at the time that the Constitution was being drafted—more than the entire population of England.[2] The framers of India's Constitution were faced with several difficult questions concerning them: Should reservations only be provided to those communities that were historically considered 'untouchables' or to others as well? To what extent should reservations be allowed—for instance, could 70 per cent of the seats in government jobs be reserved for backward classes? Were reservations a permanent feature of the republic or would they cease after some time? Would reservations extend to cabinet ministries and the judiciary? Could a court reject reservations for a community that was well-represented in public services or numerically large? Would government services become less efficient if quotas were provided for backward communities? By looking at the debates that took place in the Constituent Assembly, this chapter examines how our founding fathers attempted to answer these questions.

This chapter will, in particular, highlight a crucial speech made by Ambedkar in the Constituent Assembly, which had a lasting impact on the reservations jurisprudence of the Supreme Court in subsequent decades. In it, Ambedkar said that reservations were an exception to the principle of equality of opportunity and should be restricted to a minority of seats. This essentially gave birth to the 50 per cent rule, which we will see in subsequent chapters.

Only Two Kinds of Reservations

The Constitution, as originally drafted, only conceived of reservations in legislative bodies and government jobs.[3] In other words, a certain number of seats in the lower house of the central and state legislatures were to be reserved for Scheduled Castes and Scheduled Tribes; and some government jobs were to be kept apart for backward classes.[4] The Constitution provided no reservations in the upper house of Parliament (i.e., the Rajya Sabha) or, for that matter, in the upper house of bicameral state legislatures.[5] No quotas were prescribed in executive offices like ministries in the cabinet,[6] in the judiciary,[7] in local bodies like municipal corporations, or in educational institutions.

At the time that India's Constitution was being prepared, there were many proposals that there should be reservations in other areas as well. Dr B.R. Ambedkar had originally conceived that Scheduled Castes ought to have some 'representation in the Executive—Union and State'.[8] Similarly, some other members of the Scheduled Caste community in the Constituent Assembly, like H.J. Khandekar and Jagjivan Ram, wanted reservations in the executive and judicial branches of the government.[9] The All-India Adi-Hindu Depressed Classes Association asked for reservations in 'municipalities and all statutory local bodies'.[10] Others pointed out that by August 1949, though India had been independent for two years, and though there were two Scheduled Caste ministers in the Central government (Ambedkar[11] and Jagjivan Ram), provinces like Bombay had no Scheduled Caste ministers or parliamentary secretaries.[12] Further, no Governor or Ambassador had been appointed from among the Scheduled Castes by that time.[13]

However, the Constituent Assembly did not accept these proposals. In July 1947, the subcommittee on minorities decided, by a slim vote of 8–7, that 'no statutory provision should be made for reservation of seats' for Scheduled Castes and others in cabinets.[14] Sardar Vallabhbhai Patel said that this was the position under the Government of India Act, 1935, and it was 'constitutionally proper'.[15] Much before the Constituent Assembly had been formed, Gandhi had been opposed to cabinet representation for Scheduled Castes, calling it a 'dangerous' principle which would 'harm the country'. Ministers in the cabinet, he believed, had to be 'topmost' men 'commanding universal confidence', selected on the basis of their 'intrinsic merit and popularity'.[16]

At the initial stages of its preparation, the draft Constitution did not contain any provision which specified that there would be reservations in government jobs. The chapter on fundamental rights prepared by K.M. Munshi,[17] which was used as a template by the subcommittee on fundamental rights, only said that there would be 'equality of opportunity for all citizens . . . in matters of public employment'.[18] However, Ambedkar insisted that the Constitution itself should say that there would be reservations in government jobs, and that this 'shall not be a matter which will be left to the sweet will of the legislature or the executive'.[19]

The Constitution as originally drafted did not speak of reservations in promotions or in private sector jobs either. This was despite the fact that there were very few public sector jobs compared to jobs in the private sector. According to the 1931 census, though around 67 per cent of India's workers were involved in agriculture, a sizeable proportion of the working population was engaged in industry (10 per cent), trade (5.1 per cent), transport (1.5 per cent), and professions (1.5 per cent), compared to those engaged in public administration (0.7 per cent).[20] However, it is likely that jobs in the public sector were more prestigious and remunerative at this time. For example, the Chief Justice of the Calcutta High Court was paid more than judges in England, and such posts were very highly regarded.[21]

A Cap on Quotas?

The Constitution did not prescribe the proportion of the seats in government jobs that could be reserved for backward communities.[22] Sardar Patel felt that the constitutional provision for reservation of seats in government jobs 'should not [be] of any rigid character but should be more in the nature of a general directive'.[23] Consequently, it did not provide any ceiling on the number of seats which could be reserved either. This begged the question: could a government in the future decide to reserve 70 per cent or even 100 per cent of the positions in government departments in favour of backward classes? An important speech made by Ambedkar in the Constituent Assembly suggests that the answer to this question was in the negative—that only a minority of seats in public employment could be reserved for the backward castes.

On 30 November 1948, Ambedkar was responding to a criticism in the Constituent Assembly that the words 'backward class' used in the Constitution were vague. A provision in the Constitution said that the government would have the power to reserve seats in government jobs for the 'backward classes'. However, many asked the question: who exactly were the backward classes? Pointing out that the answer to this question was unclear, T.T. Krishnamachari, who later resigned as India's finance minister after the Mundhra scandal,[24] accused Ambedkar of preparing a Constitution that was a 'paradise for lawyers'—one that would improve their 'business prospects' on account of its many open-ended phrases.[25]

Answering this accusation, Ambedkar addressed the Constituent Assembly and said that the drafting committee had to 'produce a formula' that reconciled three points of view when it came to government jobs: (i) firstly, that there should be equality of opportunity for all citizens; (ii) secondly, that there should be 'no reservations of any sort for any class or community at all'; and (iii) thirdly, that there should be reservations for 'certain communities which have so far been outside the administration'.[26] He said that if reservations were too excessive, the first principle, of equality of opportunity, would be violated.

To illustrate his point, Ambedkar said that if a government reserved 70 per cent of the positions in government jobs, leaving only 30 per cent for the general populace, then this would violate the principle 'that there shall be equality of opportunity'. 'Therefore', he said, 'the seats to be reserved . . . must be confined to a minority of seats.'[27] In fact, at the time these provisions were being debated, the Government of India had issued a circular granting 12.5 per cent and 16.5 per cent reservations for Scheduled Castes in the 'higher services' and 'lower services' respectively.[28] Perhaps this is what Ambedkar had in mind when he spoke of a 'minority of seats'. He explained that reservations were an exception to the rule that there should be equality of opportunity in public employment, and that the exception should not 'eat up the rule altogether'.[29] He expected the courts to decide whether governments had provided reservations for 'such a large number of seats' that 'the rule regarding equality of opportunity has been destroyed', or whether governments had 'acted in a reasonable and prudent manner' in fixing quotas.[30]

These views propounded by Ambedkar, i.e., that reservations constituted an exception to the principle of equality of opportunity and that only a minority of seats should be reserved for the backward classes, were repeatedly invoked by the Supreme Court of India while evolving the 50 per cent rule which we will see in the coming chapters. Ambedkar's arguments in the Constituent Assembly on this question were uncharacteristically mild and conservative. Why did Ambedkar not ask for proportional representation instead of a 'minority of seats', i.e., why did he not insist that backward classes should get as many seats as their proportion of the population?

One wonders whether his own tenuous position in the Constituent Assembly made Ambedkar more willing to compromise on this question. No candidate from his party, the Scheduled Castes Federation, was elected to the Bombay legislature in the 1946 elections, and Ambedkar himself was appointed to the Constituent

Assembly as a goodwill gesture by the Congress party in Bombay.[31] Later, after resigning as Law Minister, Ambedkar also lost his election in the 1951–52 general elections,[32] and a bye-election in 1954.[33] In 1953, during a debate in the Rajya Sabha, Ambedkar said: 'People always keep on saying to me: "Oh, you are the maker of the Constitution." My answer is I was a hack. What I was asked to do, I did much against my will.'[34]

However, Ambedkar's views in the Constituent Assembly on this question were consistent with his earlier opinions. As we saw in Chapter 1, in his memorandum before the minorities committee at the First Round Table Conference (1930–31), Ambedkar asked the colonial government for 'adequate' (not 'proportional') reservation for the depressed classes in government jobs. Further, Ambedkar's argument that reservations should be confined to a minority of seats did not really come in the way of ensuring proportional representation for Scheduled Castes and Scheduled Tribes, who constituted a minority of the population. It did, however, get in the way of proportional representation for Other Backward Classes who Ambedkar was aware of when he made this speech.

Adequacy of Representation

As far as reservations in the lower house of legislative bodies were concerned, the Constitution prescribed that the number of seats reserved in a legislature would be commensurate with the population of Scheduled Castes and Scheduled Tribes.[35] Importantly, in fixing the size of the quotas, what mattered was not how many eligible Scheduled Castes and Scheduled Tribe voters there were, but what the total population of the community was (which included those who were not registered to vote or ineligible to do so, e.g., children).[36]

However, Scheduled Castes and Scheduled Tribes are not homogenous categories.[37] A vast number of disparate groups are included within this nomenclature. For example, in 1956, there were around 21 castes in Bihar that were considered 'Scheduled Castes' in that state.[38] There is no rule which said that each of those 21 castes had to be equally represented in legislatures and government jobs. In other words, nothing would stop the members of just one of those castes from occupying all the reserved seats in legislative bodies and public services, leaving the rest to fend for themselves.

This problem was explained in a speech made by Mahavir Tyagi in the Constituent Assembly. Tyagi, who later became the finance and defence minister in independent India,[39] said that out of around 400 communities that were considered to be Scheduled Castes, only 'two or three communities are taking advantage of the seats reserved for Scheduled Castes'.[40]

Article 16(4) of the Constitution says that the State can reserve jobs in government departments for those backward classes that in its opinion are 'not adequately represented' in the services. The use of the word 'adequate' and not 'proportionate' is important, going back to Ambedkar's speech that reservations were to be confined to a minority of seats. When this provision was being debated, Ambedkar did not want the courts to have the power to decide that a class had been adequately represented in public employment and that it did not need reservations. Courts should not be able to 'say that reservation is made for a class although in fact it is adequately represented', he believed, because it would be, in his view, 'quite impossible for a minority community' to face this kind of litigation.[41]

It was K.M. Munshi who therefore suggested that the words 'in the opinion of the State' be inserted into Article 16(4),[42] so as to take the question of the adequacy of representation of backward classes in government jobs beyond the pale of judicial review. In other words, the framers of our Constitution believed that courts should not have the power to say that certain backward communities were adequately represented in government services and did not require representation. It was only the opinion of the government, as to whether a community was adequately represented in the services or not, which mattered.

The Constitution does not say that members of the 'backward classes' who are entitled to get quotas in government jobs must constitute a minority of the population. In other words, a 'backward' community may be numerically very populous in a state, and it may yet be entitled to reservations in government jobs. A debate which took place between C. Rajagopalachari and Ambedkar in the Advisory Committee in April 1947 makes this clear. At that meeting, C. Rajagopalachari was concerned that 'in some States[,] reservation may be made for majority communities', adding that the Constitution would 'not then really [be] protecting minority communities'.[43] Ambedkar suggested that the word 'minorities' should be used instead of 'classes' in the Constitution,[44] so that it could be made clear that only minorities are entitled to reservations. However, Article 16(4) of the Constitution, which speaks of reservations for a 'backward class' citizen, does not use the word 'minorities'. In using the term 'backward classes' instead of 'minorities', the framers of the Constitution intended that reservations can be provided for backward communities regardless of how numerically large they might be. In short, reservations in government jobs were not only for Scheduled Castes and Scheduled Tribes (a minority of the population), but also Other Backward Classes (a majority of the population).

The Sunset Clause

The Constitution provided a sunset clause for reservations in legislative bodies.[45] In other words, it said that ten years after 26 January 1950, reservations for Scheduled Castes and Scheduled Tribes in legislative bodies would cease.[46] However, there was no such sunset clause for reservations in government jobs.

Ambedkar did not want there to be any sunset clause for reservations in the Constitution. In his original draft of the Constitution, reservations would go on indefinitely. In Ambedkar's vision, Parliament could decide to abolish reservations, but only 25 years after the Constitution came into force and after a vote by a two-thirds super-majority.[47] Several members of the Constituent Assembly asked for a longer duration for the sunset clause. For example, T. Channiah[48] said that he wanted reservations to continue 'for 150 years'.[49] 'Why only for ten years?' asked Santanu Kumar Dass. 'If we get equal rights within two years', he added, 'all would be on the same level after that period and there would be no need for reservations.'[50] Jaipal Singh, a noted Scheduled Tribe leader who had captained India's first hockey team at the Olympics in 1928,[51] pointed out that ten years was only the lifespan of two successive governments,[52] which was not enough to improve the conditions of the scheduled communities.[53] S. Nagappa suggested that reservations should end after 10 years only if the educational, social, and economic condition of the Scheduled Castes and Scheduled Tribes was brought to the same level as others.[54]

As the chairman of the Drafting Committee, though Ambedkar had to defend the sunset clause in the Constituent Assembly, he argued against it. He pointed out that while Muslims and Christians had enjoyed electoral privileges in India since 1892 and 1920 respectively, Scheduled Castes had received political reservations only since 1937, and even those had been interrupted by the Second World War. Though he was personally in favour of a longer duration for the sunset clause, he said that '[i]f at the end of the ten years, the Scheduled Castes find that their position has not improved or that they want further extension of this period, it will not be beyond their capacity or their intelligence to invent new ways of getting the same protection which they are promised here.'[55]

On the other hand, some in the Constituent Assembly asked for a sunset clause for reservations in government jobs as well. For instance, Pandit Hirday Nath Kunzru[56] asked that all such reservations cease after 10 years.[57] Responding to arguments such as these, Ambedkar quoted the words of Edmund Burke: 'Large Empires and small minds go ill together.'[58]

Other Backward Classes

The Constitution used three different phrases to describe those who would benefit from reservations: (i) firstly, reservations in public employment were to go to a 'backward class of citizens';[59] (ii) secondly, reservations in legislative bodies were meant only for 'Scheduled Castes' and 'Scheduled Tribes';[60] and (iii) the President had the power to appoint a Commission to look into the condition of 'socially and educationally backward classes'.[61] Further, a directive principle of state policy called on the government to promote the interests of the 'weaker sections of the people'.[62]

Several members of the Constituent Assembly pointed out that this created much confusion, and it was not clear who exactly the 'backward classes' were.[63] For example, Krishnamachari asked whether backwardness was to be measured in terms of a person's literacy,[64] economic condition, or birth.[65] Some suggested that the word 'backward' be qualified with the phrase 'economically or culturally',[66] others that the word 'backward' be deleted altogether.[67] For instance, Aziz Ahmad Khan said that deleting the word 'backward' would enable the government to grant reservations to Sikhs, Christians, and Muslims who were not backward as a group.[68] Ari Bahadur Gurung said that '90 per cent if not more of the Indian people are educationally and economically backward'.[69] Dharam Prakash pointed out that every community in India had some 'section of people which is backward whether economically or educationally or socially'.[70] R.M. Nalavade said that the phrase 'backward class' 'could be interpreted in such a way as to include so many classes which are even educationally advanced'.[71] Khandekar wished that the words 'Scheduled Caste' had been used instead.[72] He felt that the use of the term 'backward class' would prevent Scheduled Castes from getting reservations in public employment as 'people of other castes will also claim to be backward and get the chances on reserved posts'.[73]

It was the drafting committee of the Constituent Assembly, under the chairmanship of Ambedkar, which was responsible for adopting the phrase 'backward class'.[74] K.M. Munshi, one of its members, explained that they had used the 'best possible term' which was available to them. That word was not meant to convey only those communities that were considered to be 'untouchables'.[75] In Bombay, said Munshi, the term 'backward classes' meant not merely Scheduled Castes and Scheduled Tribes but also 'other backward classes who are economically, educationally, and socially backward'.[76] Since 1931, Bombay had a 'Backward Class Board' to look into the affairs of the backward classes in the province.[77] This term was not restricted to Bombay alone. In Bihar, for instance, castes like 'Gowalas, Kurmis, Nais, [and] Kandus' were considered by some to be 'backward classes', i.e., 'not Harijans and aborigines but otherwise far inferior to Brahmans, Kshatriyas, Bhumihars, and Kayasthas'.[78]

Ambedkar had been a member of the Bombay committee which had come up with the term 'Other Backward Classes' in 1930.[79] In the Constituent Assembly, he explained that they had 'left it to be determined by each local Government' what was meant by the term 'backward class',[80] perhaps in acknowledgement of the fact that there were different meanings of backwardness in places like Madras, Mysore, and Bombay, as we have seen in the previous chapter. The backward classes were numerically very large. In fact, in April 1948, before the debate in the Constituent Assembly on backward classes, Ambedkar had made a speech in Lucknow where he had said that the 'Scheduled Castes and the Backward Classes form the majority of the population of this country'.[81] In that Lucknow speech, Ambedkar had hoped that the Scheduled Castes and backward classes would unite to form a political party, even if the latter did not want to dine with or marry members of the former because of social norms.

Though Marathas and non-Brahmins had enjoyed reservations in the colonial legislatures of Bombay and Madras respectively, this was now discontinued. In other words, political reservations were only meant for Scheduled Castes and Scheduled Tribes, not for those whom Munshi had described as 'Other Backward Classes'. The Constitution gave the President, after consulting the

Governor, the power to specify which castes and tribes would be considered Scheduled Castes and Scheduled Tribes in each state.[82] Ambedkar explained that this was done in order to 'eliminate the necessity of burdening the Constitution with long lists of Scheduled Castes and Scheduled Tribes'.[83] However, V.I. Muniswami Pillai, a Congress Scheduled Caste leader,[84] explained that it was only the 'untouchables' who professed Hinduism who would be considered 'Scheduled Castes'.[85]

The definition of Scheduled Castes and Scheduled Tribes was state specific. For example, in 1956, though 'Bantar' was a Scheduled Caste in Bihar, it was not so in Bombay.[86] What happened if a person belonging to the Bantar caste left Bihar and came to Bombay— would her Scheduled Caste status travel with her? Or what if a Bantar person left Bombay and moved to Bihar—would she be considered a Scheduled Caste in Bihar though she was not one in her state of origin? The Constitution itself provided no answers.

Merit and Efficiency

Some members of the Constituent Assembly opposed reservations in government jobs on the grounds that they would interfere with the efficiency of the services. Lokanath Misra,[87] for example, argued that a quota system in public employment 'puts a premium on backwardness and inefficiency'. Appointments to public jobs, he said, were not a fundamental right but something to be decided on the basis of merit alone.[88] Similarly, Damodar Swarup Seth, a member of the Socialist Party from U.P., said that reserving posts in public services would mean 'the very negation of efficiency and good Government'.[89] He believed that though 'necessary facilities and concessions' should be given to 'backward classes for improving their educational qualifications', people should be appointed to posts in the public services on the basis of 'merit and qualification' alone.[90]

Some argued that by abolishing untouchability, the Constitution had magically wiped out the stigma faced by Scheduled Castes. For instance, in the subcommittee on minorities, Rajkumari Amrit Kaur, health minister and one of the few female members of the assembly,[91] said that Scheduled Castes ceased to exist as a separate category once untouchability was abolished by the Constitution and they became 'legally one with most of the backward and ignorant poor Hindus of this country'.[92] However, just as the abolition of slavery did not bring to an end all the prejudices faced by black people in the US, this argument ignored the fact that the formal abolition of untouchability on the books did not end it overnight in practice.

Sardar Vallabhbhai Patel argued that members of Scheduled Castes should stop harbouring an 'inferiority complex'.[93] He said that if he and H.J. Khandekar, a Scheduled Caste member of the assembly 'were to go outside India, nobody will find out whether he is a Scheduled Caste man or I am a Scheduled Caste man'.[94] This argument perhaps failed to take into account that caste discrimination is based not on a person's readily apparent physical attributes (like the colour of one's skin) but by a person's birth into a social group, the membership of which is reinforced through social norms. Caste discrimination, unlike discrimination based on colour, works in subtle ways.[95] Incidentally, Patel did not have a very high opinion of Khandekar, describing him in private correspondence as an 'undesirable person'.[96]

Some opposed reservations even in public office. Mahavir Tyagi said that elections should be all about the 'capabilities' of candidates and not their caste, and about 'who has served the country in a better way and who can represent the country in a better way'.[97] He lamented that there was 'no provision . . . in this Constitution' for poor and illiterate members of forward castes.[98] Some were worried that Scheduled Castes would be overrepresented in legislative bodies and that they should therefore not have the right to contest general unreserved seats[99]—a suggestion which was rejected by the framers of the Constitution.[100]

Perhaps the most eloquent defence in favour of reservations in the Constituent Assembly was made by H.J. Khandekar. He gave five reasons why Scheduled Castes ought to be given quotas in public employment and political office:

Firstly, he argued that reservations would constitute compensation for centuries of oppression faced by their community. 'The members of the Scheduled Castes have,' he said, 'for thousands of years, suffered cruelties and oppression in various forms at the hands of their brethren belonging to castes other than their own.' 'Now', he continued, 'reservation is being provided for us as a compensation for the atrocities we have suffered'.[101]

Secondly, he hinted that by giving the Scheduled Castes what they wanted, India was avoiding a violent revolution or popular uprising at their hands. 'I do not want to threaten anybody', he said, but if reservations were not provided to them, then 'Harijans will intensify the movements they have launched for their progress . . . though I cannot predict what may happen in the country as a result thereof.' He pointed out that '[m]embers of parties' (he did not specify which parties, but one could surmise that they were possibly communists) were mingling with Scheduled Castes and propagating views among them that 'might go against the interests of this country'. 'I warn you of this situation', he continued, 'and urge you to grant to Harijans whatever facilities they ask for to come to your level.'[102]

Thirdly, Khandekar argued that the absence of merit in Scheduled Caste candidates was the result of centuries of oppression at the hands of forward caste communities. 'You are responsible for our being unfit today', he said. For 'thousands of years', forward castes 'suppressed us to such an extent that neither our minds nor our bodies and nor even our hearts work, nor are we able to march forward'. 'You have reduced us to such a position and then you say that we are not fit and that we have not secured the requisite marks', he added. 'How can we secure them?' he asked.[103]

Fourthly, he pointed out that many Scheduled Caste students lacked 'facilities which other students get and hence they cannot stand in competition with others'.[104]

Fifthly, he said that the selection processes for government jobs were biased because those in charge of selecting candidates for public employment tended to pick students from forward caste communities. '[T]hough the candidates of the Scheduled Castes apply for certain Government posts,' he said, 'they are not selected for the posts because the people who select the candidates do not belong to that community or that section.'[105] The Federal Public Service Commission and Provincial Commissions, he said, 'are not represented by us'.[106]

To this list, Munshi added that reservations in public services gave members of backward classes 'status and an opportunity to serve the country'.[107] Both Patel and Munshi argued that while efficiency in the public services was important, there had to be some concession in favour of backward communities who 'require a little help'.[108] To balance efficiency with reservations, one provision of the Constitution said that while making appointments to services and posts, the 'claims of the members of the Scheduled Castes and the Scheduled Tribes' would be taken into account 'consistently with the maintenance of efficiency of administration'.[109] In a letter Patel later wrote to Ambedkar, he added that including Scheduled Caste candidates in the public services made the administration of those services 'more and more sympathetic' towards the Scheduled Castes.[110]

No Separate Electorates

Following the Poona Pact, Scheduled Castes were not given 'separate electorates' like Muslims under the Government of India Act, 1935. In other words, though seats were reserved for Scheduled Caste candidates standing for elections, the voters who voted in those elections belonged to all castes, and not merely Scheduled Castes.[111] This arrangement—of reserved constituencies in which a general electorate would be allowed to vote—was continued under the Constitution of independent India. K.M. Munshi went out of his way to point out that Scheduled Castes were Hindus and not 'minorities'. '[T]he Harijans are part and parcel of Hindu community,' he said, 'and the safeguards are given to them to protect their rights only till they are completely absorbed in the Hindu Community.'[112]

Ambedkar wanted a kind of veto power to be given to minorities in elections. He suggested that candidates of majority communities should not be able to get elected to office unless they secured 'a minimum number of votes' from 'the minority communities in their constituencies'. This proposal lost by a large majority, with only Ambedkar voting in its favour.[113] One of his colleagues in the Constituent Assembly, K.M. Munshi, thought that Ambedkar was 'Utopian' in his approach towards Scheduled Castes in the assembly.[114] Had the Constitution been left to Ambedkar alone to prepare, thought Munshi, the Indian government would have become 'a totalitarian apparatus run for the benefit of Scheduled Classes in which the majority would be politically reduced to the status of second-class citizens'.[115]

Continuity and Change

In the previous chapters, we saw that the Government of India Act, 1935, spoke only of 'Scheduled Castes' and non-Hindu 'backward tribes', but not of Other Backward Classes. Scheduled castes were those communities who, apart from being backward, suffered from the stigma of untouchability. Non-Hindu backward tribes, on the other hand, did not suffer from untouchability. The only reason they were granted reservations under the 1935 Act was because they were vulnerable to being taken advantage of and needed statutory protection. Their backwardness was the only reason why they were granted reservations. This then begged the question: why should Other Backward Classes (e.g., those who had been identified in 1930 by the Starte Committee in Bombay) not be granted reservations as well? If backwardness was the only criterion for reservations, why should backward tribes be granted reservations and not Other Backward

Classes? Indeed, provinces like Mysore, Madras, and Bombay granted reservations to communities other than Scheduled Castes and backward tribes even prior to Independence. The Constitution therefore recognized the claims of Other Backward Classes in Article 16(4), by permitting the State to reserve seats in government jobs for all backward classes—Scheduled Castes, backward tribes (now known as 'Scheduled Tribes' under the Constitution), and Other Backward Classes.

Out of these three communities—Scheduled Castes, Scheduled Tribes, and Other Backward Classes, one community (i.e., Scheduled Castes) got reservations because of both untouchability and backwardness, while two (i.e., Scheduled Tribes and Other Backward Classes) were given reservations only on account of backwardness. We saw in Chapter 1 that in the 1931 census, some untouchable communities were not counted as 'depressed classes' because they had ceased to be backward. In other words, backwardness was the sine qua non for reservations. This then begs the question: should reservations no longer be provided to any of these communities if their members cease to be backward? The Supreme Court grappled with this question in cases like Nagaraj and Jarnail Singh, which we will see in Chapter 6.

In the Constituent Assembly, Khandekar argued that one of the justifications for providing reservations was to compensate Scheduled Castes for the centuries of oppression they had faced. However, we saw in Chapter 1 that there was a great deal of *inter se* caste prejudice within the depressed classes as well. Census Commissioner Hutton wrote in his report in 1931 that the Mahars in Bombay refused to share lawyers with the Chamars, and both the Mahars and Chamars 'unanimously spurned the Bhangi' caste.[116] Does Khandekar's compensation theory still hold good when many castes that are beneficiaries of reservations were also those that discriminated against other castes lower down in the social order? Also, the compensation theory does not really apply to Scheduled Tribes and Other Backward Classes, which did not suffer the stigma of untouchability.

In Chapter 1, we saw that in the First Round Table Conference in London, Ambedkar had submitted a memorandum in which he had advocated that separate electorates should be granted to the depressed classes. In it, he had suggested that separate electorates for the depressed classes could only be abolished if seats continued to be reserved for them and there was universal adult franchise.[117] The Poona Pact gave the depressed classes only some reserved seats and neither separate electorates nor universal adult franchise. Under the Constitution, Ambedkar was able to secure universal adult franchise, thereby ensuring that all eligible depressed class voters would be able to vote, not only those who held property or were literate as per the Government of India Act, 1935.

The Poona Pact required the government to ensure 'fair representation' of depressed class candidates in government jobs. While not saying anything expressly about public services, Article 298 of the Government of India Act, 1935, said that the colonial government had a 'special responsibility' of ensuring that the 'legitimate interests of minorities' would be safeguarded. Article 16(4) of the Constitution now made it very clear that the State would be able to reserve seats for backward classes in government jobs, though the Constitution uses the term 'adequate representation' instead of 'fair representation' under the Poona Pact.

In the Constitution, though Ambedkar was not able to secure cabinet reservation, which had been his request ever since the First Round Table Conference, he was able to ensure that seats would now be reserved for Scheduled Castes and Scheduled Tribes in legislatures on the basis of their population. In this regard, the Constitution went beyond the Poona Pact. Though depressed classes had 18 per cent reservation of the 'general' seats under the Poona Pact, the proportion of their seats fell woefully short of their numbers in the population when one looked at the total seats on offer. For instance, the Poona Pact reserved some 148 seats for the depressed classes in the provincial legislatures, amounting to around 9 per cent of their strength. This was lower than the proportion of depressed classes in the population—in 1931, it was estimated that they constituted 14 per cent of India's population. Now, the Constitution provided that seats would be reserved for them on the basis of their population.

In 1934, though 25 per cent of the government jobs were reserved for Muslims, the colonial government did not fix any such quota for the depressed classes because it felt that their educational levels were low. Instead, it advocated that the government should ensure 'fair representation' for the depressed classes in public services. The Constitution follows this approach. Article 16(4) of the Constitution does not say that the number of seats reserved for backward classes in government jobs will be commensurate with the population of these communities. It speaks only of 'adequate' representation for the backward classes in the public services, not 'proportional' representation. This is despite the fact that the number of seats reserved for Scheduled Castes and Scheduled Tribes in legislatures is tied to their population. Interestingly, no seats are reserved for these communities in the Rajya Sabha, though there was reservation for Scheduled Castes in the Council of State under the Government of India Act, 1935.

The Poona Pact had not provided any sunset clause for political reservations. It had said that the system of reservations would continue until it was mutually agreed that it should cease. The Constitution, on the other hand, imposed a limit of ten years on political reservations (though no such limit was imposed for reservations in government jobs). However, in practice, political reservations have been extended from decade to decade, such that the Poona Pact has been followed in practice.

Interestingly, members of the Constituent Assembly were not directly elected by the people. They were elected by the provincial legislatures whose members,[118] in turn, had been elected by only about 27 per cent of the adult population of India. In other words, the Constitution of independent India was drafted by the indirectly elected representatives of only 27 per cent of the adult population,

most of whom owned property or were educated. At its opening
session in December 1946, among 296 members, the Constituent
Assembly had 33 Scheduled Caste members and 5 backward tribe
members, together constituting 12.8 per cent of the strength of the
house.[119]

4

Nehru Dislikes the Word 'Dalit'

In the early years of the republic, several questions concerning quotas cropped up. For instance, though the Constitution only spoke of reservations in public employment and legislatures, was the government allowed to reserve seats in educational institutions on the basis of caste? Who exactly were the 'Other Backward Classes'? Scheduled Castes and Scheduled Tribes could be identified with relative ease,[1] on the basis of untouchability and tribal seclusion respectively. However, who were the others? Would a Scheduled Caste person lose her caste if she converted to Christianity? Further, if an entire caste was recognized as 'backward', would well-off families who were members of those castes also be considered backward?

In this chapter, we will see how the newly independent Indian nation attempted to answer these questions. In 1951, the Supreme Court held that caste-based reservations in educational institutions were unconstitutional, prompting a constitutional amendment. In 1955, the Kaka Kalelkar Commission tried to define the term 'Other Backward Classes' but came up with criteria that were so broad-brushed as to be practically useless. For instance, the commission said that fortune-tellers and superstitious people were backward.

In a country rife with superstition, this meant anyone could be backward, even President Rajendra Prasad who wanted to change the date of India's first Republic Day because 26 January was not astrologically auspicious. We will also see in this chapter that though Prime Minister Nehru tried sincerely to improve the condition of the backward classes, he was not a vocal proponent of quotas and reservations which, he believed, prevented marginalized communities from pulling themselves up by their own bootstraps.

Educational Institutions

The Communal G.O.s

The Constitution only provided that there would be two kinds of reservations: in public employment and legislative bodies. It said nothing about reservations in educational institutions. In an early case decided in April 1951, *State of Madras* v. *Champakam Dorairajan*,[2] the Supreme Court held that caste-based reservations in colleges were unconstitutional. This eventually led to the first amendment to the Constitution.

In the academic year 1949–50, the State of Madras had only four medical colleges and four engineering institutions, with 725 total seats available for students.[3] As we have seen in Chapter 2, as a result of the non-Brahmin movement in Madras, since the 1920s, the government of Madras had issued government orders[4] or 'G.O.s', which were called 'Communal G.O.s' because they apportioned seats in educational institutions and government jobs on the basis of caste or community. One such Communal G.O. said that every 14 seats in colleges in Madras would be divided among the following groups: non-Brahmins (6), backward Hindus (2), Brahmins (2), Harijans (2), Anglo-Indians and Indian Christians (1), and Muslims (1).[5] Even groups that were not backward were entitled to a certain proportion of seats under this arrangement.

After the Constitution sprang to life, two students, Champakam Dorairajan and Srinivasan, challenged this Communal G.O. on the grounds that it violated Article 29(2) of the Constitution. That provision said that no Indian citizen could be denied admission into any educational institution maintained by the government (or receiving government funding) only on the basis of caste. Srinivasan, a Brahmin who wanted to be an engineer, would have got admission into one of the four colleges in Madras had it not been for the Communal G.O.

The Supreme Court said that a student could not complain if he was denied admission because he lacked the 'requisite academic qualifications'. However, if 'he has the academic qualifications but is refused admission only on grounds of religion, race, caste, language or any of them, then there is a clear breach of his fundamental right'.[6] 'Take the case of the petitioner Srinivasan', said the court. The State of Madras had not disputed the fact that he had obtained a much higher score than many non-Brahmin students who had secured admission in state engineering colleges. 'What is the reason for this denial of admission', asked the court, 'except that he is a Brahmin and not a non-Brahmin.'[7] In other words, Srinivasan was denied admission 'for no fault of his except that he is a Brahmin and not a member of the aforesaid communities'.[8] This, said the court, was discrimination based only on caste, which violated Article 29(2) of the Constitution.

In arriving at its conclusion, the Supreme Court relied on the fact that there was no provision akin to Article 16(4) for reservations in educational institutions. Article 16(1) of the Constitution said that all Indian citizens would have equality of opportunity in getting employment from the government. However, Article 16(4) said that the government would nonetheless be entitled to reserve jobs for any backward class of citizens it considered to be inadequately represented in the services. However, no such provision of the Constitution existed for reservations in educational institutions. This omission, said the court, was significant.[9]

The Advocate General of the State of Madras pointed out to the court that Article 46 of the Constitution, a directive principle of state policy, called upon the government to promote the educational interests of 'the weaker sections of the people', particularly the Scheduled Castes and Scheduled Tribes. However, the Supreme Court held that the directive principles could not override the fundamental rights under the Constitution, and Article 29(2), one such fundamental right, prevailed over Article 46.[10]

On the same day that the Champakam Dorairajan case was decided, the Supreme Court also delivered judgement in *B. Venkataramana* v. *State of Madras*,[11] in which it struck down a Communal G.O. which applied to government employment. The petitioner, Venkataramana, had applied for a job as a District Munsif, a subordinate judge in Madras. Though there were 83 such jobs on offer, by virtue of a Communal G.O., quotas were provided for the following groups: Harijans (19), Muslims (5), Christians (6), backward Hindus (10), non-Brahmin Hindus (32), and Brahmins (11).[12]

The Supreme Court found that though Article 16(4) allowed the government to reserve seats for backward classes, many of the communities for whom seats were reserved under the Communal G.O. were not backward at all, e.g., Brahmins or non-Brahmin Hindus.[13] The court held that Venkataramana would have secured a job as a District Munsif had it not been for his caste—he may have performed better than non-backward candidates like Christians or non-Brahmins.[14] On these grounds, the court struck down the Communal G.O.

'We Cannot Make a Fool a Wise Man'

On the day that the Supreme Court handed down these two decisions, 9 April 1951, the Chief Minister of Madras, P.S. Kumaraswami Raja, wrote a letter to Prime Minister Nehru asking him to amend the Constitution. Keeping the Communal G.O.s alive, he wrote, was 'in the interests of South India'.[15] Nehru disagreed. He believed that reservations were only meant 'for really backward classes of citizens', while the Communal G.O.s reserved seats for everyone.[16] Raja and several ministers from Madras met Nehru on 27 April to discuss the Communal G.O.s[17] and probably once again requested a constitutional amendment to keep the orders alive, but to no avail.

However, the Supreme Court's judgement in the Champakam Dorairajan case created problems for the government.[18] The court had said that caste-based reservations in educational institutions were altogether prohibited under the Constitution, whether they were meant for backward classes or not.[19] An amendment to the Constitution was therefore necessary to ensure that, just as seats could be reserved for backward classes in government jobs, quotas for marginalized communities could be put into place in colleges as well.

Therefore, in May 1951, a month after the Supreme Court's judgement, Nehru introduced a bill in Parliament to amend the Constitution for the very first time. Parliament, at that moment, was in a state of limbo. Since the Constitution had come into force in January 1950, the Constituent Assembly had ceased to function. The first general elections had not yet been held (they would only take place between December 1951 and February 1952).[20] There was, thus, no Constituent Assembly and no elected Lok Sabha. There was no upper house of Parliament either—the Rajya Sabha had not yet come into existence.

It was in this provisional Parliament that Nehru introduced the first amendment to the Constitution. The amendment also introduced several exceptions to the right to freedom of speech and expression, and most of the debates in Parliament were consumed by that subject.[21] However, while explaining the clause of the amendment that dealt with reservations in educational institutions, Nehru made it clear that the government's objective was not to revive Madras's Communal G.O.s.[22] In other words, the Constitution was not being amended to ensure that all communities (including well-off and forward castes) would get quotas. Reservations in colleges were only meant for backward classes. Nehru explained that though the principle in Article 29(2) of the Constitution continued to hold good (i.e., that Indian citizens should not be discriminated against in admissions to government educational institutions on the basis of caste), 'individual or group inequality' could not be brought about while protecting individual freedom.[23]

Ambedkar said that the Supreme Court's judgements in the Champakam Dorairajan and Venkataramana cases were the reason why the amendment was being introduced.[24] He said that these cases had been decided in an 'utterly unsatisfactory' manner.[25] The Supreme Court had, in these cases, said that caste-based reservations were forbidden. Ambedkar argued that this meant that reservations for backward classes, 'which are nothing else but a collection of certain castes', were accordingly barred.[26]

The first amendment inserted a new provision, Article 15(4), into the Constitution which said that the government had the power to make a 'special provision'[27] for the 'advancement of any socially and educationally backward classes of citizens or for the Scheduled Castes and the Scheduled Tribes'. This was meant to be a qualification to the general principle contained in Articles 15(1) and 29(2) of the Constitution, that the government would not be able to discriminate amongst its citizens on the grounds of caste. Unlike Article 16(4), which spoke only of backwardness generally, Article 15(4) said that these backward classes had to be 'socially and educationally' backward.

Many members of the provisional Parliament argued that the word 'economically' should also be inserted into the amendment.[28] In other words, classes that were 'socially and educationally' backward, but economically advanced, should not get the benefit of reservations, they suggested.[29] For example, M.A. Ayyangar, who later held the position of Speaker of the Lok Sabha,[30] argued that though Nattukkottai Chettiars in south India were often not educated in English, they were 'the richest of the lot', owning all the 'business houses and factories' like the 'Marwari community in the north'.[31] He was concerned that even they might be considered 'socially and educationally' backward, despite their financial status, and obtain reservations in colleges. Ramalingam Chettiar argued that members of the 'Vaisya caste' may be rich but 'educationally very backward' and few of them would have secured government jobs. Would they too be considered backward, he asked.[32] Some argued that it was not exactly clear who the backward classes were,[33] and that state governments would abuse educational reservations with political objectives in mind.[34]

However, in response to these criticisms, Nehru explained that the words 'socially and educationally backward' had been borrowed from Article 340 of the Constitution, which gave the President the power to appoint a Commission to investigate the conditions of socially and educationally backward classes.[35] Since those words already existed in the Constitution, they were only repeated here. He also added that social backwardness included economic backwardness. 'Therefore, I felt that "socially and educationally" really cover the ground', he said.[36] '[W]e cannot make a fool a wise-man or make a wise-man a fool', he added, but by reserving seats in educational institutions, 'we do wish to give the same opportunities to everyone'.[37]

Others spoke in favour of the amendment as well. For instance, M. Shankaraiya[38] from Mysore argued that the amendment to Article 15 furthered the objective of Article 16(4)—without reserving seats in educational institutions for backward classes, it would be impossible for those communities to get government jobs.[39]

The bill was passed on 2 June 1951 by an overwhelming majority—only 20 out of 228 members in Parliament voted against it.[40]

Who Is Backward?

Barbers, Washermen and Fortune Tellers

The Constitution now gave the government the power to reserve seats for 'backward classes' in government jobs and educational institutions. The term 'backward classes' meant Scheduled Castes, Scheduled Tribes, and 'Other Backward Classes'. In the Constituent Assembly, Munshi had suggested that 'Other Backward Classes' meant 'economically, educationally and socially backward' communities. However, the provisional Parliament had now left out the word 'economically' from the first amendment to the Constitution and said that reservations could only be given to 'socially and educationally' backward communities. Ambedkar, we have seen, said that backward classes were a collection of castes. All this gave rise to a question: who exactly were these 'Other Backward Classes'? Which castes or communities would be considered backward apart from Scheduled Castes and Scheduled Tribes?

'There is no definition in the Constitution', said President Rajendra Prasad in a letter to Home Minister K.N. Katju in January 1953, 'as to who should be treated as socially and educationally backward classes'.[41] A few days later,[42] Prasad appointed a commission headed by Rajya Sabha member and Gandhian[43] Kaka Kalelkar, the Backward Classes Commission, to figure out who the Other Backward Classes were. 'What are these backward classes?' Nehru asked the commission. 'Is there an economic yardstick to measure backwardness?' he added, because '[i]f that is so, perhaps 90 per cent of India's population will qualify as backward classes. Perhaps the number may be more'.[44]

The Kalelkar Commission was not able to clearly and precisely define who the Other Backward Classes were. It was less difficult to point out who Scheduled Castes and Scheduled Tribes were. Scheduled Castes were those who had suffered from the stigma of untouchability. Scheduled Tribes were primitive tribes that had not been assimilated into mainstream society. But it was far harder to come up with a universal rule for identifying the Other Backward Classes. The Kalelkar commission decided that backward classes were 'nothing but castes'. However, in its forwarding letter to the President, the commission said that investigating backwardness on the basis of caste had given rise to 'caste-consciousness, caste loyalties and caste aspirations', and such group identities were 'repugnant to the spirit of democracy'.[45]

The Kalelkar Commission therefore came up with a 'rough list' of non-caste-based criteria that could be used to identify backwardness. For instance, it said that women, the residents of rural areas, and those 'driven to the necessity of working with their own hands' or who 'labour[ed] under the sun and in open air' were backward.[46] Landless labourers, unskilled workers, those without 'sufficient, or any capital', clerks or menial servants were also backward.[47] Those whose parents were poor and uneducated, 'lacking ambition and having no vision', were backward.[48] Anyone who was illiterate, lacking resources, lived in 'inaccessible and backward areas', or who believed in 'magic, superstition and fate', or who did not have the 'capacity to understand modern times' was backward.[49]

Economic criteria or literacy were not sufficient for determining backwardness, said the Commission.[50] 'Brahman scholars of olden times', it said, 'though learned in the *Vedas* and *Vedangas* were unable to sign a document.' The Commission found 'many illiterate Brahmans in Himachal Pradesh, in the hilly areas of Uttar Pradesh, and in Bankura district of West Bengal' who were still 'occupying socially a top place in the caste hierarchy'.[51]

Those who had social status, influence, and wealth or the means to educate themselves were not backward. Neither were those who occupied positions of power and authority either in government service or in trade, commerce, and industry, or who employed large numbers of people.[52] On the other hand, cattle and sheep breeders, petty traders, weavers, artisans, barbers, beggars, washermen, those who lived in unsanitary surroundings, even fortune-tellers, would typically be considered backward, said the Commission.[53]

Dominant communities among backward classes, however, were not to be given reservations. For instance, in rural areas, those who owned 'large tracts of land', had 'money enough to lend'; those who had traditionally wielded governmental power, or who had the 'brains to create quarrels and factions amongst the people', were not among the backward, said the Commission. In north India, the 'AJGAR' communities (named after a boa constrictor that 'quietly swallows and leisurely digests many animals') or 'Ahir, Jat, Gujjar and Rajput' were not backward, said the Commission.[54] In Maharashtra, Marathas and Prabhus were not backward either, it found.[55] However, it acknowledged that even advanced Hindu communities had some 'extremely poor and handicapped families' that needed help.[56]

Some Muslims, not all, said the commission, were backward as well. Though Islam did not recognize castes, a 'sense of high and low' had gradually entered Muslim society in India and there were a number of communities who were 'suffering from social inferiority and consequent educational backwardness'.[57] Thus, the 'Pinjaras or carders, the Momins or the weaving communities, Kassais or butchers, Bhistis or water-carriers, Fakirs or beggars, Labbes, Moplahs and many others were found to be backward'.[58]

Similarly, many Christian converts in India, said the Commission, had not abandoned Hindu customs. For instance, Christians in Goa, it said, 'still consult caste and "gotra" in the minutest details when arranging marriages amongst themselves'.[59] Some south Indian Scheduled Caste Christian converts were 'not allowed to pray together with upper class Christians' and were 'forced to have a separate cemetery for their dead'.[60]

Taking into account all these factors, the Kalelkar Commission came up with four criteria for determining backwardness. A community would be considered backward if: (i) it occupied a '[l]ow social position in the traditional caste hierarchy of Hindu society'; (ii) the majority of its members were not educated; (iii) it had inadequate or no representation in government service; (iv) it was inadequately represented in trade, commerce, and industry.[61] It also suggested that when a member of a Scheduled Caste or Scheduled Tribe migrated from his state to another state where he was not on the list of Scheduled Castes and tribes, he could be considered a member of the Other Backward Classes because 'backwardness persists' upon migration.[62]

Nehru, Prasad, and Astrology

These criteria were incredibly broad and imprecise. Fortune tellers and even people who believed in superstition or fate were considered backward. Applying these criteria, perhaps Rajendra Prasad, an upper-caste Hindu and the first president of independent India, could have fallen within this definition. In September 1949, Prasad wrote to Nehru and asked him whether the date for India's first republic day, 26 January, could be changed, because it was not astrologically auspicious. He believed that even 15 August 1947, the date of India's independence from colonial rule, was considered by astrologers to be an inauspicious day; '[b]ut we didn't pay any heed to their warnings', he said. 'We may have no faith in astrology and may be right in considering it to be [a] remnant of superstition', he wrote, but as representatives of millions who believe in such things, he felt that there was no harm in finding out 'the most auspicious day and time for the inauguration of the new Constitution'.[63]

Nehru, on the other hand, wrote a stinging letter to Prasad in which he said: 'I am afraid I have no faith in astrology and certainly I should not like to fix up national programmes in accordance with the dictates of astrologers.' He said that changing the date would look very bad and result in a 'bitter controversy'. He doubted if millions of Indians believed in astrology, but if they did, he felt it was his duty to either 'combat this delusion' or to 'allow others, who believe in astrology, to take charge of the destiny of the nation'.[64]

Prasad was disappointed with the Kalelkar Commission's work. In a note he wrote in 1956, he said that its report was 'so discursive that hardly any criterion can be found' for scientifically determining how to identify backward classes.[65] He also felt that it was a mistake to identify entire castes as backward because even privileged members in those castes would then get benefits.

On the other hand, it was relatively easier to define who the Scheduled Castes and Scheduled Tribes were. Between 1950 and

1951,[66] the President issued lists identifying its members—lists that were subsequently modified from time to time.[67] These lists were prepared on the basis of lists furnished by the state governments to the President.[68] In 1965, the Lokur committee recommended the deletion of 171 Scheduled Castes and 131 Scheduled Tribes from these lists.[69] It maintained that Scheduled Castes were those who had suffered 'extreme social, educational and economic backwardness' on account of 'the traditional custom of untouchability'.[70]

Scheduled Tribes could be identified on the basis of their 'primitive traits, distinctive culture, geographical isolation, shyness of contact with the community at large and backwardness'.[71] However, tribes that had been 'by and large mixed up with the general population' were not eligible to be on the list.[72] Less than a third of the Scheduled Tribes lived in the so-called 'scheduled areas' under the Constitution—regions to which India's laws applied with such modifications as the Governors deemed fit.[73] According to the 1951 census, Scheduled Tribes constituted about 5.3 per cent of the population.[74] They were mostly concentrated in Madhya Pradesh, Bihar, Orissa, Gujarat, Rajasthan, Assam, Maharashtra, West Bengal, and Andhra Pradesh.[75]

So, for instance, where the members of a tribe numbered less than 100 in a state, especially when they were 'spread over several districts' and not all located in one place, it was 'safely assumed', said the Lokur committee, that they had assimilated themselves into mainstream Indian society.[76] For example, the Konda Reddi tribe had only 8 members in Madras state, of whom 3 were in Madras city while the rest were scattered over two districts. Such tribes, said the committee, should not be on the list of Scheduled Tribes.[77] Similarly, if the members of a caste in a state were less than 10, the committee assumed that such castes would probably not suffer any disabilities arising out of untouchability and would not be eligible for protection as Scheduled Castes.[78]

Caps on Quotas

The Kalelkar Commission recommended a cap on quotas in government jobs. At the time that the report was written, Scheduled Castes had around 12 per cent to 16 per cent while Scheduled Tribes around 5 per cent reservations in jobs with the Central government.[79] No seats in Central government jobs[80] were reserved for Other Backward Classes. The Kalelkar Commission recommended quotas for Other Backward Classes in government jobs and also said that reservations for all communities should not exceed 49 per cent in total.[81]

However, the Commission recommended up to 70 per cent reservations in 'higher technical institutes of learning' for all reserved communities. Justifying this recommendation, Kalelkar wrote that his intent was not to 'turn the upper classes into a new under-privileged class' but to achieve equality of opportunity with 'break-neck speed'. 'It is only when the traditionally more promising sections of society are kept out of higher learning', he added, 'that those in authority and power will shed their traditional lethargy' and set up more educational institutions so that all students will have a seat.[82] Of course, this idea was contrary to Ambedkar's argument in the Constituent Assembly that reservations are an exception to the principle of equality of opportunity and the exception should not swallow the rule. However, the Kalelkar committee recommended that reservations must be withdrawn after some time.[83]

Nehru and Reservations

'I Do Not Like This Name At All'

Though Prime Minister Nehru was in favour of improving the social and economic condition of backward classes in India, he seemed to be against reservations. He felt that there was no point in reserving seats for backward classes in government jobs at the cost of efficiency. For instance, at the chief minister's conference in 1955, Nehru pointed out that though the 'brightest person in the Indian Foreign Service' at that time was a member of the Scheduled Castes, he was an exception. By and large, it was difficult to find qualified Scheduled Caste candidates for the Indian Foreign Service. 'I cannot send a man abroad who is completely useless to me', he said.[84] In 1957, he wrote to Sankar Saran and said that though Harijans had started getting employed in government jobs, he did not 'fancy their constantly asking for reservations' as this 'means an attempt at lowering standards'. 'It is of great importance that we maintain our standards,' he added, 'or else we shall remain a second-rate nation.'[85]

In 1958, Nehru addressed the workers of the Bharat Dalit Sewak Sangh and said that he was not pleased with what they had decided to call themselves.[86] 'I do not like this name at all', he said, for '[n]obody must ever call himself "dalit"—downtrodden.' He believed that such names had the tendency of stigmatizing individuals and affecting their way of thinking.[87] Nehru said that reservations in politics were not a good thing because they tended to weaken backward classes. 'They become incapable of standing on their own feet' because of reservations, he said.[88] Though he felt that everyone needed to get employed, that did not mean 'making reservations and keeping 50 posts here or there' apart for backward classes.[89] At a speech in Rajasthan that year, Nehru added that nobody could 'progress on the basis of one's caste' and that '[w]e should discourage this practice'. 'One progresses by one's merit alone', he added.[90]

In a letter to M.R. Krishna[91] in December 1958, Nehru wrote that he was 'not generally in favour of reserved seats'.[92] Though he certainly wanted the condition of Scheduled Castes in India to improve, he was of the view that reserving seats 'does not tend to do that, but perpetuates . . . division'. It was necessary in the short term, but bad in the long run, he felt. Though he could not say how long reservations were necessary in India, he wanted people to know that reservations were 'not a good thing from the point of view of raising certain social classes'. He hoped that India would focus more on the 'positive aspects of removing inequalities' than on 'negative' matters like 'reserved seats'.[93]

By March 1950, six Scheduled Caste candidates were selected for the Indian Administrative Service (IAS).[94] By 1959, around 41 per cent of the 'total number of the seats available in the Services' were reserved for Scheduled Castes, Scheduled Tribes, and Other Backward Classes.[95] However, demands were being made that since they represented 80 per cent of India's population, they should get more posts.[96] In 1965, the Lokur committee recorded the 'extraordinary phenomenon . . . of castes and communities solemnly setting forth their desire to be considered backward and included in the Schedules for special treatment'.[97] Initially, it had been stigmatic for communities to be included in these lists. Now, many wanted to be considered backward.

In 1959, Nehru was alarmed by how far the Mysore government had taken the principle of reservations. In that state, virtually every community barring Brahmins and Mudaliars had been included in the list of backward classes. On 15 August 1959, Nehru wrote to Chief Minister B.D. Jatti and said that 'this approach of stratification and reservation for every odd group does not appeal to me at all'. 'I think this is bound to perpetuate divisions', he added, 'and lower standards all round.' 'How is any Government to be carried on like this, is not clear to me', he concluded.[98] That same day, he also wrote to Home Minister G.B. Pant about how he was 'indeed alarmed at the way reservations for appointments in Government Services have been given to a tremendous number of castes and groups'. 'This is a very bad tendency and must lead to deterioration in Government work and in public life generally', he reiterated.[99]

In 1960, Nehru turned down a suggestion that Scheduled Caste and Scheduled Tribe candidates be permitted to contribute less money to the Congress party than what others had to contribute. He said that there were several members who were not Scheduled Castes or Scheduled Tribes but were 'economically even worse off'. If the

Congress could not make an exception for them then it could not do so for Scheduled Castes and Scheduled Tribes either.[100]

The Ford Foundation's Community Hall

However, Nehru's aversion to reservations did not mean that he had no concern for the backward classes. In 1957, he was absolutely livid when he learned that a community hall in Delhi, which had been built by the Ford Foundation as a memorial to Mahatma Gandhi[101] 'for the Harijans there' was being, 'in effect', 'monopolized by middle-class folk' who had converted it into a 'club for their own use', complete with a badminton court inside.[102] 'I do not want excuses or whitewashing statements', he wrote in a sharp note to his principal Private Secretary, K. Ram, seeking an immediate solution to the problem, 'I want a job done, not explanations.'[103]

When he visited a colony for sweepers in Delhi in 1958, he was 'greatly distressed' by what he saw there. 'Human beings certainly should not live in this way', he wrote to a government official. He asked for suggestions on how the government could 'introduce a little sanitation' there. He was also 'particularly interested in the large number of children there'. 'Could they have a decent open playground?' he asked, adding that he hoped that a good school could be started there for them.[104]

Some tribes in British India were designated as 'criminal tribes'. Their members were presumed to be criminals and they were subjected to very harsh regulations. For instance, sweepers belonging to the 'Dom' tribe in parts of Bihar had to live virtually like prisoners.[105] They had to visit the police station four times each night in order to report their whereabouts. Failure to do so resulted in brutal punishment at the hands of the police. When they converted to Christianity, however, all these disabilities ceased. According to A.V. Thakkar, a social reformer who was fondly called 'Thakkar Bapa',[106] this indirectly gave Doms and other criminal tribes incentives to convert to another religion.[107]

When a law was passed in 1952 to abolish this system, Nehru wrote, in his letter to the chief ministers, that the colonial-era law, which designated entire tribes as criminals was 'a blot on our administration' and that its repeal had given him 'much pleasure'.[108]

Nehru was also particularly concerned about tribes in the northeast, in regions that shared an international border with China and East Pakistan. He admired how the Russians, after the Soviet Revolution, 'deliberately encouraged every tribal language and thus gained the goodwill of the tribes'.[109] He wanted to adopt a similar approach and tried to ensure that tribes there did not feel as though they were 'under any foreign domination'.[110]

Religious Conversions

Over the years, Nehru was asked several times about what would happen if a member of the Scheduled Castes converted to another religion—would he lose his constitutional status? For example, if a Hindu from a Scheduled Caste in Bombay converted to Christianity, would he no longer be able to contest elections in a reserved seat? The answer Nehru gave was that conversion to another religion would only result in the inability of the convert to contest a reserved seat in elections. It would not affect the ability of the convert to get a reserved seat in a government job or an educational institution. Though converts might lose their caste, Nehru wanted them, and all the backward classes, to get all the other benefits of the Scheduled Castes. He believed that the slight advantage that Scheduled Castes had over Other Backward Classes would eventually be wiped out since reservations in elections were only going to be around for the limited period of ten years. He also thought that many backward classes were as backward as (and sometimes even more backward than) Scheduled Castes.[111]

In December 1950, Nehru made this clear in one of the letters he frequently wrote to all the chief ministers in the country. In it, he said that the order made by the President under the Constitution

'declaring certain castes and tribes as Scheduled Castes and Tribes'
gave them only 'electoral privileges'. 'It does not mean', he continued,
'that other Backward Classes, whatever religion they may profess,
should not be given all necessary State aid and facilities, apart from
elections.' 'To withdraw these facilities from Christians belonging to
backward communities', he added, 'would be to go against the spirit
of the Constitution.'[112]

In October 1951, Giani Kartar Singh, a Sikh leader, wrote to
Nehru and said that he would refuse to contest India's first general
elections as a Congress candidate unless, among other things, Sikh
Scheduled Castes were given the same rights as Hindu Scheduled
Castes.[113] Nehru's response was that while Sikh Scheduled Castes
would not have a right to contest elections from reserved seats,
educational and other facilities would be extended to all backward
classes, whether they were Hindus, Sikhs, or Christians.[114] Until
1956,[115] only four castes among Sikhs were recognized as Scheduled
Castes—Kabirpanthis, Mazhabis, Ramdasis, and Sikligars.[116]

In October 1956, Ambedkar and his wife, along with
thousands of Scheduled Caste followers, converted to Buddhism.[117]
Ambedkar died a few months later, in December 1956.[118] The
question which then arose was whether Ambedkar's followers,[119]
Scheduled Caste Hindus who had converted to Buddhism, would
be entitled to their constitutional benefits. The formal answer, at
least until 1990,[120] was that they would not. Thus, in July 1957,
Nehru asked his principal private secretary to write to the Maha
Bodhi Society and inform them that the 'privileges laid down in
the Constitution for Scheduled Castes' could not be granted 'to
those who have ceased to be members of the Scheduled Castes'.
However, Scheduled Caste converts to Buddhism would be
'entitled to the other help which is given on economic grounds
to the Backward Classes'.[121] Nehru also felt that since reservations
in legislatures were going to come to an end soon (as political
reservations were confined to ten years), this would not make
much of a difference to converts.[122]

In 1958, Nehru wrote to U.N. Dhebar, President of the Indian National Congress,[123] that Harijans who had converted to Christianity would be treated like those who had not 'except in the matter of representation in the Legislatures'.[124] That year, he wrote to Thomas Pothacamury, Archbishop of Bangalore,[125] that Hindu Scheduled Castes who had converted to Christianity could no longer be considered Scheduled Castes because there was no such thing as 'Scheduled Caste Christians'. 'I have been under the impression', he said, 'that Christianity has fortunately kept itself away from these caste distinctions.'[126]

In 1950, the Central government accepted the views of an overwhelming majority[127] of India's states and laid down that Hindu Scheduled Castes who converted to other religions would lose their status as such.[128] Eventually, from 1956 and 1990 onwards, the government took the view that a person continued to be a member of his Scheduled Caste upon conversion to Sikhism or Buddhism respectively.[129] However, a Scheduled Caste person who converts to Islam or Christianity usually loses her constitutional privileges, a topic which we will explore in Chapter 7. A complicated jurisprudence has now emerged, as we shall see in that chapter, on what happens to a person's caste when she converts or reconverts to a religion.

However, the no-conversion rule was not meant to apply to Scheduled Tribes, who were supposed to be able to convert to any religion without loss of their constitutional protections. This is because many Scheduled Tribes were originally not Hindus. If conversion resulted in loss of tribal status, it would mean that even those tribals who converted to Hinduism would cease to be Scheduled Tribes. In fact, many tribal religious practices were influenced by Hinduism, and the Bhils called themselves Hindus.[130] To encourage tribals to convert to Hinduism, India's administration decided in 1950 that a person does not lose his Scheduled Tribe status upon conversion to another religion.[131]

In fact, in 1949, the Central government had asked the state governments for their opinion on whether 'a person not professing the tribal religion should be treated as a member of a Scheduled Tribe'.[132] There was a difference of opinion among the various provinces on this question. The governments of Assam, Hyderabad, Madhya Bharat, Madras, Mysore, East Punjab, Saurashtra, and West Bengal opined that religious conversion should make no difference to a person's Scheduled Tribe status. On the other hand, the governments of Bombay, CP and Berar, United Provinces, and Orissa had suggested otherwise. Eventually, the law ministry of the Central government decided to 'accept the view of the majority and provide that a member of a Scheduled Tribe shall continue to be a member of that tribe even if he does not observe the tribal religion'.[133]

The primary debate on this point was over whether conversion to another religion resulted in loss of membership of the tribe and abandonment of tribal customs. The government of Madhya Bharat had written to the Central government in January 1950 that a person who no longer professes the tribal religion but who 'is a member of the Tribe' should continue to be a member of his/her Scheduled Tribe.[134] Likewise, the Mysore government had recommended that tribal converts who continued to 'carry on the activities' of the tribe they were born in should be considered Scheduled Tribes.[135] As one bureaucrat in the law ministry of the Central government noted in March 1950, most cases of tribal conversion to Christianity involved only 'formal rather than real' conversion, and did not 'affect the allegiance of the convert to the tribal laws and customs'.[136] On the other hand, the government of the United Provinces had opined that when a tribal converts to another religion, he ceases to belong to his tribe.[137] In 2004, the Supreme Court eventually laid down a test (to determine whether religious conversion results in loss of Scheduled Tribe status) that was consistent with these views, as we will see in Chapter 7.

Interestingly, during the freedom struggle, the fear that untouchables would convert to other religions like Christianity or Islam in order to escape untouchability was a recurrent theme in speeches Indian leaders delivered towards social reform. For instance, in 1927, Vallabhbhai Patel told the farmers in Chalora village that '[t]hese untouchables embrace Islam or Christianity when they are maltreated by you and then when they become Christians, you kow-tow to them.' He added: 'When that Hindu goes out of Hinduism, you consider him your equal. But then he becomes your opponent.'[138] In a letter he wrote to Ambedkar in 1935, Patel said that asking Scheduled Castes to convert to another religion to escape untouchability was like a surgeon chopping off a patient's head in order to cure his stomach disease.[139] After the Constitution came into being, Scheduled Castes who converted to these religions usually lost their privileges.

5

Enter Mandal and Sawhney

The law of caste-based reservations started evolving with bewildering complexity in subsequent decades. A cluster of questions occupied the docket in the cases that came before the Supreme Court. For instance, the court was often asked the age-old question: how will the 'Other Backward Classes' really be identified? Can entire castes be considered backward? What about well-off families in castes that are backward—would they get to benefit from reservations as well? How far could quotas go—would Ambedkar's vision that reservations were only for a minority of seats survive vote-bank politics? In the colonial period, though the word 'class' was used in terms like 'depressed classes' and 'backward classes', 'class' was really a euphemism for caste. However, in independent India, would reservations be permissible on the basis of caste? This chapter examines the intense debates that took place among the judges of the Supreme Court—judges like Justice Gajendragadkar, Justice Subba Rao, and Justice Chinnappa Reddy—as the court attempted to answer these questions.

The 50 Per Cent Rule Is Born

In January 1960, the State of Mysore in south India set up a committee headed by a member of the legislative assembly, Dr R.

Nagan Gowda, to specify the criteria to decide who the 'socially and educationally backward classes' were.[1] The committee opined that social backwardness would be defined on the basis of caste or community.[2] For instance, if a caste was considered to have a generally low status in society, it was identified as backward.[3] For determining 'educational backwardness', the committee figured out that in 1959–60, there were 6.9 students for every 1,000 people in Mysore in the last three classes in high schools in the state. If a caste or community had a lower average than this, then it was considered educationally backward.[4]

For instance, the Voddar caste in Mysore had only 1 such student for every 1,000 people in the state—way below the state average. They were obviously educationally backward. By contrast, Brahmins had 38.8 such students for every 1,000 people in Mysore—much higher than the state average.[5] For this purpose, it did not matter how much lower than the state average a community's literacy levels were. For example, though Muslims had 5 students for every 1,000 people in the state, not substantially lower than the state average, they were still considered to be backward. The Nagan Gowda committee also grouped Other Backward Classes into two categories—backward and more backward. Those who had literacy levels that were less than 50 per cent of the state average were considered 'more backward'.[6]

The Nagan Gowda committee submitted its report in 1961. The following year, Mysore State passed an order reserving 50 per cent of the seats in medical and engineering colleges for Other Backward Classes (28 per cent were for backward classes and 22 per cent for 'more backward' classes). This was over and above the reservations for Scheduled Castes (15 per cent) and Scheduled Tribes (3 per cent). In other words, the total reservation in the state was 68 per cent.[7]

This reservation policy was challenged in the Supreme Court in the case of *M.R. Balaji* v. *State of Mysore*. Speaking for the court, Justice Gajendragadkar found fault with the approach of the Nagan Gowda committee. He said that though caste could be a factor in deciding social backwardness, it could not be the only factor.[8] Its importance, said the court, should not be exaggerated,[9] and caste could not be the 'sole or the dominant test' for deciding whether a community was socially backward.[10] The economic status of a community, the court felt, was as important, and those who are 'deplorably poor automatically become socially backward'.[11] Other factors, like occupation or place of habitation, were also relevant.[12] On the other hand, the Nagan Gowda committee had adopted caste as 'the predominant, if not the sole, test', which was wrong.[13]

The Supreme Court said that the committee ought to have only considered those communities that were 'well below the State average' in terms of literacy to be 'educationally backward', e.g., those with less than 50 per cent of the state's literacy rate.[14] It felt that the literacy levels of Muslims in the state were not so low as would justify their being included in the category of educationally backward classes.[15] It said that in order to be considered eligible for reservations, a community had to be both socially *and* educationally backward, not socially *or* educationally backward.[16] The backwardness of these communities, said the court, also had to be comparable to that of Scheduled Castes and Scheduled Tribes,[17] which is what the colonial Bombay government had opined in 1933, as we have seen in Chapter 2. The Supreme Court found that the categorization of communities into 'backward' and 'more backward' was not permissible.[18]

However, the court was particularly alarmed by the fact that a very large chunk of seats in Mysore had been reserved for backward communities. Nearly 90 per cent of the state was now treated as backward.[19] Article 15(4) of the Constitution, which allowed the government to reserve seats in educational institutions, was considered at that time to be an exception to the principle of equality of opportunity. The exception cannot 'completely [exclude] the rest of the society', said the court.[20] This would lower the standards of higher education in universities and was against the 'national interest' because the country's need for 'technicians, scientists, doctors, economists, engineers and experts' was far too great.[21]

Justice Gajendragadkar then went on to do something quite unexpected. He said that reservations should be lower than 50 per cent of the total number of available seats. How much lower depended on the 'prevailing circumstances in each case',[22] adding that reservations had to be within reasonable limits.[23] He concluded by finding that Mysore's 68 per cent reservations were a fraud on the Constitution.[24]

The Creamy Layer and the Cake

A year later, the Supreme Court decided another case[25] involving a principle called the 'carry-forward rule'. At this time, around 12.5 per cent and 5 per cent of the posts in Central government jobs were being reserved for Scheduled Caste and Scheduled Tribe candidates respectively. However, it often happened that the government was not able to find enough candidates to fill up the reserved seats. In such cases, general candidates were recruited to the reserved seats, and the reservation was 'carried forward' to a subsequent year. Reservations could be carried forward for a total of two years. As a result of this, 65 per cent of the positions that were filled up in 1961 went to reserved candidates. In *T. Devadasan* v. *Union of India*, the question was whether this violated the 50 per cent rule articulated by Justice Gajendragadkar in M.R. Balaji's case.

The carry-forward rule can be explained with an interesting example that the court came up with. Let us assume, it said, that there are 100 posts which become vacant in Year 1, that another 100 positions are available in Year 2, but only 50 posts are advertised in Year 3. Since reservations for Scheduled Castes and Scheduled Tribes are 12.5 per cent and 5 per cent respectively, this means that 18 posts will be set apart for them in Year 1 and another 18 posts in Year 2. If these posts are all carried forward into Year 3, this will mean that there will be 18 + 18 + 9[26] posts reserved for Scheduled Castes and Scheduled Tribes in Year 3, adding up to 45 posts. In short, there will be only 5 posts vacant for general candidates in Year 3.[27]

This, said the court, violated the 50 per cent rule and was unconstitutional. The reservations were 'so excessive' that they 'practically [denied] a reasonable opportunity for employment to members of other communities'.[28] Reservations had to be within reasonable limits,[29] especially since Article 16(4), the provision dealing with reservations, was an exception to Article 16(1), i.e., the principle of equality of opportunity.[30]

The government's lawyers tried to argue that in computing 50 per cent, the court should look at the total strength of the cadre and not the total number of available posts in any given year. For example, let us say that there are 1,000 posts in a government department, out of which only 100 are presently occupied by Scheduled Castes and Scheduled Tribes. Let's say that 100 vacant posts are now advertised in that department this year, but 75 of those new seats are reserved for Scheduled Castes and Scheduled Tribes. Though 75 per cent of the advertised seats have been reserved (much higher than the 50 per cent cap laid down in M.R. Balaji's case), only 17.5 per cent of the total cadre strength (i.e., 175 out of 1,000 posts) would be occupied by reserved category candidates at the end of the year. The state argued that if one looked at the total number of employees in the organization, not the total number of seats that became vacant in the year, the 50 per cent rule was not being violated. However, the court rejected this argument. It held that 'each year of recruitment will have to be considered by itself'[31] for the purposes of the 50 per cent rule.

However, in a dissenting judgement, one of the 42 solo dissents that he would write in his career,[32] Justice K. Subba Rao said that the carry forward rule was valid. He wrote that India's reservation policy was like a race with two horses in it—one, a 'first class race horse', the other, an 'ordinary' one. To make both horses start from the same position would be unfair—the first-class horse would easily defeat the ordinary one. Allowing the ordinary horse to run a shorter distance or fixing a weight on the first-class horse makes the race a level playing field.[33] Of course, this was very unfair towards the first-class horse. However, 'injustice to individuals', he said, was 'inherent in any scheme of reservation'.[34]

For perhaps the first time in the court's history, Justice Subba Rao said that Article 16(4) was not an exception to Article 16(1). In Chapter 3, we saw that Ambedkar had said that reservations were an exception to the rule of equality of opportunity. Justice Subba Rao, however, felt that this was not so.[35] He thought that the 50 per cent rule laid down in M.R. Balaji's case was 'intended only to be a workable guide but not an inflexible rule of law'.[36] In any event, he believed that the rule applied to the total cadre strength as the state had argued and not to each recruitment cycle.[37]

Thereafter, in 1975, the Supreme Court was called on to decide whether a service rule in Kerala was valid. Lower division clerks employed in that state had to pass a test within two years of getting promoted in order to keep their promotions. The rule allowed the government to give Scheduled Caste and Scheduled Tribe clerks who had been promoted a longer period of time to pass the test.[38] In *State of Kerala* v. *NM Thomas*,[39] the Supreme Court found that this rule was fine.

However, while arriving at that conclusion, one judge, Justice Krishna Iyer, said something quite interesting. In his judgement, he wrote that reservations had many dangers. One of them was that its benefits were, 'by and large . . . snatched away by the top creamy layer of the "backward" caste or class'. This was the first time that the words 'creamy layer' had been used in a Supreme Court judgement. Justice Krishna Iyer believed that the well-off, affluent members of the backward classes were the ones who were getting to 'consume the whole cake', while those genuinely in need, the 'weakest among the weak', were left with nothing.[40]

There were 'vocal groups', said Justice Krishna Iyer, who had ceased to be backward thanks to employment and education. These groups, he said, wished to 'wear the "weaker section" label' even though they were nearly as advanced as socially forward communities.[41] He felt that it was necessary for the government to constantly reevaluate the progress made by backward classes in order to ensure that reservations would not become 'reverse discrimination' against forward communities.[42] In fact, he wrote, research conducted at an institute of social studies in Patna 'revealed a dual society among harijans'—'a tiny elite gobbling up the benefits and the darker layers sleeping distances away from the special concessions'. For the latter, the provisions of India's constitution were a 'noble romance'. The reservations 'bonanza', the study said, went 'to the "higher harijans"'.[43] In another case, Justice Krishna Iyer wrote that India had a somewhat 'dubious obsession with "backwardness"' and that the 'politicking' that went on with 'castes labelled backward' was something which demanded 'judicial examination'.[44]

Many judges who decided the N.M. Thomas case said things that were contrary to the principles that had been laid down previously. For instance, some said that in deciding whether reservations were reasonable, the entire cadre strength must be looked at, and not each recruitment cycle.[45] Adopting Justice Subba Rao's reasoning in T. Devadasan's case, some said that the 50 per cent cap was not a hard-and-fast rule[46] at all and that Article 16(4) of the Constitution was not an exception to Article 16(1).[47] For instance, Justice Fazal Ali said that if the backward classes constituted 80 per cent of the population, reserving 80 per cent of all posts and seats was reasonable.[48]

The state of Kerala soon adopted a creamy layer test for backward classes. Though the Ezhava community was recognized as a backward class in the state, its members who had an income above Rs 10,000 could not seek admissions in medical colleges. The Supreme Court found that this rule was perfectly valid.[49]

'The Constitution Does Not Permit Us to Be Arbitrary'

In the years that followed, the Supreme Court started diluting the principles laid down by Justice Gajendragadkar in the M.R. Balaji case. For instance, the court found that it was okay for governments to identify backward classes using caste as the primary criterion.[50] The

50 per cent cap began to be seen as a rule of thumb, not an inflexible norm.[51] The idea that reservations in educational institutions affected the excellence of colleges started being questioned.[52]

For instance, in one case decided in 1981, the Supreme Court had to consider the legality of a decision taken by Madhya Pradesh concerning medical admissions. Around 216 out of 720 seats in government medical colleges in that state were reserved for Scheduled Castes and Scheduled Tribes. However, no such student could seek admission into one of those colleges without securing the minimum number of marks: 40 per cent in all subjects and 30 per cent in each subject.[53] Due to this rule, hardly any reserved category students got admission into medical colleges. The state of Madhya Pradesh therefore decided to do away with the rule altogether. In other words, it was no longer necessary for reserved category students to secure a minimum score in their exams in order to get admitted into a medical college in the state. As a result of this, all the 216 reserved seats were likely to be filled up by Scheduled Caste and Scheduled Tribe candidates.

The Supreme Court said that there was nothing wrong with what Madhya Pradesh had done. The court did not accept the argument that this would lower the standards of the medical profession in the state. After all, the court said, 'the curriculum remains the same for all'.[54] The government had not made it any easier for backward class students to become doctors—it had only relaxed the requirements for getting admission into a college. The court was cognizant of the fact that many such students who had not even secured the minimum number of marks would probably not be able to survive in college and might drop out.[55] This was a risk that the court was willing to take. It was no longer acceptable to argue, as Justice Gajendragadkar had done in M.R. Balaji's case, that giving seats away to unmeritorious students would result in a waste of the state's resources. Madhya Pradesh might get fewer doctors because many of the reserved category students might not be able to graduate, but that was okay.

A few years later, in another case, Justice Chinnappa Reddy, a judge of the Supreme Court, launched an attack on the very idea of merit. '[W]hat is merit?' he asked. A backward class child 'brought up in an atmosphere of penury [and] illiteracy . . . looked down upon by tradition and Society' could not fairly compete with others. Such a child had 'no books and magazines to read at home, no radio to listen [to], no TV to watch, no one to help him with his homework', and had parents who were 'either illiterate or so ignorant and ill-informed that he cannot even hope to seek their advice'. Such a boy, the judge said, had to 'trudge to the nearest public reading room to read a newspaper to know what is happening in the world'. How could such children be said to have no merit if they, with all their disadvantages, were able to score 40 per cent or 50 per cent marks in an examination, though the 'children of the upper classes who have all the advantages, who go to St Paul's High School and St. Stephen's College, and who have perhaps been specially coached for the examination may secure 70, 80 or even 90 per cent', he asked.[56]

According to Justice Reddy, merely securing high marks in an exam did not necessarily make a person a good administrator. Efficient administrators, he thought, needed other qualities like 'the capacity to understand with sympathy' and to 'tackle bravely the problems of a large segment of [the] population'. Though efficiency in government service was important, the argument that reservations would breed inefficiency in government was being used as a 'camouflage' by the upper classes 'to monopolise the services', he added.[57]

In his judgement, Justice Reddy contradicted virtually every principle which had been laid down by Justice Gajendragadkar in the M.R. Balaji case. So, for instance, he found that caste could be used as the 'primary index' to determine social backwardness.[58] Mere poverty was not a criterion for determining backwardness,[59] he felt, though the poor certainly needed help. He found the idea of poor Brahmins being given reservations 'too grotesque even to be considered'.[60] Since agricultural income was not taxed, he believed that rich landowners would be able to establish that they were backward if a person's finances were made an indicator of backwardness.[61]

Contrary to M.R. Balaji's case, Justice Reddy said that Other Backward Classes need not be as backward as Scheduled Castes and Scheduled Tribes.[62] Any other rule, he said, would 'practically nullify' the reservations in favour of Other Backward Classes, since it would be hard to find communities that were as backward as Scheduled Castes and Scheduled Tribes.[63] Unlike what Justice Gajendragadkar had said, Justice Reddy thought it was okay to classify Other Backward Classes into backward and more backward.[64] Perhaps most importantly, he said that the court could not put any cap on the quantum of reservations. Justice Gajendragadkar's 50 per cent rule, he said, was arbitrary, and 'the Constitution does not permit us to be arbitrary'.[65] Though reservations for backward classes might be used as a 'vote-catching device' by unscrupulous political parties, he thought that this was a price that India would have to pay. '[O]ut of evil cometh good', he said.[66]

However, all the five judges in that case wrote separate judgements, and Justice Reddy's views did not have the support of the majority. Interestingly, unlike Justice Gajendragadkar, who was a high-caste Hindu, Justice Reddy was the son of a fifth-generation Roman Catholic. An atheist, Reddy refused to 'be classified to any religion or any community' preferring to be considered 'a human being and an Indian'.[67]

Mandal and Sawhney

Over twenty years after the Kalelkar Commission submitted its report attempting to define who the Other Backward Classes were, in January 1979,[68] Prime Minister Morarji Desai appointed a commission headed by a former Chief Minister of Bihar, Bindhyeshwari Prasad Mandal,[69] to objectively identify Other Backward Classes. The new commission noted that the Kalelkar committee had 'not formulated any objective criteria for classifying Other Backward Classes.'[70]

Determined not to make the same mistake, the Mandal Commission came up with eleven criteria for figuring out who the Other Backward Classes were.[71]

There were four criteria for social backwardness: castes that were considered to be socially backward by others, those that depended primarily on manual labour for their livelihood, those whose members got married below 17 years at a rate higher than the state average,[72] and, interestingly, castes whose women entered the workforce at a rate 25 per cent higher than the state average were socially backward.

The Mandal Commission identified three factors for educational backwardness: castes whose children between the ages of 5–15 years never attended school at a rate 25 per cent more than the state average, those whose students of that age dropped out of school at the same rate, or castes who had a proportion of 'matriculates' (i.e., those who finished high school) 25 per cent lower than the state average were educationally backward.

Similarly, there were four criteria for economic backwardness: castes whose average value of family assets was 25 per cent below the state average, those whose families lived in 'kuccha houses' 25 per cent more often than the state average, castes whose source of drinking water was beyond half a kilometre away for more than 50 per cent of their households, and those where the number of families that had 'consumption loans' was 25 per cent above the state average were economically backward.

The commission came up with a points system[73] for its eleven criteria, in which social backwardness was given the highest weightage—12 out of 22 points were allotted to this category. On the other hand, 6 points and 4 points were allocated to educational and economic backwardness respectively. Any caste that earned 11 out of 22 points on this scale was considered to be socially and educationally backward. According to the commission's calculations, the Other Backward Classes accounted for 52 per cent of the population of India.[74]

The Mandal Commission avoided the mistakes made by the Nagan Gowda committee. Now, only communities that were well below or above the state average in certain indices were considered backward. Further, though caste was an important factor in its calculations, it was not the only measure of social backwardness. The Nagan Gowda committee had said that castes that were thought to have a low status were, for this reason alone, socially backward. For the Mandal Commission, this was only one of many factors that went into social backwardness. However, though Justice Gajendragadkar in M.R. Balaji's case had said that economic criteria must be as important as social criteria for determining social backwardness, the Mandal Commission gave economic criteria the least importance.

The Mandal Commission recommended 27 per cent reservation for Other Backward Classes. This figure, 27 per cent, was calculated in order to avoid violating the 50 per cent rule laid down by the Supreme Court in M.R. Balaji's case. Reservations for Scheduled Castes and Scheduled Tribes at this time were 22.5 per cent of the total available seats. Though the Mandal Commission believed that Other Backward Classes constituted 52 per cent of India's population, the highest representation that could be given to them was therefore 27 per cent.[75] Thus, though the reservations given to Scheduled Castes and Scheduled Tribes of 15 per cent and 7.5 per cent was roughly proportionate to their numbers in the population, Other Backward Class reservations fell substantially short of proportional representation.[76]

By the time the Mandal Commission submitted its report, the Janata Government had been defeated by Indira Gandhi's Congress in the elections. The report was shelved for ten years, until 13 August 1990, when the government of Prime Minister V.P. Singh issued an office memorandum which, for the first time in India's history, gave reservations to Other Backward Classes in Central government jobs. Until then, only Scheduled Castes and Scheduled Tribes had posts reserved for them in Central government services. After this office memorandum was issued, 27 per cent of the vacancies in civil posts and services under the Central government were reserved for socially and educationally backward classes.[77] It was perhaps no small coincidence that at this time, regional backward caste parties entered national politics, about a fourth of India's parliament had Other Backward Class MPs, and 20 per cent of Prime Minister V.P. Singh's cabinet had backward caste members.[78]

Thereafter, once Prime Minister Narasimha Rao came to power, another office memorandum was issued on 25 September 1991. This provided that preference in reservations would be given to the poorer sections of the socially and educationally backward classes. It also said that 10 per cent of the vacancies in Central government jobs would be reserved for economically backward communities.[79]

Several people filed cases in the Supreme Court challenging these office memoranda issued by the V.P. Singh and Narasimha Rao governments. Included among them was a lawyer by the name of Indra Sawhney.[80] These cases, which were decided by a bench of nine judges of the Supreme Court,[81] would be known by her name.[82]

The Supreme Court in Indra Sawhney's case said that the criteria formulated by the Mandal Commission were okay.[83] While caste could be an important factor to determine backwardness, it could not be the only factor.[84] It was always open to a government to identify Other Backward Classes without reference to caste altogether, by looking at factors like occupation, income, and other criteria.[85] Social backwardness was essential.[86] However, Justice Jeevan Reddy relied on colonial history and found that in pre-independence India, 'the expressions "class" and "caste" were used interchangeably' and 'caste was understood as an enclosed class'.[87] It was held that a caste could be a class as well.[88]

Disagreeing with Justice Gajendragadkar's view in M.R. Balaji's case, the view which was also taken by the government of colonial Bombay in 1933, the court held that the Other Backward Classes did not have to be as backward as Scheduled Castes and Scheduled Tribes.[89] In fact, the phrase 'backward classes' in Article 16(4) of the

Constitution was wider than the phrase 'socially and educationally backward classes' used in Article 15(4).[90] In other words, said the court, a caste could qualify for reservations in government jobs even if it was educationally forward, though it would not qualify for reservations in educational institutions. It was okay for a government to classify other backward communities into backward and more backward.[91]

However, the court held that backwardness could not be decided on the basis of economic criteria alone.[92] For instance, Justice Sawant felt that the high-caste poor were not socially backward and if they were given reservations along with Other Backward Classes then all the seats would be monopolized by them.[93] The court therefore struck down the 10 per cent reservations for economically backward communities that had been provided by Prime Minister Narasimha Rao's government.[94]

Far-Flung and Remote Areas

Perhaps the greatest disagreement among the nine judges in Indra Sawhney's case took place over the question of whether to accept Justice Gajendragadkar's 50 per cent cap on reservations. The judges held, contrary to what Ambedkar had said in the Constituent Assembly, that Article 16(4) of the Constitution was not an exception to Article 16(1)—in other words, that reservations were not an exception to the principle of equality of opportunity.[95] However, the judges disagreed with each other about whether this meant that there could be a cap on reservations.

The majority of the court agreed that the 50 per cent rule would be sacrosanct and could only be violated in 'certain extraordinary situations' to provide for backward communities in far-flung or remote areas of the country.[96] In other words, reservations could not be provided to backward classes in proportion to their population—the Constitution prescribed 'adequate', not 'proportional' representation in government jobs.[97] On the carry-forward rule, the judges agreed that the 50 per cent cap would apply to each year and would not be fixed on the basis of the strength of the cadre.[98]

In perhaps the most significant move, the court decided that the 'creamy layer' would have to be mandatorily excluded from the Other Backward Classes. How were members of the creamy layer to be identified? According to Justice Jeevan Reddy, economic criteria alone would not do.[99] A migrant worker who goes to the UAE might have more money than the other members of his caste, but he might still be backward. Further, money could not be used as a uniform measure of the creamy layer throughout the country either—a sum of Rs 10,000 would go much further in rural India than in the cities. Justice Reddy said that people like factory owners (who were in a position to employ many people) and government servants were a part of the creamy layer.[100]

Justice Sawant wrote that a family was a part of the creamy layer if it had the capacity to compete with the forward castes, not just if it were relatively better off compared to the other members of its own caste. In other words, a creamy layer family was one which had 'cross[ed] the Rubicon of backwardness'. He said that it could hardly be argued that 'once a backward class, always a backward class.'[101] Justice Pandian was perhaps the only one who felt that even the creamy layer should be included in the Other Backward Classes.[102] However, the court agreed that Scheduled Castes and Scheduled Tribes were presumed to be backward[103]—courts could not investigate whether the castes included in those categories were backward or not.[104]

Finally, the court decided, by a majority, that reservations could not be allowed in promotions,[105] reversing decades of jurisprudence on this point.[106] Justice Jeevan Reddy felt that if reservations were allowed in promotions, the members of reserved classes would feel as though they 'need not have to compete with others but only among themselves'. As a result of this, they will not feel any need to 'work, compete and excel', as they would think that 'their promotion is assured'. This would also create a sense of frustration amongst those from the general categories. 'Crutches cannot be provided throughout one's career', he said. He added that this would not prevent backward classes from reaching the upper echelons of government service, since direct recruitments often took place in those positions, where reservations were permitted. District judges, for instance, are often directly recruited and not promoted from the lower judiciary.[107]

In short, the court in the Indra Sawhney case accepted the Mandal Commission report but asked the government to exclude the creamy layer from the Other Backward Classes. It accepted the 50 per cent rule but said that it could be exceeded in rare cases. It refused to allow 10 per cent reservations for economically backward communities and rejected reservations in promotions.[108]

Ambedkar, Gajendragadkar, or Chinnappa Reddy?

At the time that the Indra Sawhney case was decided, there were three different points of view on reservations. The first approach, a conservative one, was that of India's founding fathers like Nehru and Ambedkar. Nehru frowned on quotas while Ambedkar wanted them to be restricted to a minority of seats. The supporters of this approach believed that reservations were an exception to the principle of equality of opportunity and that an exception cannot swallow the rule.

The second viewpoint, a centrist one, was of judges like Justice Gajendragadkar, who suggested that reservations should extend to no more than 50 per cent of the available seats or posts. They drew on the arguments made by Ambedkar in the Constituent Assembly and said that Article 16(4) was an exception to Article 16(1). Giving backward classes too large a share of the pie, they suggested, would be unfair to the other communities. The Constitution itself only spoke of 'adequate' (not 'proportional') representation for the backward classes, they pointed out. Allowing sub-standard students to get reserved seats in educational institutions, they said, would mean that many of them would be unable to complete their courses and India would be deprived of the doctors, scientists, and economists that she desperately needed. Yet, they recognized that reservations could not be restricted to a tiny minority of seats.

The third viewpoint, a liberal one, was of judges like Justice Subba Rao, Justice Fazal Ali, and Justice Chinnappa Reddy who said that there should be no hard-and-fast rule restricting reservations to 50 per cent. They argued that backward classes should be entitled to a share commensurate with their numbers in the population. Where did the 50 per cent cap come from, they asked. It was an arbitrary formulation picked out of a hat by an over-zealous court. What is merit, they asked. A boy from a socially disadvantaged community who scored 40 marks had as much merit as someone from St Stephen's college who scored 70. Allowing them to enter medical colleges, they said, did not lower the standard of medical education, since the curriculum remained the same for one and all.

The solution that the Supreme Court eventually came up with in the Indra Sawhney case attempted to balance these different viewpoints. Reservations would not be restricted to a minority of seats as Ambedkar had said. They could not extend to 70 per cent either, contrary to what liberals like Justice Subba Rao would have preferred. Yet, at the same time, they recognized that Justice Gajendragadkar's 50 per cent cap required exceptions in extraordinary cases. On the other hand, in deciding that reservations would not be permissible in promotions, the court swung towards the conservative view adopted by the founding fathers. Even Justice Gajendragadkar had not taken such an extreme position. In fact, one of the first judgements of the Supreme Court recognizing reservations in promotions was authored by him.[109]

When Justice Krishna Iyer first spoke of the 'creamy layer', he applied it to 'Harijans'. The word 'Harijan', as we have seen, was originally used for the 'depressed classes', those who had suffered from the stigma of untouchability, whom the Constitution now called Scheduled Castes. However, the Supreme Court in Indra Sawhney's case did not apply the concept of the creamy layer to

Scheduled Castes or even the Scheduled Tribes. It was meant to weed out well-off or forward sections of the Other Backward Classes. The question which then arises is: why should the creamy layer concept not apply to Scheduled Castes and Scheduled Tribes as well?[110] One answer might be that reservations were meant to compensate castes that had suffered the stigma of untouchability for centuries. However, as we saw in the first chapter, Scheduled Tribes were usually not untouchable communities. Why should the creamy layer doctrine not apply to them? The reason Scheduled Tribes were considered to deserve reservations was because of their backwardness. If that is so, then why should those who have come out of their backwardness continue to benefit from reservations, especially when their counterparts in the Other Backward Classes cannot do so? The creamy layer concept was eventually taken to its logical conclusion by the Supreme Court in the Jarnail Singh case, which we will see in the next chapter.

We now know with some more clarity who the 'Other Backward Classes' are. The answer depends on the kind of reservation that is being spoken about. The Constitution grants reservations in educational institutions to 'socially and educationally backward classes'. Unlike in government jobs, here, both social *and* educational backwardness are essential. Reservations in government jobs, on the other hand, are provided to those who primarily suffer from some kind of social disability—typically castes (Hindu or otherwise) that are backward (e.g.,manual labourers, those who marry early, castes considered low), minus their creamy layer. The Mandal Commission had said that a caste whose women are in the workforce is socially backward for that reason, because upper-caste women would usually not want to work out of choice. Perhaps such criteria now need revision.

6

An Era of Constitutional Amendments

In the years that followed the judgement of the Supreme Court in Indra Sawhney's case, Parliament enacted a series of constitutional amendments to essentially wipe out judgements delivered by the Supreme Court in quota cases. Many of these amendments were passed by governments as they neared the end of their terms, with an eye towards the elections. These amendments can broadly be classified into three groups: amendments which sought to dilute the 50 per cent rule, amendments that allowed the government to reserve seats for Scheduled Castes and Scheduled Tribes in promotions, and amendments that extended reservations beyond their traditional domains, i.e., reservations in private colleges and for poor upper-caste communities. Each such amendment was passed almost unanimously by Parliament with hardly any legislators who argued against the bill. Often, some members of Parliament argued that high-caste judges sitting in the Supreme Court were insensitive to the needs of the backward classes, and that there should be reservations in the higher judiciary.[1] It was the Supreme Court that played the role of the opposition in these cases, accepting Parliament's power to undo its judgements, but imposing or reiterating limits on that power through devices like the creamy layer test, the 50 per cent rule,[2] and the new 'quantifiable data' requirement.[3] This chapter examines the tug-of-war that took place between Parliament and the Supreme Court in the years following the Indra Sawhney case.

The 50 Per Cent Rule Relaxed

The Ninth Schedule

In 1994, around two years after the Supreme Court's judgement in Indra Sawhney's case, Parliament amended the Constitution to allow the state of Tamil Nadu to exceed the 50 per cent cap on reservations. Tamil Nadu had 69 per cent reservations—50 per cent of posts and seats were reserved for Other Backward Classes alone, while 18 per cent and 1 per cent were reserved for Scheduled Castes and Scheduled Tribes respectively.[4] After the Supreme Court's decision, the state enacted a law reiterating its resolve to breach the 50 per cent rule.[5] Then, through the 76th amendment to the Constitution, Parliament inserted that law into the 9th Schedule to the Indian Constitution. In the pages of the *Times of India*, the legendary lawyer Nani Palkhivala called the government 'an unabashed prisoner of political expediency' for doing so.[6] When a law is inserted into the 9th Schedule to the Constitution, it becomes nearly invulnerable and can be challenged on very limited grounds, i.e., if it violates the basic structure of the Constitution.[7]

The bill to amend the Constitution was passed by a majority of 348 to 0 in the Lok Sabha.[8] No member of the house voted against it. This is particularly significant given the fact that Prime Minister Narasimha Rao was running a minority government at this time. Reservation for backward classes seemed to be a consensus issue which was easy to get through Parliament. There was almost no engagement in Parliament with the ideological questions concerning the 50 per cent rule. For instance, hardly any discussion took place in the Lok Sabha on whether reservations were an exception to the principle of equality of opportunity, as Ambedkar had argued in the Constituent

Assembly. Parliamentarians insisted that like political reservations, reservations in government jobs and educational institutions should be proportional to the population of backward communities.

However, after this amendment was passed, the Supreme Court played the role of the opposition and issued an interim order restraining reservations in excess of 50 per cent in Tamil Nadu, by directing the state government to temporarily create additional seats for general category candidates.[9]

Quantifiable Data or Extreme Caution

Eventually, the case against the insertion of the Tamil Nadu law into the 9th Schedule was dismissed because the Supreme Court relaxed the 50 per cent rule.[10] In a cryptic order passed in 2010, the Supreme Court seemingly introduced a new exception to the 50 per cent rule. In *S.V. Joshi* v. *State of Karnataka*,[11] it said that 'if a State wants to exceed fifty per cent reservation, then it is required to base its decision on the quantifiable data'.[12] In support of this proposition, the court relied on two of its own judgements in the cases of *M. Nagaraj* v. *Union of India*[13] and *Ashoka Kumar Thakur* v. *Union of India*.[14]

Oddly, neither of these two cases had said anything about exceeding the 50 per cent cap on quotas. In fact, in M. Nagaraj's case, the Supreme Court had said that exceeding the 'cut-off point' of 50 per cent would result in 'reverse discrimination' and that 'a numerical benchmark is the surest immunity against charges of discrimination'.[15] What the court had said in that case was that if the government wanted to reserve seats in government jobs for backward classes, it had to have 'quantifiable data' that those classes were backward and were inadequately represented in public service.[16] However, the court had said nothing about breaching the 50 per cent rule. In fact, it had reiterated that rule, referring to it as 'the ceiling limit of 50% (the numerical benchmark)'.[17]

Similarly, Ashoka Kumar Thakur's case had said nothing about violating the 50 per cent rule either. Yet, the Supreme Court in S.V.

Joshi's case misconstrued its earlier decisions and laid down the proposition that a government could exceed the 50 per cent cap on quotas if it had 'quantifiable data' that the class for which the rule was being violated is backward and that it is inadequately represented in the services.

Relying on this judgement, the Bombay High Court recently upheld the decision of the Maharashtra government to exceed the 50 per cent rule in order to provide reservations in colleges and government jobs to the Maratha community.[18] In Maharashtra, the term 'SEBC', or socially and educationally backward classes, is virtually a code-word for 'Maratha'. The High Court said that the burden was on the government in such cases to justify a violation of the 50 per cent rule through quantifiable data.[19] It found that since 85 per cent of the population of Maharashtra was considered backward, it would be a travesty of justice if the 50 per cent cap were to be observed.[20] This was despite the fact that the Bombay High Court had itself, a few years previously, held that the Supreme Court had not really modified the 50 per cent rule in S.V. Joshi's case.[21]

On appeal, however, the Supreme Court reversed the decision of the Bombay High Court.[22] The Supreme Court held that the S.V. Joshi judgment does not allow the government to breach the 50 per cent rule with quantifiable data.[23] The 50 per cent cap on quotas, said the Supreme Court, can only be breached in extraordinary situations in accordance with the Indra Sawhney judgment.[24] The 'far-flung' areas test articulated by the Supreme Court in Indra Sawhney's case (discussed in the previous chapter), however, was only an illustrative and not an exhaustive test.[25] Since Marathas in Maharashtra were in the mainstream of social life, the court found that reservations for Marathas were not permissible in violation of the 50 per cent cap.[26] The court also found that Marathas in Maharashtra were adequately represented in government services—the mere fact that they were not proportionately represented (i.e., in proportion to their population) in government jobs was irrelevant.[27]

The Supreme Court in *Chebrolu Leela Prasad Rao* v. *State of AP*[28] held that the government can breach the 50 per cent rule to some extent, but 'extreme caution' was to be exercised in such cases and a 'special case' had to be made out by the government to justify violating the quota cap.[29] In that case, it found that 100 per cent reservations given to Scheduled Tribes by the State of Andhra Pradesh in scheduled areas for the posts of teachers in schools were 'unreasonable and unfair'.[30] The government's justification, viz., that there was a great deal of teacher absenteeism in scheduled areas, was found not to be an 'extraordinary circumstance' justifying a breach of the 50 per cent cap on quotas.[31] It also directed the government to revise the lists of Scheduled Castes and Scheduled Tribes so that affluent groups within them could be excluded.[32]

The Roster System

In Indra Sawhney's case, the Supreme Court had said that the 50 per cent cap had to be calculated on the basis of the number of vacancies arising in the year and not on the basis of the total strength of the cadre. For example, let's say that there are 100 sanctioned posts in a government department, of which 20 are supposed to be reserved. Let's say that as of now, none of the seats are occupied by members of the backward classes. Assume that 20 vacancies are advertised this year in the department. If the 50 per cent cap were to be calculated on the basis of the strength of the cadre, then all 20 vacancies could go to backward class candidates, amounting to 100 per cent reservation for that year. However, the Supreme Court in Indra Sawhney's case had held that the 50 per cent cap would have to be calculated on the basis of the total vacancies arising in any year, not the strength of the cadre. In other words, only 10 seats can be reserved for backward class candidates this year out of the 20 vacancies that have arisen this year.

In 1995, the Supreme Court diluted this principle and held that it would not apply to a 'roster system'.[33] This requires an example.

Let's say that there are 15 posts in a government department of which 6 are reserved for backward class candidates. The reserved posts are at serial numbers 4, 7, 8, 12, 14, and 15 of the roster. Let's assume that all 15 seats have been filled with general and reserved candidates in the appropriate numbers. In other words, all the initial appointments have been made. Now, let's assume that there is a vacancy which subsequently arises at serial numbers 4, 7, and 8 of the roster this year. All of these seats are reserved in the roster. Therefore, they will have to be filled by backward class candidates. This is despite the fact that this would theoretically mean that there will be 100 per cent reservation this year.

However, reservation is not permissible if the entire cadre consists of only a single post.[34]

Broadly speaking, there are two kinds of roster systems which are now prevalent for recruiting government employees: the '200-point roster' and the '13-point roster'.[35] The 200-point roster system applies to cadres in which there are 14 or more employees, while the 13-point roster applies where there are between 2 and 13 employees in the cadre.

Table 1 sets out how the 200-point roster system is composed in a department of, say, 21 employees. The percentage of reservation is: 15 per cent (SC), 7.5 per cent (ST), 27 per cent (OBC), and 10 per cent for economically weaker sections or 'EWS' which we will see below. These figures are divided by 100, and then multiples are worked out until one of these categories crosses a natural number, upon which it obtains a reserved seat.[36] For instance, let's take the example of the Scheduled Caste category, which starts off with the number 0.15 [15/100]. Since the 7th multiple of 0.15 gets past a natural number [15/100 x 7 = 1.05], the 7th seat on the roster is reserved for Scheduled Castes. The first three seats in this system are unreserved (UR). This method is called the '200 point' roster because one entire loop or pattern is complete at the 200th post,[37] and the entire pattern repeats itself starting with the 201st post.[38] What is important is that each seat is earmarked for a certain category and recruitments to those seats can only be made in accordance with the category for which they are earmarked.

This can be explained with the following example. Let's assume that a government department has 21 employees in it. Since it has more than 13 employees, the 200-point roster applies to it. The 21 employees of the government will be recruited in the following pattern:

1. UR
2. UR
3. UR
4. OBC
5. UR
6. UR
7. SC
8. OBC
9. UR
10. EWS
11. UR
12. OBC
13. UR
14. ST
15. SC
16. OBC
17. UR
18. UR
19. OBC
20. SC
21. EWS

If the employees at serial numbers 4, 7, 10, and 12 of the roster all retire this year, the vacancies will have to be filled up by the categories for which these seats have been earmarked (i.e., OBC, SC, EWS, OBC).

Table 1: The '200-point' roster in a government department of 21 employees

Sr. No. of Post.	Share of Entitlement				Category for which the posts should be earmarked
	SC @ 15per cent	ST @ 7.5per cent	OBC @ 27per cent	EWS @ 10per cent	
1	0.15	0.08	0.27	0.10	UR
2	0.30	0.15	0.54	0.20	UR
3	0.45	0.23	0.81	0.30	UR
4	0.60	0.30	1.08	0.40	OBC-1
5	0.75	0.38	1.35	0.50	UR
6	0.90	0.45	1.62	0.60	UR
7	1.05	0.53	1.89	0.70	SC-1
8	1.20	0.60	2.16	0.80	OBC-2
9	1.35	0.68	2.43	0.90	UR
10	1.50	0.75	2.70	1.00	EWS-1
11	1.65	0.83	2.97	1.10	UR
12	1.80	0.90	3.24	1.20	OBC-3
13	1.95	0.98	3.51	1.30	UR
14	2.10	1.05	3.78	1.40	ST
15	2.25	1.13	4.05	1.50	SC-2
16	2.40	1.20	4.32	1.60	OBC-4
17	2.55	1.28	4.59	1.70	UR
18	2.70	1.35	4.86	1.80	UR
19	2.85	1.43	5.13	1.90	OBC-5
20	3.00	1.50	5.40	2.00	SC-3
21	3.15	1.58	5.67	2.10	EWS-2

Note: The shaded portions reflect the points at which the multiple of a category crosses a natural number, upon which the category gets a reserved seat.

In the 200-point roster, all the reserved categories get seats by the 14th post. In other words, the last reserved category to get a seat is Scheduled Tribes, which gets a post at the 14th point in the roster.

This means that the 200-point roster cannot work in a government department which has 13 employees or less. For example, if a government department has only three employees in it, then if the 200-point roster were to be followed, all the posts would go to the unreserved category and there would be no reservation. In order to remedy this problem, the '13-point' roster system is followed for departments which have 13 employees or less.

Table 2 explains how the 13-point roster system works. All employees in the 13-point roster are recruited in the same pattern as the first 14 points of the 200-point roster, i.e., UR, UR, UR, OBC, UR, UR, SC, OBC, UR, EWS, UR, OBC, UR, ST, after which the pattern repeats itself (unlike the 200-point roster where the pattern repeats itself at the 201st point in the roster). Since there can be no reservation for a single post cadre, the 13-point roster system only applies for cadres of between 2 and 13 employees.

This can be explained with the following example. Let's assume that there is a government department which has 5 employees in it. The five employees will be recruited on the basis of the shaded portion of the 13-point roster in Table 2 below. The pattern will repeat itself after every 14 appointments. So, for example, the 5th vacancy will be recruited from the economically weaker section category, the 9th vacancy from the Scheduled Tribe category, and the 10th vacancy from the unreserved category. This is called an 'L' shaped roster because the initial recruitments are made in the vertical pattern and the subsequent appointments follow the horizontal pattern (forming the shape 'L'), until the loop repeats itself. Since there are only 5 employees, in order to maintain the 50 per cent rule, at no point in time can more than 2 employees belong to the reserved categories. Unlike the 200-point roster, reservation takes place by rotation and posts are not earmarked for any category.

The problem with the 13-point roster is that reserved categories have to wait a long time in order to get their turn. In the 5-employee example given above, a Scheduled Caste candidate will be entitled to reservation when the 2nd vacancy arises, while a Scheduled Tribe candidate will have to wait until the 9th vacancy. This may take a long time.

Table 2: The 'L' Shaped 13-Point Roster:

Cadre Strength	Initial Recruitment	1st	2nd	3rd	4th	5th	6th	7th	8th	9th	10th	11th	12th	13th
														Replacement No.
1	UR	UR	UR	OBC	UR	UR	SC	OBC	UR	EWS	UR	OBC	UR	ST
2	UR	UR	OBC	UR	UR	SC	OBC	UR	EWS	UR	OBC	UR	ST	
3	UR	OBC	UR	UR	SC	OBC	UR	EWS	UR	OBC	UR	ST		
4	OBC	UR	UR	SC	OBC	UR	EWS	UR	OBC	UR	ST			
5	UR	UR	SC	OBC	UR	EWS	UR	OBC	UR	ST				
6	UR	SC	OBC	UR	EWS	UR	OBC	UR	ST					
7	SC	OBC	UR	EWS	UR	OBC	UR	ST						
8	OBC	UR	EWS	UR	OBC	UR	ST							
9	UR	EWS	UR	OBC	UR	ST								
10	EWS	UR	OBC	UR	ST									
11	UR	OBC	UR	ST										
12	OBC	UR	ST											
13	UR	ST												

Note: The shaded portion reflects the recruitment pattern in a government department of 5 employees. The pattern repeats itself after the 9th replacement (i.e., after a cycle of 14 appointments is complete).

There has recently been some controversy over the application of the 13-point roster system in teaching departments at universities run by the Central government.[39] The question which arose some years back was: how should the 50 per cent rule be calculated in such universities—with all the teaching departments taken together, or each department separately? For instance, let's assume that a Central government university has 20 teaching departments (e.g., history, sociology, economics, etc.), and each department has five teachers in it. The total number of teachers in the university is therefore 100. If all the departments taken together are to be considered as one unit for the purpose of the 50 per cent rule, then there can be as many as 50 reserved positions.[40] The 200-point roster will apply since the entire unit has over 13 employees. However, if each department is to be treated as a unit separately for the purpose of the 50 per cent rule, then the number of reserved posts will be 40; since there are only 5 teachers in each department, the number of reserved posts in each department can't exceed 2. In other words, if each department is treated as a unit for the purpose of the 50 per cent rule, then the total number of reserved positions will be 20 x 2 = 40. Further, since each department has less than 14 employees, the 13-point roster will apply, which means that reserved categories will have to wait a long time in order to get appointed.

In 2017, the Allahabad High Court held that each department has to be treated as a unit for the purpose of the 50 per cent rule.[41] As a result of this, the University Grants Commission imposed the 13-point roster instead of the 200-point roster for recruitment at Central government universities.[42] However, the government issued an ordinance and later a statute saying that each Central government educational institution has to be treated as a unit for the purpose of reservation,[43] essentially overruling the Allahabad High Court judgement. While this book was being written, the Supreme Court had not opined on the validity of this new law.

The Carry-Forward Rule

In the year 2000, during Prime Minister Vajpayee's tenure, Parliament passed the 81st constitutional amendment which obliterated the 50 per cent cap on quotas when it came to the 'carry-forward rule'.[44] This rule can be explained with an example. Let's say that there's a department in the government which has 100 vacancies each year, of which 20 are reserved for Scheduled Castes and Scheduled Tribes. Let's assume that no candidate was available to occupy a reserved seat in the first year. As a result, the 20 unfilled reserved seats (called 'backlog vacancies') are filled up by general candidates and are 'carried forward' to the next year. However, in the second year, there are now 40 reserved seats out of the 100 vacancies which arise that year, since 20 reserved seats from the first year have been 'carried forward' into the second year. Let's say that none of those seats are filled in the second year either. Carrying all the unfilled reserved seats forward into the third year, however, will breach the 50 per cent rule, since that year, a total of 60 out of 100 seats will be reserved (i.e., 20 seats from the first year, 20 from the second year, and 20 fresh reserved seats in the third year). In the Indra Sawhney judgement, the Supreme Court had held that the 'carry-forward' rule could not violate the 50 per cent cap on quotas. In short, the court had said that while seats can be carried forward to subsequent years, the total number of reserved seats cannot exceed 50 per cent of the available vacancies in any year.

The 81st amendment to the Constitution overruled the Indra Sawhney judgement on this point. It inserted a new provision, Article 16(4B), into the Constitution, which said that the government could consider the backlog vacancies that were carried forward to subsequent years as a separate class of vacancies for calculating the 50 per cent rule.[45] In other words, using the example above, in the third year, the government could, if it wanted to, fill all 60 reserved seats, since the 40 carried forward seats from two previous years were to be considered a separate class from the 20 fresh reserved seats for that year. Once again, the 81st amendment was passed by a whopping majority of 418 to 1 in the Lok Sabha.[46] In other words, only one member of Parliament[47] voted against it.

In the debate on the constitutional amendment, one member of the Lok Sabha, Santosh Choudhary, pointed out why reserved seats were not being filled in government jobs. She said that many government officials preferred to hire temporary (or 'ad-hoc') employees from the forward communities to do the jobs reserved for backward classes. Further, even when backward class candidates were selected for jobs, they would be prevented from joining their posts in several ways: e.g., they would be sent their appointment letters late, so that they could not join on time; they would be declared medically unfit, though they were perfectly fit for the job; or they would be posted to remote areas which are akin to 'mental torture'.[48] She ended her speech with an Urdu couplet, saying: 'do not remove the thorns from the garden, O gardener, we have also bloomed with the flowers in spring'.[49]

MRCs, Migrations and Interlocking Reservations

The 50 per cent rule does not really ensure that general category candidates actually get 50 per cent of all available seats or positions. This is for three reasons.

Firstly, a reserved category candidate is not precluded from competing for a seat or a post in the general category. In other words, if a student or an applicant from a backward class gets a seat on her own merit, she is counted in the general category and her seat will not be counted towards the 50 per cent cap on quotas.[50] The idea behind this rule is that seats cannot be reserved for forward classes, and if backward class students are not permitted to compete for general seats, then this would amount to reservations for forward classes as well, akin to the Communal G.O. that was struck down by the Supreme Court in M.R. Balaji's case.[51] However, what this also essentially means is that the proportion of backward class candidates is theoretically likely to be higher than 50 per cent. Since 'meritorious reserved candidates', or 'MRCs' as they are legally called, are counted towards general seats, this enables more backward class candidates to take up places within the 50 per cent reserved quota.

Secondly, in college admissions, it may sometimes happen that an MRC, i.e., a backward class student who gets in on her own merit, does not obtain a sufficiently high rank in the merit list and as a result is unable to pick the college of her choice. In such cases, the MRC is allowed to 'migrate' to a reserved seat in a better ranked college. In other words, rather than picking a college lower down the order, the MRC is allowed to pick a superior college by opting for a reserved seat instead of a general seat. In these cases, the MRC is not counted within the 50 per cent quota and is still considered a general category student.[52] Further, the general seats that are thereby vacated by migrating MRCs are not given to general category students but to reserved students.

This can be explained with the following example. Let's assume that there are 100 seats available in all medical colleges in a state, of which 49 are reserved for backward classes. In the entrance exam, 21 backward class students get a rank on the general list, i.e., they are 'MRCs'. However, the 21 MRCs are not able to get the college of their choice on the general list—they are only able to get into the 10th ranked college in the state. They therefore opt to 'migrate' to reserved seats, which allows them to get into a college that is ranked third. However, the 21 general seats that are now available in the college ranked tenth are given to reserved category students, not to general students. In a sense, therefore, 70 [i.e., 49 + 21] out of 100 seats now appear to be reserved.

The idea behind this rule is that it only fixes *inter se* merit amongst students in the backward classes. Had this rule not been in place then the irony would be that MRCs would get poorer college choices than reserved category students despite the MRCs having done better in the entrance exam. In our example, in the absence of this rule, MRCs would get into the tenth-best college, while less deserving reserved students would get into the third-best college. As a result of the rule, the total number of students from the backward classes who get seats in colleges does not really change. To use our example above, had the rule not been in place, 70 out of 100 students would still be from the backward classes. However, at the same time, this rule really allows a reserved category student to obtain a general category seat. Perhaps for this reason, this rule is not followed in government employment cases, only in college admissions.[53]

Thirdly, 'horizontal' or 'interlocking' reservations, i.e., reservations that are not based on caste, are not part of the 50 per cent rule.[54] For instance, reservations in favour of women,[55] differently abled students, children of freedom fighters or members of the army—these are not considered part of the 50 per cent cap on quotas. The reason they are called 'horizontal' or 'interlocking' reservations is that they are applied in a compartmentalized manner across all caste categories.[56] In other words, if 5 per cent seats are reserved for women, this usually means that 5 per cent of backward class seats are reserved for women and 5 per cent of general category seats are also reserved for women. In other words, the quota for the horizontal category does not only come from the general seats. However, in the ultimate analysis, the seats available in the general category get further reduced by horizontal reservations.

Let's take the same example from above. There are 100 seats available in medical colleges in a state this year, of which 49 are reserved for backward class students. Let's say that another 10 per cent are reserved for women, differently abled students, children of freedom fighters and members of the army. This means that 5 seats reserved for backward class students will go to those backward class students who are either women, differently abled, children of freedom fighters or members of the army. Similarly, 5 seats will go to those students who are able to obtain a seat on their own merit in the general category and who are either women, differently abled students, children of freedom fighters or members of the army. This eventually means that for a person who does not belong to any of these categories (i.e., one who is not a backward class student, a woman, differently abled, or the child of a freedom fighter or member of the armed forces), the actual number of seats that he or she can compete for is only 46.

To add to this complicated jurisprudence, the Supreme Court has held that horizontal reservations are self-liquidating.[57] In other words, in the example above, if 5 students from horizontal categories (i.e., women, differently abled students, children of freedom fighters and members of the army) obtain general seats on their own merit, then they will be considered as occupying the 5 horizontally reserved seats. This is unlike MRCs who are counted in the general category in vertical reservations.

Promotions

The 77th Amendment

Indra Sawhney's case, at its heart, was about the Mandal Commission and OBC reservations. It was not directly concerned with reservations for Scheduled Castes and Scheduled Tribes. Yet, many things that the Supreme Court said in that case affected Scheduled Castes and Scheduled Tribes as well. The 50 per cent cap on quotas, for instance, affected not merely Other Backward Classes, but also Scheduled Castes and Scheduled Tribes, especially in its application to the 'carry-forward rule' (for which, as we have seen, a constitutional amendment was passed to overrule Indra Sawhney's judgement). Perhaps most importantly, in Indra Sawhney's case, the Supreme Court said that no reservations are permissible for even Scheduled Castes and Scheduled Tribes in promotions, as this would hamper the efficiency of the services.

In 1995, Parliament enacted the 77th amendment to the Constitution which essentially overruled[58] Indra Sawhney's case on this point. It inserted Article 16(4A) into the Constitution, which gives governments the power of reserving seats for Scheduled Castes and Scheduled Tribes in promotions in government services.

However, the amendment did not include Other Backward Classes within its ambit. In other words, no reservations are permissible in promotions in government jobs for Other Backward Classes. When the bill to amend the Constitution was being debated in Parliament, there was a great demand to include Other Backward Classes in it as well. In the discussion that took place in the Lok Sabha, nobody really opposed reservations for Other Backward Classes in promotions. However, Sita Ram Kesari, the Congress leader who moved the bill in the Lok Sabha, said that while all parties in Parliament had agreed on reservations in promotions for Scheduled Castes and Scheduled Tribes, apparently there had not been unanimous agreement on including Other Backward Classes.[59] Talks had been held on this subject on three separate occasions with opposition parties, but there was no consensus on the question of OBC reservation in promotions.[60] It is not entirely clear which party was opposed to providing reservations for Other Backward Classes in promotions.[61] One legislator in the Lok Sabha suggested that the opposition to OBC reservations in promotions came 'from the rank and file of the Congress Party itself'.[62]

Many in Parliament suggested that the 77th amendment was being enacted with an eye towards the elections.[63] The Indra Sawhney judgement, as far as it applied to promotions, was not going to take effect until November 1997.[64] Many asked why the bill was being passed in 1995, with two years left for the Supreme Court's decision to take effect, especially when there were only two days left for the Lok Sabha session to end, with elections around the corner. Perhaps the minority government of Prime Minister Narasimha Rao did not believe that any substantial political gains would accrue to it by including Other Backward Classes in the amendment. Perhaps OBC reservations had, by then, become a very contentious issue. In fact, though the constitution was amended several times on matters involving quotas, it was only during the regime of UPA-1, as we will see below, that an amendment included Other Backward Classes within its fold.

In response to the charge of electoral opportunism, Congress leaders in Parliament argued that though the Indra Sawhney judgement's view on promotions was formally supposed to take effect only in November 1997, many government departments had already started implementing it, and this was affecting the morale of Scheduled Caste/Scheduled Tribe government servants.[65] Some like Nitish Kumar also pointed out that backward class representation was very thin in the higher levels of government service at this time. By January 1994, the Central government had instituted reservations of 15 per cent for Scheduled Castes, 7.5 per cent for Scheduled Tribes, and 27 per cent for Other Backward Classes. Yet, Class A services had only 10.25 per cent Scheduled Castes, 2.9 per cent Scheduled Tribes, and 4.69 per cent Other Backward Classes in them. There was a backlog even in Class B services. On the other hand, Scheduled Castes had exceeded their 15 per cent quota in Class C and Class D services of the government, which were the lower levels of public employment.[66] According to the 1991 census, the Scheduled Caste and Scheduled Tribe population of India was 16.48 per cent and 8.08 per cent respectively.[67]

The bill was passed by a vote of 319 to 1 in the Lok Sabha.[68] Only one member of the house, Mohan Rawale from the Shiv Sena, voted against it. He argued that reservations in promotions would reduce the efficiency of the services because those who were entitled to reservations would 'be sure of getting [a] promotion'.[69] 'How can a person work in Banks, Indian Airlines, LIC and other public sector undertakings,' he asked, 'if [a] promoted officer does not possess quality, if he does not know anything.'[70]

Relaxations

In 1996, the Supreme Court decided a case that eventually prompted yet another constitutional amendment. In *S. Vinod Kumar* v. *Union of India*,[71] the court was asked to determine whether a government memorandum issued in 1977 was valid. The memorandum said that when promotions are handed out to government servants on the basis of seniority and fitness, a qualifying exam must be held to determine whether a candidate is fit for the promotion. The standard which applied to Scheduled Caste/Scheduled Tribe employees in the qualifying exam, however, was lower than that for other candidates. The question was whether this was lawful. Justice B.P. Jeevan Reddy, the judge who had written a judgement for 4 out of 9 judges in the Indra Sawhney case, answered this question by saying that the memorandum violated Article 335 of the Constitution, which required governments to maintain the efficiency of the services. In other words, by allowing Scheduled Caste and Scheduled Tribe candidates to be promoted on relaxed evaluation criteria, the government was hurting the efficiency of the government department, which was impermissible.

Consequently, in the year 2000, Prime Minister Atal Bihari Vajpayee's government amended the Constitution for the 82nd time and inserted a proviso to Article 335, which essentially said that the government could relax the qualifying marks in any exam or lower the standards of evaluation for Scheduled Castes/Scheduled Tribes in matters of promotion. Unsurprisingly, the bill was passed by a vote of 340 to 0 in the Lok Sabha, i.e., nobody voted against it.[72]

The Catch-Up Rule and Consequential Seniority

After the 77th constitutional amendment, Scheduled Castes and Scheduled Tribes who were government employees got reservations in promotions. However, the Supreme Court thereafter applied a peculiar rule to these promoted Scheduled Caste/Scheduled Tribe candidates called the 'catch-up rule'. This rule essentially said that when a junior Scheduled Caste/Scheduled Tribe candidate was promoted over the head of his senior, the senior would regain his seniority upon being promoted to the same level.

This can be explained through the following example. Let's say that X and Y are both employees in Level 1 of a government department. X is a Scheduled Caste employee, while Y is a general category employee. Y is senior to X. However, because of reservations in promotions, X is promoted to Level 2 before Y, and is therefore now senior to Y. However, once Y is promoted to Level 2, if X is still at Level 2, Y will once again be considered senior to X. In other words, Y would have 'caught up' to X. This rule will not apply, however, if X is promoted to Level 3 before Y reaches Level 2.

The Supreme Court first applied this rule in the case of *Union of India* v. *Virpal Singh Chauhan*,[73] in which it said that though an 'accelerated promotion' was being given to Scheduled Caste/ Scheduled Tribe candidates, the 77th constitutional amendment did not confer 'accelerated—or what may be called, the consequential— seniority' on them.[74] This rule was reiterated by the court in *Ajit Singh Januja* v. *State of Punjab*.[75]

The 85th amendment to the Constitution, enacted in 2001, amended Article 16(4A) of the Constitution,[76] to ensure that a Scheduled Caste/Scheduled Tribe candidate who had received an 'accelerated promotion' on account of reservation also got 'consequential seniority'. In other words, in our example above, Y would no longer be able to claim seniority over X upon being promoted to Level 2 after X was promoted to Level 2. Once again, the bill was passed by 355 to 0 in the Lok Sabha, i.e., nobody voted against it.[77]

Quantitative and Qualitative Limits

The Supreme Court was asked to decide the validity of the 77th, 82nd, and 85th amendments to the Constitution in *M. Nagaraj* v. *Union of India*,[78] which we have briefly seen above. In India, a constitutional amendment can only be set aside if it violates the 'basic structure' of the Constitution. In that case, the court found that those amendments did not violate the basic structure of the Constitution and were therefore validly enacted.[79] However, the Supreme Court held that before any reservations could be brought about by the government in public services, whether at the promotion stage or otherwise,[80] three criteria had to be met, viz. there had to be 'quantifiable data' that the class for which the reservation was being provided was: (i) backward, and (ii) inadequately represented in the services; and (iii) the government had to bear in mind that such reservations should not hamper the overall efficiency of the services.[81] Relaxations of marks given to Scheduled Caste/Scheduled Tribe candidates under the 82nd amendment could not be very excessive.[82] Further, the 50 per cent rule had to be observed and the creamy layer[83] had to be excluded from the backward class to which reservations were being provided.[84]

The court in M. Nagaraj's case also said that there was no fundamental right to reservation in government jobs—clauses like Articles 16(4), 16(4A), 16(4B), and the proviso to Article 335 are enabling provisions.[85] In other words, the government can—but is not obliged to—provide reservations under those articles of the Constitution. However, this seems to conflict with the proposition laid down in the Indra Sawhney case that reservations are not an exception to the principle of equality of opportunity. If reservations are a part and parcel of equality of opportunity, then that would, by implication, mean that there is a fundamental right to reserved seats.[86]

However, after the M. Nagaraj case was decided,[87] a new question arose: what portion of the principles laid down in that case would apply to Scheduled Castes and Scheduled Tribes? For instance, would the government have to collect data to show that a caste included in the list of Scheduled Castes is backward before that caste could obtain the benefit of reservations? In an earlier case, the Supreme Court had held that Scheduled Castes and Scheduled Tribes (unlike Other Backward Classes) cannot be bifurcated into backward and more backward communities.[88] But would this mean that the creamy layer concept would not apply to Scheduled Castes and Scheduled Tribes? These questions were answered by the Supreme Court in the case of *Jarnail Singh* v. *Lachhmi Narain Gupta*.[89] In that case, the Supreme Court held that Scheduled Castes and Scheduled Tribes are presumed to be backward and no quantifiable data showing backwardness are required to be collected by the government before providing reservations to them.[90] However, all the other criteria laid down in M. Nagaraj's case, including the creamy layer principle and the requirement that the government must collect quantifiable data concerning inadequacy in services, apply to Scheduled Castes and Scheduled Tribes with equal vigour.[91] The court will, however, apply a light-touch approach while examining the question of whether the government had sufficient quantifiable data showing the inadequacy of the backward classes in government jobs.[92]

In short, when a government wants to reserve posts in government departments for Scheduled Castes, Scheduled Tribes, or Other Backward Classes, it has to satisfy the following requirements: (i) it cannot violate the 50 per cent rule, barring exceptional circumstances; (ii) it must exclude the 'creamy layer' from the reservation;[93] (iii) it must obtain quantifiable data that the community for which the reservation is being provided is inadequately represented in the department;[94] (iv) it must ensure that efficiency in services will not be compromised; and (v) for Other Backward Classes, the government must have quantifiable data that the community for whom reservations are being provided is backward.[95]

Mandal II:

In 2006, Parliament passed the 93rd constitutional amendment which inserted Article 15(5) into the Constitution. This amendment was unique for two reasons. Firstly, it brought about reservations in the private sphere for the first time—casting the quota net over private non-minority colleges, even those that had not received any financial aid from the government. This was in recognition of the fact that education in India had, to a vast extent, been privatized. By 2011, nearly 85 per cent of the engineering seats and 50 per cent of the medical seats were in the private sector.[96] Secondly, for the first time since Prime Minister V.P. Singh's government resurrected the Mandal Commission report in 1990, Other Backward Classes were included within its ambit. For this reason, the press referred to this quota regime as Mandal-II.[97]

The immediate cause for the amendment was the decision of the Supreme Court in *P.A. Inamdar* v. *State of Maharashtra*[98] in which the court had said that reservations were not permissible in private non-minority educational institutions that received no financial assistance from the government. However, in the debate on the amendment bill, several members of Parliament asked for minority institutions to be included within its scope as well. Some, like C.K. Chandrappan, argued that the vast majority of educational institutions in parts of the country were owned by minorities.[99] In reply, HRD Minister Arjun Singh answered that the consensus at an all-party meeting was that minority rights should not be trampled upon by virtue of this amendment.[100]

Once again, the bill was passed by a majority of 379 to 1 in the Lok Sabha.[101] Hardly anyone argued against it. Some suggested that it was a political move, that the Congress minister who moved the amendment, Arjun Singh, was vying for the post of Prime Minister. It was perhaps a Freudian slip when a Congress MP, Dr Chinta Mohan, thanked Sonia Gandhi and Arjun Singh for the amendment bill but left out any mention of Prime Minister Manmohan Singh,[102] something which did not go unnoticed.[103] BJP MP Dharmendra Pradhan said that the amendment was part of the 'internal politics of the Congress for the post of Prime Minister'.[104] At the conclusion of the debate, Arjun Singh made it a point to acknowledge both Sonia Gandhi and Prime Minister Manmohan Singh for creating the right 'ambience' for the amendment.[105]

There had long been a chorus of demands in Parliament for reservations in the private sector.[106] Many MPs had argued, over the years, that privatization had meant fewer jobs in the public sector, and that caste-based quotas should be extended to the private sphere as well. Some serious steps started being taken during the UPA-1 regime in this direction. A Group of Ministers (GoM), headed by the Agriculture Minister Sharad Pawar, was set up to determine whether reservations should be extended beyond government jobs. However, this was met with a volley of opposition in the private sector. Titans of industry like Ratan Tata, Narayana Murthy, and Rahul Bajaj were quoted in the press as being opposed to reservations in private jobs,[107] though they promised to do more for the cause of social justice.[108] In an editorial piece in April 2006, the *Indian Express* wrote that 'businesses are in the business of making money and the right and freedom to decide whom they should hire is intrinsic to that mandate.'[109] Eventually, the GoM decided against reservations in the private sector, saying that 'sensitive issues' were involved and that the 'political desirability, political feasibility and legality of amending the Constitution need to be carefully considered in consultation with UPA constituents.'[110]

The Supreme Court upheld the constitutional validity of the 93rd amendment.[111] However, in doing so, it reiterated that the creamy layer must be excluded from Other Backward Classes.[112]

Gated Communities of Exclusion

In cases concerning reservations, the Supreme Court often had to ask itself whether merit or efficiency would suffer if quotas were allowed to proliferate. Should meritorious candidates not be rewarded— those who had worked hard and done well in exams or in their performance reviews as employees of the government? By giving a boost to unmeritorious reserved candidates, would reservations not bring the level of colleges and government departments down, the court was asked. In the years since the Indra Sawhney case, several judges of the Supreme Court have come up with some answers to these questions.

For instance, in *Ajay Kumar Singh* v. *State of Bihar*,[113] the question before the Supreme Court was whether reservation should be permitted in post-graduate medical institutions. The opponents of reservation argued that the level of post-graduate education would be brought down if quotas continued, which would be a disastrous consequence at that level of specialization. However, rejecting this argument, Justice B.P. Jeevan Reddy held that since all candidates—belonging to both the general and reserved categories—would eventually have to pass the same exam and be tested on the same standards in order to obtain a post-graduate medical degree, it could not be said that reservations lowered educational standards.[114] He also added that academic performance was 'no guarantee of efficiency in practice'.[115] It often happened, he said, that lawyers and doctors who did poorly in academics excelled in their professional careers and vice versa.[116]

In another case,[117] the Supreme Court held that reservations were permissible in both 'speciality' and 'super-speciality' courses. Speaking for the bench, Justice K. Ramaswamy wrote that marks could not be a measure of 'higher proficiency, efficiency or excellence'.[118] He even added that in internal examinations, marks are awarded by examiners 'on the basis of caste, creed, colour, religion etc'.[119]

However, these judgements were later overruled by the Supreme Court in *Dr Preeti Srivastava* v. *State of MP*.[120] The question in that case was whether the government could relax the minimum qualifying marks that backward class students needed in order to get admission into post-graduate medical programmes. The cut-off in the entrance exam in the state of Uttar Pradesh for admission into these courses was 45 per cent for general students and 35 per cent for reserved category students. However, since no reserved category students could be found who had obtained a minimum of 35 per cent in the qualifying exam, the state of Uttar Pradesh reduced the minimum qualifying marks to 20 per cent for reserved category students. The question was whether this was legally permissible.[121]

Answering that it was not,[122] the court held that reservation policies could not be designed in a manner that undermined 'other vital public interests or the general good of all'.[123] The court said that it was in the national interest for a large percentage of reservations to be implemented at the primary school level.[124] Reasonable reservations, said the court, were also permissible at the university level up to graduation.[125] However, at the postgraduate level, considerations apart from 'the individual self-interest of the candidate' came into play. The 'facilities for training or education at this level', said the court, 'are not available in abundance'. The scarce resources of the state, it added, must therefore be given only to high-calibre students 'possessing the highest degree of merit'.[126] The court did not express any opinion on whether reservations were valid in post-graduate medical courses.[127]

In other words, reservations at the post-graduate level had to be minimal.[128] The court added that no reservations were permissible at the super-specialization level as doing otherwise, said the court, would be 'detrimental to the national interest', since students at this level would be expected to make an original contribution to the field.[129]

Speaking for the bench in Dr Preeti Srivastava's case, Justice Sujata Manohar came up with three answers to the propositions put forward by Justices Jeevan Reddy and Ramaswamy in the earlier cases. Firstly, she said that facilities for training were limited at the post-graduate and super-speciality levels of medical education, and these had to be given only to the best students, so that India would gain by the creation of high-quality doctors and researchers.[130] Secondly, admitting unmeritorious students into these colleges would lower the educational level there, since the quality of teaching would have to cater to the lowest common denominator.[131] Thirdly, according to Justice Manohar, it was no answer, as Justice Jeevan Reddy had written, to say that the passing standard would be the same for all students—general and reserved. India needs students who pass with flying colours at that level,[132] she said.[133]

In 2011, the Supreme Court said that a medical college in Delhi could not reserve all its seats for the children of members of the army or their widows.[134] In arriving at this conclusion, however, Justice B. Sudershan Reddy presented an eloquent argument in favour of reservations. He said that quotas were necessary in order to ensure that India's marginalized youth did not rise up in rebellion against the state—in order to avoid 'a state of social emergency with a potential for conflagration that would be on an unimaginable scale'.[135]

This was not an unfamiliar argument—the fear that backward communities would rise up and revolt was repeatedly cited as justification for reservations in India's Parliament,[136] and even earlier. In 1915, Gandhi told a member of the Servants of India Society in Poona that their activities would 'make Harijans rise in rebellion against society'.[137] In 1995, Prime Minister V.P. Singh made a speech at Harvard in which he said that not having reservations might 'not only cost our government, but our lives as well'.[138]

Justice Sudershan Reddy added that merit could not be measured on the basis of marks alone. '[G]reat universities' now admitted students on the basis of recommendation letters, statements of purpose, and the willingness of students to undertake social service.[139] Further, 'having a diverse student body' enhances the learning environment at colleges, as students from different backgrounds bring their own unique perspectives to the academic community.[140] He wrote that many Indian 'upper crust' students would not be able to study at such universities (probably universities abroad) had marks been the sole criterion for admission.[141] Knowledge, he concluded, could not be confined to 'gated communities of exclusion'.[142]

These justifications for quotas were not restricted to education alone. In the sphere of public employment, Justice K. Ramaswamy in *Ashok Kumar Gupta* v. *State of U.P.*[143] equated reservations with socialism. Unlike capitalist countries, India's socialist state believed in the redistribution of wealth. Justice Ramaswamy argued that public jobs were like national wealth and had to be redistributed in order to correct social imbalances.[144] Reservations in government employment enabled marginalized communities to share power.[145] He suggested that unless the backward classes were permitted to serve in government jobs, they would not be able to prove their efficiency which, in turn, would be used as an argument to prevent them from getting reserved seats. He compared this vicious cycle to the parable that 'insanity cannot be cured until married and marriage cannot be celebrated till insanity is cured'.[146] He referred to Scheduled Castes as 'dalits'.[147]

Finally, in *B.K. Pavitra* v. *Union of India*,[148] the Supreme Court provided three answers to the argument that reservations reduce the efficiency of the services. Firstly, it held that there was no empirical evidence to show that reserved category candidates performed poorly in their jobs.[149] Secondly, 'merit' can hardly ever be measured through neutral criteria. For instance, success in an entrance exam requires, among other things, (i) economic resources (e.g., access to coaching classes), (ii) social and cultural resources (networks of contacts, guidance from seniors, etc.), and (iii) intrinsic ability and hard work.[150] Of these, (i) and (ii) have nothing to do with merit. Thirdly, diversity itself is merit—a meritorious candidate is not merely one who is talented, but one 'whose appointment [fulfils] the constitutional goals of uplifting members of the Scheduled Castes and Scheduled Tribes and ensuring a diverse and representative administration'.[151]

From OBC to EWS

In 2019, Parliament passed the 103rd amendment[152] to the Constitution which introduced reservations in government jobs and higher educational institutions for 'economically weaker sections of citizens' or EWS. The amendment breached the 50 per cent rule and enabled the government to provide up to 10 per cent reservations for the EWS. EWS communities would be identified by the government on the basis of 'family income and other indicators of economic disadvantage'.

The government has said that those who do not belong to the Scheduled Caste, Scheduled Tribe or Other Backward Class categories and whose family (i.e., parents, siblings below the age of 18, spouse, and children below the age of 18): (i) has a gross annual income below Rs 8 lakh (which is also the income limit for determining creamy layer status for the backward classes[153]); and (ii) does not own property of a certain size (e.g., 5 acres of agricultural land, a residential flat of 1,000 square feet, etc.) would be EWS communities for the purpose of the amendment.[154] It has been estimated that 80 per cent of Indian households would fall within the definition of EWS communities.[155]

This amendment, enacted by Prime Minister Modi's BJP government at the end of its first term, was significant for at least three reasons. Firstly, until this point in time, social backwardness was the sine qua non for reservations.[156] Reservations in public employment required social backwardness, while quotas in education required both social and educational backwardness. Though economic criteria were used, even by the Mandal Commission, to evaluate a community's backwardness, they were never sufficient, by themselves, to make a group eligible to receive reservations. In the previous chapter, we saw that Justice Chinnappa Reddy considered the idea of poor Brahmins receiving reservations to be 'too grotesque even to be considered'.[157] However, now, for the first time in India's history, economic criteria alone were going to be constitutionally sufficient to enable a community to get quotas, and social backwardness was irrelevant. Further, the government has excluded Scheduled Castes, Scheduled Tribes, and Other Backward Classes from EWS reservations, essentially implying that this is only upper-caste reservation. In this sense, the 103rd Constitutional amendment marks a substantial departure from the scheme of the Constitution. However, the term 'weaker sections' in the amendment was borrowed from Article 46 of the Constitution—a directive principle of state policy which calls on the government to promote the 'educational and economic interests of the weaker sections of the people'.

Secondly, the amendment increased the limit of reservations by 10 per cent, violating the 50 per cent rule laid down in M.R. Balaji's case, a rule which was reiterated, with exceptions, since the Indra Sawhney case. We have seen that the Supreme Court upheld the constitutional amendments in the Nagaraj case partly because the 50 per cent rule had not been violated.[158] However, reservations based on economic criteria had long been demanded in India's parliament.[159]

Thirdly, as one scholar points out,[160] it is now potentially easier for the government to provide reservations for EWS in government jobs than for Scheduled Castes, Scheduled Tribes, and Other Backward Classes. For Scheduled Castes, Scheduled Tribes, and Other Backward Classes, the government has to have 'quantifiable data' that these communities are inadequately represented in the services. However, there is no such requirement before providing reservations for the EWS group, though the EWS group gets only 10 per cent whereas the others get 50 per cent. This is particularly relevant for two reasons: (i) Available quantitative data suggest that EWS communities already have a share of around 28 per cent in 445 higher educational institutions ranked by the National Institutional Ranking Framework in India.[161] In other words, EWS communities already have 'adequate' representation in colleges, though not 'proportional' representation. (ii) Further, backward classes are below the poverty line at a rate which is much higher than the rest of the population.[162]

The Supreme Court has recently upheld the validity of the 103rd constitutional amendment in Janhit Abhiyan v. Union of India (2022).

7

Marriage, Conversion, Migration

Does a Scheduled Caste, Scheduled Tribe or Other Backward Class person lose her caste when she converts to another religion? Does a third-generation Christian who converts to Hinduism get back the caste of her Hindu forefathers? Does a Brahmin woman who marries a Scheduled Caste man acquire his caste? Can a person who has a Scheduled Tribe certificate in Nagaland seek a seat reserved for Scheduled Tribes in the public services in Uttar Pradesh? What would happen to a student occupying a reserved seat in a medical college if it turned out that she was not actually a Scheduled Caste, Scheduled Tribe or Other Backward Class person—would she be allowed to graduate? These are the kinds of fascinating questions that came before the Supreme Court in the several decades since India's independence, and a complex body of law has emerged to answer them.

Conversion

Does a Hindu who converts to Christianity, Islam, or any other religion automatically lose her caste? Not necessarily. If three circumstances exist, then a convert is still considered to belong to her original caste: (i) firstly, members of the convert's original caste must continue to consider her to be a part of that caste[1]; (ii) secondly, the convert herself should still want to be a part of her caste[2]; and (iii) thirdly, the new religion should permit the convert to retain her caste (which is often seen in south India and the north-east).[3] For instance, the Supreme Court has observed that in Andhra Pradesh and Tamil Nadu there are 'Christian Reddies, Christian Kammas, Christian Nadars, Christian Adi Andhras, [and] Christian Adi Dravidas'.[4]

Additionally, a Hindu may be able to show that she never converted to another religion at all and therefore never lost her caste. For instance, in 1974, a person elected to the Maharashtra legislative assembly in a seat reserved for Scheduled Castes proved that he had not really converted to Buddhism—something which his electoral opponent accused him of doing. The Supreme Court in that case held that a Hindu who merely visits other houses of worship like Buddhist temples, churches, or dargas, without changing her habits and customs, cannot be said to have converted to another religion. In a town called Nagapatnam in Tamil Nadu, said the court, there was a Muslim dargah where most pilgrims were Hindus. In Andhra Pradesh, the court added, Hindus had names like Mastan Ayya or Hussain Amma, after Muslim saints whose dargahs were nearby.[5] On the other hand, a person who makes a public declaration that she has ceased to be a Hindu and is following another religion like Buddhism can no longer be considered a Hindu.[6]

However, it is not necessary to change one's name in order to convert from a religion to another.[7] A man with a Muslim-sounding name, Mohammad Sadique, was elected to the Punjab legislative assembly on a seat reserved for Scheduled Castes. His opponent alleged that he was not really a Sikh, but a Muslim—after all, his name was 'Sadique', which sounds like a Muslim name. However, Sadique said he was now a Sikh. He pointed out that he was a famous singer, his fans knew him by his name, which is why he did not adopt a Sikh name after converting to Sikhism. The Supreme Court accepted his argument and found that Sadique was observing all the rites of the Sikh religion, even though his family members were still Muslims.[8]

In Chapter 4, we saw that the Indian administration decided in 1950 that Scheduled Tribes should be allowed to convert without loss of Scheduled Tribe status. This was because many Scheduled Tribes subscribed to tribal religions and preventing them from converting without losing their constitutional privileges would have meant discouraging them from converting even to Hinduism. However, in a judgement delivered in 2004, the Supreme Court rejected the idea that Scheduled Tribes can freely convert without losing their privileges.[9] In that case, the court said that a Scheduled Tribe person who converts to another religion can only be considered to still belong to that Scheduled Tribe if three conditions are satisfied: (i) firstly, she must continue to be a part of her original tribe, despite her religious conversion[10]; (ii) secondly, she should go on following the 'customs, rituals and other traits' of the tribe, including customary laws of succession, inheritance, and marriage[11]; (iii) thirdly, it has to be shown that the convert is 'still suffering from social disability' despite her conversion to another religion.[12] The first and second conditions were consistent with what the Madhya Bharat and Mysore governments had suggested to the central government in January 1950, as we saw in Chapter 4.

Reconversion

What happens to a Hindu who converts to another religion and then reconverts back to Hinduism—does her caste revive? What about those who were born Christians or Muslims, but whose forefathers were Hindus—if they convert to Hinduism, do they revert to the caste of their Hindu ancestors? The Supreme Court in such cases has said yes, provided that two conditions are satisfied: (i) firstly, a person who reconverts to Hinduism must do so because she genuinely wants to be a Hindu and not because she wants to benefit from reservations[13]; (ii) secondly, the members of the caste to which the reconvert reverts must accept the reconvert or at least not object to her becoming a member of their caste.[14] However, reversion of the old caste is less likely when a descendant of a family that has been non-Hindu for several generations converts to Hinduism.[15] Further, a person cannot simply convert to Hinduism by making a declaration. She has to intend to be converted to the Hindu faith, conduct herself as a Hindu, and be accepted back into the Hindu community.[16]

Marriage

An upper-caste woman who marries a lower-caste man cannot acquire her husband's Scheduled Caste, Scheduled Tribe or Other Backward Class status for getting constitutional benefits.[17] For instance, in one case, a woman called Valsamma Paul, who was Syrian Catholic by birth, married a Latin Catholic man. Latin Catholics were a backward class fishing community in Kerala. Paul then applied for a job as a law lecturer at Cochin University in a reserved seat. The court held that Paul was born into a forward community and had all its advantages growing up. She was a fully educated adult when she got married, and was therefore not entitled to her husband's Other Backward Class status.[18] Conversely, a Scheduled Caste man who marries an upper-caste woman does not automatically lose his status unless his community excommunicates him. So, in one case, a Scheduled Caste man who married a Christian woman was still held to belong to his caste.[19]

When a lower-caste woman marries an upper-caste man, the presumption is that her children get the caste of their father. However, if the children show that they were brought up by their mother and suffered social disabilities associated with her caste, that they were considered to be members of their mother's caste both by that caste and by outsiders, then they can claim to have their mother's caste.[20]

In 2016, when a student at Hyderabad University by the name of Rohith Vemula committed suicide, the question which arose was whether he had acquired the Other Backward Class caste of his father or the Scheduled Caste of his mother.[21] The commission which was appointed to inquire into his suicide eventually found that though Rohith had been brought up by his divorced mother, she had no proof to show that she belonged to the 'Mala' Scheduled Caste community.[22]

Migration

The list of Scheduled Castes and Scheduled Tribes is different for the many states in India. What happens when a Scheduled Caste, Scheduled Tribe, or Other Backward Class[23] person migrates from one state to another—does she get the benefit of reservations even in the state to which she has migrated? The answer depends on whether reservation is being sought in colleges or jobs controlled by the central government or state government. The rule of thumb is that if the job or college seat is under the control of the central government, then migration makes no difference to a person's caste status.[24] In other words, if a Scheduled Caste person in, say, Maharashtra wants to apply for a central government job in Delhi, or for admission into an engineering college controlled by the central government in Bihar, then she can apply for a reserved seat.[25] This may be despite the fact that she may not be on the list of Scheduled Castes in Delhi or Bihar.

However, if the job or college is under the control of the state government, then migration results in loss of status. This could arise in three situations. The first[26] could be a scenario in which a Scheduled Caste, Scheduled Tribe, or Other Backward Class person migrates from State A to State B and her caste or tribe is only on the list in State A.[27] Secondly, there could also be a situation where the caste of this person is on the list in both State A and State B.[28] In neither of these cases is the migrant entitled to the benefit of reservations. In other words, a Scheduled Caste person belonging to 'Caste X' in Maharashtra cannot apply under the reserved category for a job or college seat controlled by the Uttar Pradesh government, whether or not 'Caste X' is on the list of Scheduled Castes in Uttar Pradesh. Thirdly, a person who migrates from State A to State B, but whose caste is on the Scheduled Caste list in State B but not State A, will probably not get the benefit of Scheduled Caste status by migrating to State B.

The idea behind the no-migration-rule[29] is that social disabilities are not the same everywhere. A caste or community might suffer from a very severe social handicap in State A but may not have any such problems in State B. A person who migrates from State A to State B may not therefore face the same social stigma that she would have faced in State A for belonging to her caste. Further, allowing outsiders to take up reserved seats in State B will deprive the reserved communities in State B that suffer from serious social disabilities.[30] Even where a caste is on the list in both states, the Supreme Court has held that the conditions for including that caste on the list might be different in each state and the degree of disadvantages might be varied.[31]

The no-migration-rule may sometimes yield unfair results. As the Supreme Court has itself pointed out in one case, a Scheduled Caste or Scheduled Tribe person might have migrated to another state for work, and might be suffering from the stigma of untouchability there—the law, as it stands, does not protect her.[32]

Sub-castes and Synonyms

Articles 341 and 342 of the Constitution give the President the power of setting out a list of Scheduled Castes and Scheduled Tribes in the different states in India. Once that list is issued, only Parliament can amend or modify it. In 1950, the President issued a list of Scheduled Castes and Scheduled Tribes, and that list has been amended from time to time.[33]

The question that often came up before the Supreme Court was: what if the name of your caste is not on the Presidential list, but you claim that your caste is actually a sub-caste of or a synonym for one of the names actually contained in the list? For instance, in Maharashtra, the Presidential list said that a tribe known as 'Halba' (also referred to as 'Halbi') was a Scheduled Tribe. Members of a tribe called 'Halba-Koshti' claimed that they were actually a sub-tribe of the Halba group and were therefore entitled to reserved seats. Similarly, members of the 'Mahadeo-Koli' community argued that they too were members of a tribe known as 'Koli' in that state, a Scheduled Tribe on the list. In Bihar, members of the 'Lohar' community said that their caste name was a synonym for 'Lohara' or 'Lohra' which was on the Scheduled Tribe list in Bihar.

The Supreme Court rejected these arguments. It held that the Presidential lists were actually quite comprehensive[34]—they specified sub-tribes, sub-castes, and synonyms. Since 'Halba-Koshti'[35] and 'Mahadeo-Koli'[36] were not specified as sub-tribes of 'Halba' and 'Koli' in Maharashtra respectively, and since 'Lohar'[37] was not specifically set out as a synonym of 'Lohara' (as 'Lohra' was) in Bihar, these groups could not claim Scheduled Tribe status. The same principles apply to Other Backward Classes. For example, the 'Namdeo Shimpi' community could not claim to be a sub-caste of the 'Shimpi' Other Backward Class in Maharashtra.[38]

The answer became a little more complicated when the government tried to say that not all members of a named caste or tribe in the list deserved to be protected. For instance, the 'Thakur' community was notified as a Scheduled Tribe in Maharashtra. However, the government there said that there were 'Thakur' Kshatriyas in the state who should not get constitutional benefits. Similarly, in Manipur, though the caste called 'Lois' was considered to be an a Scheduled Caste, the government there believed that only 'Lois' who resided in 8 villages in that state were actually backward. Likewise, the Kerala government wanted to exclude 'Ezhavas' and 'Thiyyas' from Scheduled Caste status, though they were part of the 'Thandan' community, which was on the list. The Supreme Court has not been able to give a decisive answer in these cases. More often than not, the court has said that it cannot investigate whether a subgroup should be excluded from the benefits of Scheduled Caste or Scheduled Tribe status (e.g., the 'Thandans' in Kerala).[39] However, in some cases, the Supreme Court allowed such exclusions to take place (e.g., in the case involving 'Lois' in Manipur).[40] The Supreme Court has, in the past, categorically said that a state cannot divide Scheduled Castes or Scheduled Tribes into backward and more backward classes,[41] though this question has now been referred to a larger bench for reconsideration.[42]

What happens if the Presidential list contains a name of a caste or tribe which does not actually exist in that state? For instance, the lists for Mysore and Orissa said that 'Bhovi' and 'Kulis' were Scheduled Castes and Scheduled Tribes in that state respectively. However, there were no such communities in those states. In these cases, the Supreme Court looked at evidence to figure out which communities were actually intended to be given benefits instead of the named communities. After all, the President must have intended to benefit some community when he said that the 'Bhovi' in Mysore were Scheduled Castes. The court found that in government records, the 'Bhovi' caste was often referred to as 'Vodda', and therefore concluded that the 'Voddar' community was a Scheduled Caste in that state though it was not on the list.[43] Similarly, the court came to the conclusion that Parliament meant to say 'Kuli' (without an 's') when it said that 'Kulis' were a Scheduled Tribe in Orissa.[44]

On the other hand, the Supreme Court took a seemingly different view in the recent 'Gond Gowari' case.[45] In 1956, Parliament had added 'Gond Gowari' to the presidential list as a sub-tribe of the 'Gond' scheduled tribe. Members of the Gowari community in Maharashtra contended that the 'Gond Gowari' community had become extinct since 1911, and that Parliament meant to refer to the 'Gowari' community when it added 'Gond Gowari' to the presidential list. Disagreeing with this submission, the Supreme Court held that the Maharashtra government strongly believed that the 'Gond Gowari' community was in existence in Maharashtra, and several caste certificates, duly verified by the scrutiny committee, had been issued to members of that community in the state. This was unlike the Mysore government, which, several decades ago, had not disputed that there was no 'Bhovi' community in the state. However, to add to the confusion, the 'Kuli' case was not noticed by the Supreme Court in its 'Gond Gowari' judgement.

False Caste Claims

In 1994, the Supreme Court had to decide an interesting case.[46] Two sisters, Madhuri and Suchita Patil, had secured admission in medical colleges claiming to be members of a Scheduled Tribe. However, it turned out that they did not actually belong to a Scheduled Tribe community. The question which then arose was: should the sisters be allowed to continue their studies and occupy reserved seats? The Supreme Court said that one of them, Suchita, had nearly completed her degree and should be allowed to sit for her final exam. However, after graduating, Suchita would not be entitled to get any reserved jobs or other benefits a Scheduled Tribe. Her sister, Madhuri, on the other hand, was still in the second year of her programme, and the Supreme Court did not allow her to continue her education unless she could get admitted in the open category.

The rule which was thereafter followed in some cases was that if a student in a professional college had completed or nearly completed her studies,[47] had not falsified or fabricated her records in claiming backward class status, and been under the honest impression that she did, in fact, belong to the community she claimed to be a part of, she would be permitted to get her degree or complete her programme even if her status as a Scheduled Caste or Scheduled Tribe person was found to be false.[48] The idea behind this was that nobody would gain by forcing that student to drop out, and the investment made by the government in that student's education would otherwise go to waste.[49] On the other hand, government employees who were found to be wrongly occupying reserved posts were usually not shown the same indulgence,[50] though there were some exceptions.[51]

However, in a recent case,[52] the Supreme Court has now clarified that where a person is found to be wrongly holding on to a reserved seat in a college or post in a government job, she must be forced to give up that seat or post. It does not matter if she is a student in the final year of the programme. It is also irrelevant that she had no dishonest intent in claiming to be a Scheduled Caste or Scheduled Tribe person. In other words, a final-year student occupying a reserved seat in a medical college can no longer continue in the reserved seat, and an employee who has served for several years in a government job as a reserved candidate must be asked to quit, if it is found that their caste claims were false, even if they did not commit any fraud in claiming to be reserved category candidates.

The court gave three reasons for arriving at this conclusion: (i) firstly, when a person who does not belong to a Scheduled Caste or Scheduled Tribe obtains a seat reserved for those communities, she violates the rights of members of those communities; (ii) secondly, she wrongfully gains access to scarce public resources; and (iii) thirdly, an illegality would be perpetrated by 'bestowing benefits upon an imposter undeservingly'. Allowing a general category student to occupy a reserved seat, said the court, is itself a fraud on the Constitution.[53]

In Madhuri and Suchita Patil's case, the Supreme Court prescribed a procedure for governments to follow for verifying caste certificates.[54] Under these directions, governments were required to hire 'vigilance officers' to investigate whether a person's claim of belonging to a Scheduled Caste or Scheduled Tribe community was valid. Vigilance officers are expected to examine all the documents provided by candidates (e.g., school leaving certificates, ration cards, etc.). Documents that are dated prior to India's independence (e.g., a grandparent's school leaving certificate, which might say what his or her caste was) are regarded as having a higher evidentiary value than those that came thereafter.[55] This is because courts think that people would have had fewer reasons to lie about their caste (i.e., by falsely claiming to belong to a Scheduled Caste or Scheduled Tribe) before Indian independence than thereafter. However, as we have seen in previous chapters, affirmative action policies based on caste came into being prior to India's independence as well. There may therefore have been reasons for people to lie about their caste even before India attained independence.

Vigilance officers are also required to conduct an 'affinity test' to verify a person's caste.[56] An affinity test is essentially when the applicant is asked questions about the caste or tribe which she claims to belong to— questions like which deities are worshipped by the community, what ceremonies are performed at marriages and deaths, how the dead are buried, etc. However, the Supreme Court has held that the 'affinity test' is not conclusive. Members of Scheduled Tribes, for instance, may now have come into contact with others thanks to migration and modernization—they may have developed 'new traits' that do not match the tribes' 'traditional characteristics'.[57]

Is All of This Fair?

This complicated body of law, laid down by the Supreme Court in various cases over the years is, in some areas, quite problematic.

For instance, a Scheduled Tribe person who converts to Christianity has to prove several things that any other Scheduled Tribe person does not have to. A Christian Scheduled Tribe convert has to show that she is still a member of her original tribe, that she follows the customs and traditions of the tribe, and that she still suffers from social disabilities. A Scheduled Tribe person who has not converted to another religion will remain a Scheduled Tribe person despite having left her tribe, abandoned her traditions, and ceased to suffer from social handicaps (unless the entire Scheduled Tribe community is denotified from the list). The additional burden that has been imposed by the Supreme Court on the Scheduled Tribe convert therefore has an adverse impact on her liberty of conscience. A member of a Scheduled Caste, Scheduled Tribe, or Other Backward Class community will think ten times before converting to another religion, or attempt to conceal her conversion, because conversion would very often imply loss of attractive constitutional benefits.[58] What is this if not an infringement of the freedom to profess, practise, and propagate the religion of one's choice guaranteed to every person by Article 25 of the Constitution?

When it comes to migration and loss of caste status, the distinction drawn by the Supreme Court between the central government and state government is quite artificial. A Scheduled Tribe person in Tamil Nadu can apply under the reserved category for a central government job in Bihar despite the fact that her tribe is not considered a Scheduled Tribe in Bihar. Yet, she would be disqualified from applying for a comparable job with the state government in Bihar. A Scheduled Tribe girl in Tamil Nadu has suffered substantial social disabilities. She has been brought up in an environment of deprivation and discrimination. The disadvantages with which she grew up do not magically cease to exist upon her migration to another state, even though her tribe may not be recognized as a Scheduled Tribe there. There is no reason why she should be considered a Scheduled Tribe person for the central government, but a general category candidate for the state government. This is even more so in cases where the migrant's caste or tribe is recognized as a Scheduled Caste or Scheduled Tribe in both states. This policy favours domestic candidates over migrants and discourages inter-state migration.

The Supreme Court has said that upper-caste women who marry lower-caste men cannot take advantage of their husbands' caste status. However, one wonders why the court does not apply the tests that it adopts in cases of religious conversion to cases of marriage. An upper-caste woman who marries, say, a Scheduled Caste or Scheduled Tribe man might be shunned by the members of her original caste. She might completely be accepted into the fold by the members of her husband's community. She may follow the customs and traditions of her husband's family. After twenty long years of marriage, she may be discriminated against in government service, on grounds of caste, and denied a promotion because she is a Scheduled Caste person. Yet, the law laid down by the Supreme Court turns a blind eye towards her.

At first blush, the Supreme Court's judgements on this subject seem to abandon the patriarchal notion that a woman derives her identity (in this case, her caste) from her husband. However, on closer inspection, one realizes that what the court's judgements actually do is deprive a married woman of her ability to decide her own identity—the freedom to choose whether she wants to retain the caste of the family she was born into, or to adopt the caste of her husband's family.

Finally, the Supreme Court has, until recently, said that governments cannot classify Scheduled Castes and Scheduled Tribes into backward and more backward.[59] All Scheduled Castes and Scheduled Tribes are therefore artificially presumed to be as backward as one another respectively, which is absolutely not true. Some Scheduled Caste groups are better off than others.[60] Relatively well-off Scheduled Caste communities might capture all the reserved seats and positions, leaving nothing for the really backward Scheduled Castes. Yet, the Supreme Court does not permit the government to come to the aid of the latter.[61] This is despite the fact that governments have the absolute freedom to classify Other Backward Classes into backward and more backward. This double standard between Other Backward Classes, on the one hand, and Scheduled Castes and Scheduled Tribes, on the other, is puzzling.

Conclusion

The framers of India's Constitution were accused of plagiarizing from other countries. 'We wanted the music of *Veena* or *Sitar*', said K. Hanumanthaiya in the Constituent Assembly, 'but here we have the music of an English band.'[1] Indeed, many parts of the Constitution were inspired by the Constitutions of other countries. The right to life under Article 21 used the phrase 'procedure established by law' from the Constitution of Japan. The freedom of speech and expression under Article 19(1)(a) was based on the Irish Constitution. The words 'equal protection of the laws' under Article 14 were copied from the fourteenth amendment to the US Constitution. However, when it came to reservations, the provisions of the Constitution were uniquely derived from India's own history and experiences.

'Affirmative action' in the US as we now know it really started in the 1960s during the civil rights movement.[2] Race-based quotas are considered unconstitutional there, though admissions departments at colleges can give some 'preference' to under-represented racial minorities provided that race is only one of the factors in the decision.[3] Affirmative action policies are viewed by courts with extreme suspicion and tested on the touchstone of the lethal 'strict scrutiny' test—where laws are upheld only if they are narrowly tailored to meet a compelling state interest.[4] Affirmative action policies are adopted by only a tiny minority of colleges in the US—most colleges admit almost anyone who applies.[5] Affirmative action is certainly not unique to India alone and is followed in some form or the other in countries like South Africa, Brazil, Colombia, Israel, Malaysia, Nigeria, and the US.[6] However, the quota provisions of the Indian Constitution were not borrowed from a foreign jurisdiction. The 50 per cent rule, the creamy layer concept, the constitutional bifurcation of backward communities into Scheduled Castes, Scheduled Tribes, and Other Backward Classes, the carry-forward rule, consequential seniority, interlocking reservations—these are among India's many original contributions to constitutional law.

It is important to bear in mind that reservations in government jobs and educational institutions actually affect only a minority of the population. About 9.5 per cent of the country's population aged 20 and above has attained graduate level education and only 4.8 per cent Scheduled Castes and 3.1 per cent Scheduled Tribes, aged 20 and above, have acquired a graduate degree.[7] Only 4.8 per cent of the approximately 600 million Indians between the ages of 20 and 59 are actually employed in any capacity in the public sector, where there is a chance of getting a reserved job.[8] It is, therefore, abundantly clear that reservations alone will not be able to improve the socio-economic condition of the backward classes.

Despite the fact that India has been independent for over seventy years, backward classes lag behind the rest of the population on several social indicators. For instance, Scheduled Caste and Scheduled Tribe babies are born with a lower weight than the national average.[9] Scheduled Caste, Scheduled Tribe, and Other Backward Class children are shorter than general caste children.[10] As a group, between 36–39 per cent of Scheduled Castes are below the poverty line in India, as against 26–31 per cent of Other Backward Classes, and 16 per cent of others.[11] The literacy rate among the Scheduled Caste and Scheduled Tribe population is lower than the national average. Scheduled Caste students drop out from school at a rate greater than most Indian schoolchildren do.[12] According to the 2011 census, though 63 per cent of India is considered literate, only 56 per cent of the Scheduled Castes and 49 per cent of the Scheduled Tribes are literate. As the table below indicates, Scheduled Castes and Scheduled Tribes have lower access than the national average to electricity, toilets, drinking water at home, banking services, television sets, the Internet, and cell phones.

Table 1: Access of Scheduled Castes and Scheduled Tribes to certain assets

	Electricity	Latrines at home	Drinking water at home	Banking services	Television sets	Computer / laptop with Internet	Mobile phone
Scheduled Castes	59	33.9	35.4	50.9	39.1	1.3	50.2
Scheduled Tribes	50	20.6	18	44.2	19.9	0.7	31.3
India	67	47	47	59	47	3	59

Source: Census of India (2011). All figures are expressed in percentages.

Even reservations have not been able to ensure that backward classes reach the very highest levels of government service and educational achievement. Between 2004 and 2014, the representation of Scheduled Castes and Other Backward Classes in central government services has generally gone up.[13] However, available data suggest that despite reservations, Scheduled Castes have not yet fully penetrated the highest levels of government service, Scheduled Tribes have failed to do so at the higher and mid-tier levels, while Other Backward Classes lag behind at all echelons of government service. The civil services of the central government are roughly divided into four groups which correspond with their rank, status, and degree of responsibility[14] (e.g., administrative, clerical, or menial work[15]): Groups A, B, C, and D, with Group A being the highest and D the lowest. The official reservations quota in central government jobs is 15 per cent for Scheduled Castes, 7.5 per cent for Scheduled Tribes and 27 per cent for Other Backward Classes. In 2015, Scheduled Castes went past these quotas in Groups B and C of government service—16.2 per cent of Group B posts and 17.3 per cent of Group C posts (excluding Safai Karmacharis) were held by Scheduled Castes. They were only marginally below the Scheduled Caste quota in Group A services with 13.3 per cent of these jobs being held by Scheduled Castes.[16] Scheduled Tribes were below their quota in Groups A (5.8 per cent) and B (6.7 per cent), and only exceeded their quota in Group C (excluding Safai Karmacharis) (8.6 per cent). Other Backward Classes were well below their 27 per cent quota in central government jobs at all levels of the service: Group A (11.7 per cent), Group B (12.3 per cent), and Group C (excluding Safai Karmacharis) (18.9 per cent).[17]

Reservations seem to have benefited the backward classes in higher educational institutions,[18] though not enough. A 2019 government report found that the gross enrollment ratio of Scheduled Castes and Scheduled Tribes in these institutions was 23 per cent and 17.2 per cent respectively,[19] which exceeds their reservation quotas. However, a deeper investigation reveals that while backward class students have enrolled in large numbers in BA and MA programmes, they lag behind their quotas in PhDs and professional schools like medicine, engineering, and law.[20] So, for instance, in the academic year 2018–19, enrollment in the BA programme for Scheduled Castes (18 per cent), Scheduled Tribes (7.5 per cent), and Other Backward Classes (36 per cent) exceeded their quotas. However, enrollment in the MBBS programme for Scheduled Castes (8.6 per cent), Scheduled Tribes (3.8 per cent), and Other Backward Classes (25 per cent) was low despite reservations. Generally, Other Backward Classes do better in terms of their enrollment numbers than Scheduled Castes and Scheduled Tribes, while Scheduled Tribes do the worst. For example, in the MBA programmes in the academic year 2018–19, Scheduled Tribe enrollment was only 1.8 per cent, while Other

Backward Class and Scheduled Caste enrollment was 33.9 per cent and 11 per cent respectively.[21] While updated statistics are not easily available on how many of these students actually graduate, some scholars have suggested that like high-school drop-out rates, backward class students in higher education fail to graduate more than their advanced class peers.[22]

* * *

Under the Constitution, reservations in government jobs and educational institutions can be made in favour of a 'backward class of citizens' [Article 16(4)] or 'socially and educationally backward classes' [Articles 15(4)–(5)]. The word 'class' has been used in these provisions instead of caste. For a long time, the Supreme Court was concerned with the question of whether caste can be used as a criterion for determining eligibility for reservations, since the Constitution says 'class', not 'caste'. In M.R. Balaji's case, the Supreme Court held that caste could not be the 'sole or the dominant' test for determining whether a community was backward. Contrary to what one scholar has argued,[23] this principle still continues to hold the field today. Even now, caste cannot be used as the sole factor for deciding whether a community is backward or not. The Mandal Commission used caste in two ways. Firstly, it used caste as a unit of analysis[24] or a tool of administrative division—Hindu society was, for administrative reasons, categorized into various caste groupings, in order to determine which of those groups was actually backward. Secondly, caste was then used as only one out of several factors by the Mandal Commission in measuring social backwardness. This is not what the Nagan Gowda committee had done in Mysore, where caste was used not merely as a unit of analysis but also as the sole factor for determining social backwardness—which the Supreme Court found fault with in M.R. Balaji's case. The Mandal Commission's method, on the other hand, of using caste as only one out of many criteria in measuring backwardness, was largely accepted in Indra

Sawhney's case (albeit with the exclusion of the creamy layer), where the Supreme Court held that a caste can be a class,[25] though the word 'class' is much broader than caste.

The history of the terms 'depressed classes' and 'backward classes' in Chapters 1-2 now sheds light on this controversy. The words 'depressed classes' and 'backward classes' came to colonial India from 19th-century England, where society was divided into economic classes, not castes. The really poor and downtrodden sections of society there were called the 'depressed classes', while 'backward classes' was a broader term which included middling people. However, when these terms were imported into India, they acquired technical meanings that were virtually synonymous with caste. The nomenclature 'depressed classes' was a synonym for untouchable Hindu castes, and that label was eventually replaced by 'scheduled castes', substituting 'class' with 'caste'. The term 'backward classes' in 1933 colonial Bombay meant untouchable Hindu castes, backward tribes, and other backward castes/tribes (the communities that were enumerated by the Bombay government as 'other backward classes' were all castes/tribes). During the debate on the first amendment in the provisional parliament, Ambedkar referred to the backward classes as a 'collection of certain castes'. There is therefore no doubt that India's founding fathers and mothers intended for the word 'class' in the reservations provisions of the Constitution to be used as a synonym for 'caste' or 'tribe'.

* * *

Is the 50 per cent rule, which has been developed by the Supreme Court, fair? In the 1980s, Justice Chinnappa Reddy was absolutely right when he said that the limit of 50 per cent was an arbitrary rule and the Constitution does not permit the Supreme Court to be arbitrary. However, where should the line be drawn if not at 50 per cent? The Constitution consciously chose the formula of 'adequate' representation instead of 'proportional' representation for the backward classes in government jobs, and as Ambedkar explained, the framers intended quotas in government jobs to be limited to a minority of seats, though reservations in legislative bodies were proportional to the population of Scheduled Castes and Scheduled Tribes. Should courts ignore the word 'adequate' in Article 16(4) of the Constitution and permit governments to grant proportional reservations to the backward classes in government jobs?

If the answer to this question is in the affirmative, then one will need to know exactly how many Other Backward Classes there are in the country in order to ensure that they get proportional seats in government services. This will be no easy task. No census since 1931 has reliably contained information about caste, apart from data on Scheduled Castes and Scheduled Tribes. The Mandal Commission referred to the 1931 census to estimate that Other Backward Classes constituted 52 per cent of the population. A new census will have to be held in order to determine what their numbers now are in the population. However, the figures which emerge from such a census will be suspect, just as the 1941 census was considered to be unreliable. Different caste groups may inflate their numbers while answering census officials in order to attract greater sops from the government. At some level, the 50 per cent rule recognizes that the actual number of Other Backward Classes in the country is empirically unknowable, that the line has to be drawn somewhere, and therefore why not at 50 per cent. Though proportional representation may be a more just solution for the backward classes, in the absence of a quantitative ascertainment of the number of Other Backward Classes in the country, there may be no better alternative to the 50 per cent rule (with its limited exceptions).

As far as reservations in educational institutions are concerned, it is interesting that Articles 15(4)–(5) of the Constitution do not use the word 'adequate' as Article 16(4) does. In other words, Articles 15(4)–(5) are drafted in such a broad manner that they enable the government to confer reservations on any socially and educationally backward communities, even if they are already adequately represented in educational institutions. Can the absence of the word 'adequate' in Articles 15(4)–(5) mean that reservations in educational institutions must be proportional to the population of the backward classes? Does this mean that the state can do away with the *Nagaraj* requirement of carrying out a data collection exercise to determine whether socially and educationally backward classes are adequately represented in educational institutions prior to implementing a policy of reservations in colleges? The answer appears to be in the negative. In cases like *Ashoka Kumar Thakur*,[26] *M.R. Balaji*,[27] *S.V. Joshi*,[28] and *Preeti Srivastava*,[29] the Supreme Court has nearly dissolved the distinction between Articles 15 and 16 of the Constitution when it comes to reservation. The creamy layer test, the 50 per cent rule, the quantifiable data requirement, and the principle that 'merit' and 'efficiency' must not be harmed by reservations, have been applied by the Supreme Court with nearly equal vigour in both educational institutions and government jobs.

* * *

The Supreme Court has applied the creamy layer concept not merely to Other Backward Classes and Scheduled Tribes but also to Scheduled Castes.[30] This is problematic because the reasons for providing reservations to these communities are different. Scheduled Tribes and Other Backward Classes were given reservations purely because of their backwardness, while Scheduled Castes are entitled to quotas not merely because of backwardness but also untouchability. The creamy layer concept relies on the proposition that an individual who is no longer backward (e.g., one who is well off, or whose family members have attained high positions in the government) should not be able to get a seat reserved for herself. However, creamy layer status does not necessarily wipe out the stigma of untouchability. A Scheduled Caste person may be relatively well off, her family members might have attained high posts in the government, and she might still be subjected to invidious forms of untouchability in India.

Atrocities continue to be committed against Scheduled Castes on the basis of caste. In 1978, in Varanasi, when Jagjivan Ram, who had been a minister in the central government for several years, unveiled a statue of Dr Sampurnanand (a former Chief Minister of UP) at the Sanskrit university there, high-caste Hindus later washed that statue with the water of the Ganges in order to 'purify' it.[31] To deny a creamy-layer-Scheduled Caste person reservations without investigating whether her community has ceased to suffer from the stigma of untouchability would be constitutionally unjust. Scheduled Tribes and Other Backward Classes who have attained creamy layer status may arguably be said to have come out of their backwardness, but creamy layer Scheduled Castes may still suffer from the stigma of untouchability.

Oddly, the Supreme Court applies the creamy layer concept to reservations in education and employment, but not to reservations in legislative bodies. In other words, though members of the backward classes who have attained 'creamy layer' status cannot obtain reserved seats in educational institutions or government jobs, 'creamy layer' Scheduled Castes and Scheduled Tribes can contest elections to the Lok Sabha or state legislative assemblies in reserved constituencies. Creamy layer Other Backward Classes can similarly contest reserved seats in panchayats and municipalities.[32] In a judgement written in 2010, Chief Justice K.G. Balakrishnan explained the rationale for this inconsistency.[33] He suggested that when a backward class person is elected to political office in a reserved constituency, the benefit goes to the community as a whole, and not just to her as an individual. By contrast, he hinted, when a person gets a reserved seat in an educational institution or government job, that individual alone benefits.

However, this reasoning is flawed. When a backward class person gets a reserved seat in a government job or educational institution, the entire community may sometimes benefit along with the candidate in question. Consider the case of a Scheduled Caste student who becomes a medical doctor thanks to reservations. The fact that she has qualified as a doctor now means that networks have been opened up within her community—members of her community who might have found it difficult to even get a doctor's appointment now have easy access to a doctor within the community. It would be incorrect to say that reservations in education or employment only benefit the individual who avails of the reserved seat.

Further, there is an inherent tension between the Supreme Court's failure to apply the creamy layer test to political reservations and the court's judgements on inter-caste marriages. When an upper-caste woman marries a lower-caste man, the Supreme Court says that the peremptory rule is that the married woman cannot seek a reserved seat (whether in a job, college, or elected office) on the basis of her husband's caste. Once an upper-caste woman, always an upper-caste woman, says the court. Now, in its application of the creamy layer rule, the Supreme Court says that there is a difference between reservations in government jobs and educational institutions, on the one hand, and in political office on the other. Creamy layer candidates can avail of reservations in political office, says the Supreme Court, because the entire community benefits from the reserved candidate's election, and not the individual alone. Creamy layer candidates cannot, however, seek reserved seats in government jobs and educational institutions, since the assumption is that the individual candidate alone benefits in such cases.

On the same logic, it would be possible for an upper-caste woman who marries a lower-caste man to argue that she should be entitled to contest an election in a reserved constituency, even if she is not permitted to seek reservations in government jobs or educational institutions. After all, if she is elected to office, according to the Supreme Court's own reasoning, the benefit of that election would go not to her alone but to the entire community. As a legislator holding a reserved seat, she might be able to competently represent the interests of the backward community which she has married into, and which might have accepted her as one of their own. However, while political reservation is considered to be different from reservation in education and employment when it comes to the creamy layer rule, these concepts are thought of as indistinguishable when it comes to inter-caste marriages.

* * *

Should the Supreme Court allow state governments to distinguish *inter se* among different Scheduled Caste communities on the basis that some are more backward than others? It is true that there are some Scheduled Caste communities that have done better than other Scheduled Castes. Though there may be 20 recognized Scheduled Castes in a state, nothing stops the members of only one of those Scheduled Castes from occupying all the reserved seats. Though states can distinguish between Other Backward Classes on the basis that some are more backward than others, no such lines can, at least for now, be drawn within the Scheduled Caste or Scheduled Tribe communities.

The idea behind this appears to be that if state governments are permitted to draw lines within the Scheduled Caste and Scheduled Tribe communities respectively, then they may do so for narrow political gains, e.g., by conferring more benefits on a Scheduled Caste community that is numerically larger than the others. However, this concern can easily be met by introducing a quantifiable data requirement for sub-categorizing Scheduled Castes or Scheduled Tribes. In other words, if state governments wish to classify Scheduled Castes or Scheduled Tribes as 'backward' and 'most backward' (as they can categorize Other Backward Classes), then they should be required to have quantifiable data that demonstrate that some Scheduled Caste or Scheduled Tribe communities are *inter se* more backward than others.[34]

The sub-classification question has a long history. In 1962,[35] the State of Mysore issued an order reserving 50 per cent of seats in medical and engineering colleges for Other Backward Classes. However, within this 50 per cent quota, 22 per cent of the seats were reserved only for those Other Backward Classes who were 'more backward' than others. Communities which were far below the average educational levels of the state were entitled to opt for this 'more backward' sub-quota. In *M.R. Balaji* v. *State of Mysore*,[36] the Supreme Court held that this sub-classification of Other Backward Classes into backward and more backward was illegal. The court said that Article 15(4) of the Constitution only allows reservation for the 'really backward classes', while Mysore had given reservations to nearly 90 per cent of its population by including not-so-backward communities in the list of Other Backward Classes. Later, however, this view was overruled by the Supreme Court in Indra Sawhney's case, where it was held that sub-classification was permissible among Other Backward Classes.[37] In other words, governments are now free to create sub-quotas within the Other Backward Class quota.

However, in *E.V. Chinnaiah* v. *State of AP*,[38] the Supreme Court said that this could not be done for Scheduled Castes and Scheduled Tribes. In this case, the court was considering the legality of a law enacted in Andhra Pradesh. Under Article 341 of the Constitution, the President notifies a list of Scheduled Castes for each state, which can thereafter only be modified by Parliament. What the state of Andhra Pradesh did in its law was that it divided this presidential list of Scheduled Castes into four categories and conferred separate quotas on each group based on their relative backwardness to one another—Group A (1 per cent), Group B (7 per cent), Group C (6 per cent), and Group D (1 per cent). The Supreme Court said that the state government could not do this. There was only one presidential list of Scheduled Castes for the entire state of Andhra Pradesh, and since the state government could not add or remove a caste from the list, it could not allot separate sub-quotas to various castes in the list either.

Relying on Ambedkar's speech in the Constituent Assembly, the Supreme Court in *Chinnaiah* hinted that if governments are given the power to sub-classify within the list of Scheduled Castes specified by the President under Article 341, they might do so for political reasons—e.g., by conferring a generous sub-quota on a numerically large and politically important Scheduled Caste, to the exclusion of others. The court said that the object of Article 341 was to eliminate political factors in the identification of Scheduled Castes, and the government had no power to 'disturb' the presidential list. It was held that the Scheduled Castes and Scheduled Tribes specified in their respective lists formed a class by themselves, and regrouping or reclassifying them violated the Constitution.

However, the problem with Chinnaiah's case was that it treated the entire list of Scheduled Castes in a state as a homogenous category and presumed that each caste within the list was as backward as the other Scheduled Castes. This is simply not true. There are several castes included within the presidential list of Scheduled Castes in a state, but some of them may be ahead of others. Chinnaiah's case did not allow governments to take this into account and introduce sub-quotas for the more backward Scheduled Castes and Scheduled Tribes.

All this has been brought into the limelight by the Supreme Court in the recent case of *State of Punjab* v. *Davinder Singh (2020)*.[39] Here, the court was examining the validity of a law in the state of Punjab. The law created a sub-classification within the Scheduled Caste community and said that 50 per cent of the Scheduled Caste quota would go to the Balmikis and Mazhabi Sikhs in Punjab. A bench of five judges in Davinder Singh's case has now asked for the question of the law's legality to be referred to a larger bench of the court.

Interestingly, while making its reference to a larger bench, the Supreme Court in Davinder Singh's case referred to the 102nd amendment to the Constitution, passed in 2018, which introduced Article 342A into the Constitution. This provision says that the President must, in consultation with the governors, prepare a list of socially and educationally backward classes (SEBCs) for each state, a list which can thereafter only be modified by Parliament. Reading this amendment, the Supreme Court said that the constitutional provisions which deal with identifying Scheduled Castes, Scheduled

Tribes, and SEBCs (i.e., Articles 341, 342, and 342A) are now 'pari materia' or virtually identical—each group has a constitutionally recognized list which can only be modified by Parliament, and therefore, the court cannot disallow sub-classification within the Scheduled Caste and Scheduled Tribe lists on the one hand, while allowing it in the SEBC list on the other. Instead, held the court, governments ought to be able to use rational criteria to create a sub-quota within the Scheduled Caste or Scheduled Tribe list as well.

However, the Davinder Singh judgement of the Supreme Court raises some important questions:

Firstly, does the Davinder Singh judgement of the Supreme Court dilute its earlier established precedent in cases like *M. Nagaraj* v. *Union of India*[40] and *Jarnail Singh* v. *Lachhmi Narain Gupta*[41]? In *Nagaraj* and *Jarnail Singh*, we have seen that the Supreme Court held that before the government introduces any reservations for Other Backward Classes, it must collect quantifiable data which show that those communities are, in fact, backward. No such data collection exercise is necessary for Scheduled Castes and Scheduled Tribes who are presumed to be backward once they are included within the presidential lists under Articles 341 and 342 of the Constitution. After *Davinder Singh*, a view may be taken that once a community is set out in the list of SEBCs under Article 342A of the Constitution, it too is presumed to be backward and no such data collection exercise is thereafter necessary to show that the community continues to be backward.

Secondly, in the recent Maratha reservations case,[42] the Bombay High Court had held that Article 342A(2) of the Constitution actually contemplates two lists of SEBCs—a central list and a state list, and that the state list of SEBCs is unaffected by the 102nd constitutional amendment. In other words, Article 342A only requires the President to prepare a list of SEBCs for the central government— state governments are free to prepare and modify their own list of SEBCs. If this view were to be considered correct, then Article 342A would not really be considered 'pari materia' with Articles 341–342, contrary to what was held in *Davinder Singh*. There is no separate central and state list of Scheduled Castes and Scheduled Tribes. According to this interpretation of Article 342A, the *Chinnaiah* court would have reasoned that sub-classification is permissible within the state list of SEBCs, but not in the central list under Article 342A, because states are free to modify their own lists of SEBCs, but not the central list constitutionally prepared by the President. The court in *Davinder Singh* did not take this complex legal argument into account. However, this problem has now become academic since the Supreme Court in the recent Maratha reservations case has overruled the judgment of the Bombay High Court and held that even Article 342A of the Constitution contemplates only one list of SEBCs.[43]

Thirdly, the Supreme Court's judgement in *Davinder Singh* seems to have said that sub-classification within the list of Scheduled Castes and Scheduled Tribes should only be carried out by state legislatures, not by the executive government. We have seen that it has been a well-settled principle of constitutional law, since Indra Sawhney's case, that reservations can be brought about not merely through legislation but also by executive order. In *Indra Sawhney*, the Supreme Court mostly upheld an executive order which gave effect to the Mandal Commission report. However, in the Davinder Singh judgement, the Supreme Court has said that state legislatures are competent to create sub-classifications within the lists of Scheduled Castes, Scheduled Tribes, and SEBCs. Did the court mean to say that sub-classification is not permitted by executive order? This may require clarification by the larger bench.

* * *

The question of whether reservations constitute an exception to the principle of equality of opportunity has occupied much of the Supreme Court's time. Article 16(1) of the Constitution says that all citizens have the fundamental right to equality for the opportunity of getting a job with the government. However, Article 16(4) says that the government can reserve seats for the backward classes. If Article 16(4) is not an exception to Article 16(1), then three consequences are usually believed to follow:

(i) Firstly, there can be no 50 per cent rule. It was because reservations constituted an exception to the principle of equality of opportunity that Ambedkar, in the Constituent Assembly, said that quotas must be confined to a minority of seats. If reservations are a part of the equality of opportunity, then no such limits can apply.

(ii) Secondly, reservations can be provided to those who are not backward classes, e.g., horizontal reservations in favour of groups like women, the differently abled, children of freedom fighters, local candidates, etc. Unlike Article 16(4), there is no specific provision of the Constitution which gives the government the power to reserve seats for such groups. However, if reservations are a part of the equality of opportunity, then they can be provided under Article 16(1) itself.

(iii) Thirdly, if reservations are inherent in the principle of equality of opportunity and not an exception to it, then reservations are a fundamental right.[44] No government can refuse to provide reservations for the backward classes (if the requisite conditions for reservations are met, like backwardness, inadequacy of representation, creamy layer exclusion, etc.).

While the Supreme Court has rejected Ambedkar's view that reservations constitute an exception to the principle of equality of opportunity, it has not taken this principle to its logical conclusion. Though the court has held that horizontal reservations can be provided under Article 16(1) of the Constitution since reservations are a part and parcel of the equality of opportunity, it has not abandoned the 50 per cent rule and it continues to hold that the reservations provisions of the Constitution are 'enabling provisions', i.e., that there is no fundamental right to reservations.[45] In other words, if a government refuses to provide reservations, no backward class citizen can compel it to do so, even if there is substantial empirical material to show that there are backward communities in the state which require assistance. Even now, though reservations in legislative bodies are compulsory, quotas in government jobs and educational institutions are considered optional for the government. This is despite the fact that in the NALSA judgement,[46] the Supreme Court essentially directed the government to provide reservations to transgender persons.

* * *

The Supreme Court's differential treatment of 'vertical' and 'horizontal' reservations is, at times, quite baffling. 'Vertical' reservations are meant for the backward classes, i.e., Scheduled Castes, Scheduled Tribes, and Other Backward Classes. 'Horizontal' reservations are meant for others, e.g., women, sportspersons, orphans, the differently abled, the children of members of the armed forces, etc. There are at least four ways in which the Supreme Court treats these two categories of reservation differently:

Firstly, when a 'vertical' candidate secures a seat on his or her own merit, that candidate is not considered to occupy a reserved seat. So, if a Scheduled Caste, Scheduled Tribe, or Other Backward Class student cracks an entrance exam and gets on the merit list in the open category, he or she will not be considered as having occupied a seat reserved for the backward classes. On the other hand, if a horizontal candidate gets a seat on his or her own merit, he or she is counted towards the horizontal reservations quota. Thus, if an orphan gets on the merit list in the open category, he or she will nonetheless be counted towards the orphan quota (if there is one). Consider another example. Let us say that there is a government department which has 100 posts in it. Assume that the government has implemented a 10 per cent quota for Scheduled Castes (vertical reservation) and a 10 per cent quota for women (horizontal reservation). Now, if 10

Scheduled Caste candidates get jobs in the department on their own merit, they will be considered as part of the open category. In other words, 10 more Scheduled Caste candidates (apart from those who got in on their own credentials) can avail of the reserved seats. On the other hand, if 10 women get seats on their own capabilities, they will be counted towards the reserved quota for women, and 10 more women who were unable to get in on their own steam will not be able to take up the reserved seats.[47]

Secondly, unlike vertical reservations, there is no 'quantifiable data' requirement when a government wants to introduce horizontal reservations. According to the principles laid down by the Supreme Court in *Nagaraj* and *Jarnail Singh*, a government which wishes to reserve seats for Scheduled Castes, Scheduled Tribes, or Other Backward Classes has to collect quantifiable data to show that those communities are inadequately represented in the services (and, as far as Other Backward Classes are concerned, to also establish that the community in question is actually backward). This is not necessary when the government wants to reserve seats for 'horizontal' candidates. In other words, it is much easier for a government to institute horizontal reservations as against vertical reservations.

Thirdly, there is no 'creamy layer' requirement for horizontal reservations either. In other words, if a government decides to reserve seats in educational institutions or government jobs for women, even women who have achieved 'creamy layer' status will be entitled to avail of those reservations. On the other hand, the 'creamy layer' concept applies in vertical reservations. If the idea is to keep out of the quota ecosphere those candidates who, through their economic or social position, have gained the ability to compete with general category candidates, then the Supreme Court's failure to apply the creamy layer test to horizontal reservations is puzzling.

Finally, the 50 per cent rule does not seem to apply to horizontal reservations.[48] In other words, governments can have quotas in excess of 50 per cent if the reserved seats are meant for candidates other than Scheduled Castes, Scheduled Tribes, and Other Backward

Classes. For example, state governments are free to violate the 50 per cent rule while reserving seats in educational institutions in favour of candidates domiciled within their own territories.[49] If the 50 per cent rule is designed to safeguard merit and equality of opportunity, then why should it only apply to reservation for the backward classes?

* * *

On the basis of debates that have taken place in arenas like the Miller Committee, Simon Commission, Constituent Assembly, provisional parliament, and Supreme Court, we now have a catalogue of arguments that may be presented for and against reservations.[50] Those who oppose reservations may argue that:

i   They undermine merit and disincentivize hard work by awarding undeserving candidates.
ii   They are unfair to the displaced candidate who has not discriminated against anyone on the basis of caste.
iii It is unjust to confer benefits on reserved category candidates who might not have themselves suffered any caste-based discrimination.
iv   Reservations ignore those who might have faced non-caste based discrimination (e.g., discrimination based on sexual orientation or race, or handicaps like the loss of a parent, a serious illness in the family, etc.). Though the Supreme Court directed the government to confer SEBC status on transgender persons in the NALSA judgement,[51] the government did not follow through with this in the Transgender Persons (Protection of Rights) Act, 2019. Under the Right of Children to Free and Compulsory Education Act, 2009, a 'disadvantaged group' (whose children are entitled to reservations in elementary education, from Class 1 to Class 8), can be determined not merely on the basis of caste, but also other factors like language, gender, region, or culture.[52]

v   They are a waste of resources: India has a limited number of seats in educational institutions, and undeserving, unmeritorious backward class students might drop out, wasting their seats. Reservations might actually harm reserved category students by putting them in situations with which they cannot cope—some might succumb to the pressure and commit suicide. This is often called the 'mismatch theory', i.e., that it is better to let students go to inferior schools where they will do well than superior schools where they will struggle.[53]

vi   India loses if she does not get the best doctors and engineers.

vii By introducing unmeritorious students into educational institutions, reservations lower the quality of education by reducing the level of pedagogy to the lowest common denominator.

viii Caste-based reservations entrench the very caste system that India had set out to obliterate by reminding every new generation to think about their identities in terms of caste. They may also have the effect of stigmatizing reserved category candidates with the label of being unqualified or underqualified,[54] or give rise to resentment against the beneficiaries of quotas.[55]

ix   Efficiency in government services suffers if unmeritorious candidates are appointed and promoted based on caste.

These arguments can be met with the following responses, which are based on arguments that have been made by those like Ambedkar, Khandekar, Justice Chinnappa Reddy, and Justice B. Sudershan Reddy:

i   'Merit' cannot be determined neutrally. A student's success in an entrance exam might be the result not merely of hard work and intelligence but other factors like the ability to pay for coaching classes, having supporting parents and a good infrastructure at home, access to networks for guidance, etc. Awarding seats or jobs purely on the basis of 'merit' is unfair to those who have innate intelligence and work hard but lack other factors like 'cultural capital', e.g., having educated family members, being brought up in an environment conducive to learning, and having an excellent command over the English language.[56] Potential employees are not always selected on the basis of merit—the interview process might have inherent (sometimes subconscious) biases, which reservations correct. At some level, rewarding only merit is unfair—those who lack innate intelligence cannot be penalized for their poor genes.

ii   Though reservations may be unfair to advanced category students who have not discriminated against anyone on the basis of caste, they are nearly as unfair as other forms of redistribution of wealth. A taxpayer, for instance, who pays Rs 100 in tax does not get back services from the government worth exactly Rs 100 in return—while some part of her tax money might be used for infrastructure which she might use, part of her tax contribution may be utilized in social welfare schemes which may not benefit her at all. In other words, through taxation, the government is essentially taking a portion of a taxpayer's earnings and giving her nothing in return, but that is the price of citizenship in a fair and just state. Similarly, in reservations policies, without any fault on the part of the advanced category student, the state redistributes its scarce resources to those it considers to be in need of them. Reservations are necessary in order to ensure that marginalized communities do not rise up in revolt against the country.

iii   A Scheduled Caste or Scheduled Tribe candidate might not have suffered personal discrimination, but centuries of oppression might have affected the collective self-esteem and self-confidence of her community. Further, despite the formal abolition of untouchability in the Constitution, untouchability is still very much prevalent, overtly in rural India, and in subtle forms in urban areas.

iv   Those who suffer non-caste-based discrimination are not merely found in the advanced castes. There may be many candidates in backward communities who have suffered discrimination based on sexual orientation, or handicaps like the loss of a parent or a serious illness in the family, etc. Caste-based reservations do not single out members of the advanced communities who have suffered these disadvantages.

v In order to ensure that reserved students do not drop out, the affirmative action policy of the state should not begin and end with reservations—steps should be taken to provide counselling, training, support, etc., in order to ensure that reserved category students are able to cope with their new environment.

vi There is no guarantee that a student who passes an entrance exam with flying colours will necessarily excel in the programme in which she has secured admission. The law entrance exam, for instance, tests a student's skills in mathematics and general knowledge among other things, neither of which are essential to the toolkit of a successful lawyer. Further, there is no guarantee that a student who excels in her exams in a medical or engineering college will be an excellent doctor or engineer or that a poor student will necessarily be a bad practitioner.

vii Reservations enhance the intellectual environment of the classroom by exposing students from diverse backgrounds to each other. However, the 'diversity'[57] argument does not fully apply in India since reservations only reward some kinds of diversity (based on caste or gender) but not others (e.g., based on race, sexual orientation, geographical region, or even extra-curricular activities, interests, etc.).

viii Though caste-based reservations keep caste-consciousness alive, they have beneficial effects as well. Knowing that there are jobs reserved for them enhances the academic performance of reserved category students. Caste groups are able to politically mobilize in order to secure benefits for themselves.

ix There is no empirical evidence that efficiency in government departments suffers due to reservations. Reserved category government servants ensure that their backward communities are not left behind in government policies.[58] Efficient administrators require not merely bookish knowledge but also other qualities like empathy. An efficient government is not necessarily a just one. Further, reservations help create role models and social capital for marginalized communities.

Acknowledgements

This book was mostly written in 2020 during the lockdown that was imposed in India with the arrival of the COVID-19 pandemic. I owe a debt of gratitude to many people for making this book possible. Anurag Bhaskar, a brilliant young scholar of outstanding achievements, painstakingly went through each chapter to give me his comments, from which this book has benefited a great deal. I am deeply grateful to Mark Tushnet, Lawrence Friedman, Tarunabh Khaitan, Rohit De, Stefan Vogenauer, Nick Robinson and Vasujith Ram for going through some of the chapters of this book and offering comments. I am grateful to Abhinav Prakash and Vinay Sitapati for offering some useful insights in connection with this book. I am grateful to Vinayak Chitale, Ranga Mohan, Shreyas Narla, Anant Sangal, Unnati Ghia, and M.A. Rashid for helping me gain access to law reports, archives and materials that I was otherwise unable to access during the pandemic. In Fall 2020, I taught an elective course at the Nalsar University of Law, Hyderabad, on affirmative action and the Constitution of India. Some of the discussions I had with students in that course served as a springboard for a few of the ideas that are discussed in this book, especially in the concluding chapter. I am grateful to the students who took the class and especially to those who participated so very enthusiastically in class discussions. I presented the themes discussed in this book to the students of a course I co-taught at Cornell Law School in Spring 2021 along with Professor Sital Kalantry, and I am grateful to the students of the class and Professor Kalantry for their insightful comments. I also discussed some of the themes presented in this book in a webinar conducted by the Jharkhand Legal Literacy Forum, and I am grateful to its organizers and participants. My erstwhile column in *Bloomberg Quint* served as an incubator for the ideas presented in this book. Fernan Restrepo, a dear friend and a brilliant scholar, helped me find research resources without which this book could not have been written. I am grateful to Saanchi Dhulla and Anushka Shah, who proof-read the book meticulously. Many thanks to Professor K.L. Daswani for recommending them to me. I am deeply indebted to my senior, Mr. Darius Khambata, and to Mr. Abad Ponda, from whom I have learned a great deal. Last, but not in the least, this book could not have been written without the love and support of my family. Thank you, Dad, Kalpana, Aai, Baba, Neema Atya, Dilda, Chintan, Disha, Shloka, Sharda, Gaurav, Diya, Uday, and Aparna.

Notes

Introduction

1   According to instructions issued by the Department of Personnel and Training, the EWS scheme does not apply to those who belong to Scheduled Castes, Scheduled Tribes or Other Backward Classes. See Office Memorandum dated 31 January 2019, available at: https://dopt.gov.in/sites/default/files/ewsf28fT.PDF (last visited 2 May 2020).

2   Several state governments attempted to introduce economic quotas, but in vain. See Dhavan (2019).

3   However, in National Legal Services Authority v. Union of India, (2014) 5 SCC 438 (paragraph 135.3), the Supreme Court directed the government to grant 'socially and educationally backward' status to transgender persons. This was not on the basis of caste either. This was not done, though, in the Transgender Persons (Protection of Rights) Act, 2019.

4   However, the Right of Children to Free and Compulsory Education Act, 2009, requires unaided schools to reserve at least 25 per cent of their seats in Class 1 (or pre-school) to 'children belonging to weaker section and disadvantaged group in the neighbourhood' and to provide free and compulsory elementary education from Class 1 to Class 8. The term 'weaker section' can be identified on the basis of economic criteria

alone. Sections 2(d), 2(e), 12. In Pramati Educational and Cultural Trust v. Union of India, (2014) 8 SCC 1 (5 judges) (paragraph 56), the Supreme Court upheld the constitutional validity of the Act except in minority institutions (aided and unaided).

5　　K.C. Vasanth Kumar v. State of Karnataka, (1985) Supp SCC 714 (paragraph 79). The same applied to the 'Patels of Gujarat, Reddys and Kammas of Andhra Pradesh, [and] the Kayasthas of Bengal', though many of them were 'poor farmers and agricultural labourers'.

6　　See Dhavan (2019).

7　　See *JEE (Advanced) 2020, Information Brochure*, available at: http://www.jeeadv.ac.in/brochure.php (last visited 20 May 2020); 'Important Information', IIM-A website, available at: https://www.iima.ac.in/web/pgp/apply/domestic/important-information (last visited 20 May 2020).

8　　Horizontal reservations, as we shall see, apply across all categories and are not only taken from the general quota.

9　　Galanter came up with the term 'compensatory discrimination' for affirmative action policies in India as these policies involve departures from formal 'norms of equality', i.e., 'merit, evenhandedness, and indifference to ascriptive characteristics'. Galanter (1984), p. xxv.

10　Weisskopf (2006), p. 717.

11　Weisskopf (2004), pp. 4344–45.

12　See Bhatia (2019), p. 90. Referring to the concurring judgments of Justice Mathew and Justice Krishna Iyer of the Supreme Court in N.M. Thomas's case, which viewed reservations as an allocation of scarce resources.

13　See http://censusindia.gov.in/pca/pca.aspx (last visited 29 April 2020).

14　See 'World Population Prospects 2019', United Nations Department of Economic and Social Affairs website, available at: https://population.un.org/wpp/Download/Standard/Population/ (last visited 29 April 2020); 'Demographic balance sheet 2019', INSEE website, available at: https://www.insee.fr/en/statistiques/2382597?sommaire=2382613 (last visited 20 May 2020); 'Current Population', Statistisches Bundesamt website, available at: https://www.destatis.de/EN/Themes/Society-Environment/Population/Current-Population/_node.html (last visited 20 May 2020); 'Population estimates', Office

for National Statistics website, available at: https://www.ons.gov.
uk/peoplepopulationandcommunity/populationandmigration/
populationestimates (last visited 20 May 2020); 'Latest Press Releases',
Instituto Nacional de Estadistica website, available at: https://www.
ine.es/dyngs/INEbase/en/operacion.htm?c=Estadistica_C&cid=
1254736176951&menu=ultiDatos&idp=1254735572981 (last visited
20 May 2020).

15 Speech of Winston Churchill in the House of Commons (18 July 1946),
available at: https://api.parliament.uk/historic-hansard/commons/1946/
jul/18/india-cabinet-mission (last visited 27 March 2020).

16 Mandal 1980, Part 1, p. 64. However, as Sitapati and Jayal point out,
the Mandal Commission relied on data from the 1931 census. Sitapati
(2016), p. 724; Jayal (2013), p. 248. The Kalelkar Commission had
estimated India's Other Backward Class population to be 32 per cent.
Jayal (2013), p. 246.

17 See Choudhry (2015), p. 41.

18 As Sujit Choudhry points out, Scheduled Caste/Scheduled Tribe
reservation was less contentious because: (i) Scheduled Castes and
Scheduled Tribes were unthreatening minorities; and (ii) there was a
widespread belief that reservations were justified for them since they
had suffered substantial discrimination. Choudhry (2015), p. 31.

19 Sitapati (2016), p. 724; Jayal (2013), p. 248. The census did not
collect data on caste after Independence, except on Scheduled Castes
and Scheduled Tribes. See Galanter (1984), p. 259.

20 Panagariya and Mukim (2013). The National Sample Survey Office,
which relies on samples, has been collecting data on Other Backward
Classes since 1999–2000. See Panagariya and Mukim (2013). See
further, Deshpande (2013), p. 267.

21 The Marathas in Maharashtra are the 'numerically dominant' caste,
constituting about 30 per cent of the population. Zelliot (1969), p. 12.
In the 1920s and 1930s, they dominated the Congress party because
of their large proportion in the electorate. Zelliot (1969), pp. 134–35.
However, in a book titled *Thoughts on Linguistic States*, published
in 1955, Ambedkar said that Marathas were 'politically the most
backward community' and their leaders required political training,
which he felt would be possible if Maharashtra were divided up into

three states. Ambedkar (1955). M.N. Srinivas considered Marathas to be the 'dominant' caste in Maharashtra. Srinivas (1968), p. 21.

22 See Central Educational Institutions (Reservation in Admission) Act, 2006. Even Scheduled Caste and Scheduled Tribe reservations in IITs started in the early 1970s. See Weisskopf (2004), p. 4341 and Subramanian (2019), p. 229.

23 See https://www.nls.ac.in/admissions/undergraduate/ (last visited 29 April 2020).

24 See Sagar (2020).

25 *Master Balachandar Krishnan* v. *State of Karnataka*, Writ Petition No. 8788 of 2020, judgment dated 29 September 2020. See Section 2, National Law School of India (Amendment) Act, 2020 (received the assent of the Governor on 27 April 2020). There is 25 per cent horizontal reservation for local candidates.

26 See Deshpande (2013), p. 268; Coffey et al. (2018), pp. 49–51.

27 Thorat and Attewell (2007), p. 4144; Deshpande (2013), p. 269.

28 See Deshpande and Newman (2007), p. 4138; Jodhka and Newman (2007), p. 4127.

29 Thorat et al. (2015).

30 Guha (2007), p. 3306.

31 Guha (2007), p. 3308. In 2022, President Droupadi Murmu made history when she was elected President of India—the first from a Scheduled Tribe community.

32 See, for example, Galanter (1984). There is an impressive literature on the law of caste-based reservations in India outside the genre of legal history. Jayal (2013) briefly discussed backward tribes and Other Backward Classes in the context of defining Indian citizenship. Anup Surendranath developed a normative framework for analyzing the affirmative action judgments of the Supreme Court. His central arguments were: (i) Scheduled Castes and Muslim Other Backward Classes persons, on account of their empirically ascertainable extreme backwardness, deserve reservations more than others; (ii) the Supreme Court has not taken the principle that reservations are not an exception to equality of opportunity to its logical conclusion (for example, by doing away with the 50 per cent rule); (iii) reservations and concessions cannot be treated in the same manner; (iv) by permitting reservations under Article 16(1), the Supreme Court has made it easier for governments

to provide reservations under that provision than for backward classes under Article 16(4); (v) Scheduled Castes and Other Backward Classes are not homogenous groups and the state must account for differing levels of backwardness within these groups. Surendranath (2013), pp. 163, 167, 174, 189, 190, 213. This book engages with some of the arguments made in Surendranath's dissertation.

In 2016, Vinay Sitapati wrote perhaps one of the best recent articles on reservations in India. Sitapati (2016), pp. 720–41. However, Sitapati's analysis begins with the enactment of the Constitution and does not look at colonial history to shed light on the reservations provisions of the Constitution, which this book does. This book is also a deeper dive into the subjects that Sitapati has covered. Given the constantly evolving nature of reservations law in India, Sitapati's article is also beginning to get somewhat dated—it was written, for instance, before the Supreme Court's judgment in Jarnail Singh's case, which we will see in Chapter 6.

33   In his monumental book, Marc Galanter set out various arguments for and against reservations. Galanter (1984), p. 80.

34   This is not a book about the politics of caste in India. As Sujit Choudhry points out, scholarship on reservations exists in separate disciplinary 'silos': legal scholarship and political science. Choudhry (2015), p. 34. For studies on caste and politics in India, see the work of Christophe Jaffrelot, for example, Jaffrelot (2012). This book attempts to reconcile the silos of law and history.

Chapter 1: The Depressed Classes

1   Channing (1837), pp. 39–40.
2   Stanton (1849), p. 15. Henry B. Stanton was an American politician, abolitionist and journalist. See 'Harriot Eaton Stanton Blatch', *Encyclopaedia Britannica*, available at: https://www.britannica.com/biography/Harriot-Eaton-Stanton-Blatch#ref668804 (last visited 26 March 2020).
3   Peters (1866), p. 3.
4   Cordner (1868), p. 299. Cordner was an Irish preacher who moved to Canada. See *Dictionary of Canadian Biography*, vol. 12, pp. 213–15.
5   Rev. W.B. Boggs (2 March 1894) in Moorhead (ed.) (1894), p. 270.
6   Brown. His father, Henry James Lee-Warner, was the canon of Norwich.

7   W. Lee Warner (Acting Director of Public Instruction, Bombay) to
     Chief Secretary to Government of Bombay, letter dated 9 May 1885,
     p. 361, at p. 375, in *Proceedings of the Government of India in the Home
     Department for the Month of July 1888: Education.*

8   Thoburn (1894), p. 46.

9   Eddy (1895), p. 27.

10   Speech delivered by Gokhale at the Students' Brotherhood, Bombay
     on 9 October 1909. Karve and Ambekar (eds.) (1967), pp. 191, 198.

11   Ambedkar (1945), p. 3.

12   Ambedkar (1945), p. 4.

13   Sir Herbert Risley, commissioner of the 1901 census, is usually given
     credit for coming up with the word 'untouchable'. Surendranath
     (2013), p. 245. However, Risley was unable to complete the census,
     and E.A. Gait authored the 1901 report. Gait (1901), pp. xvi–xvii.
     According to Galanter, the word 'untouchable' started being used in
     1909. Galanter (1984), p. 24 (fn 21).

14   *Progress of Education in India, 1907–1912* (1914), p. 259.

15   Letter from H. Wheeler, Secretary to the Government of India, to
     the Chief Secretaries of the Provinces, dated 12 May 1916. National
     Archives of India, Home Department, Public 'A', July 1916, p. 36
     [Identifier: PR_000005003470] (available on the Abilekh Patal
     website).

16   *Indian Franchise Committee* (1932), vol. 1, p. 109.

17   'Speech at Aligarh College', 28 November 1917, *Collected
     Works of Mahatma Gandhi*, vol. 16, available at: https://www.
     gandhiashramsevagram.org/gandhi-literature/mahatma-gandhi-
     collected-works-volume-16.pdf (last visited 26 March 2020).

18   See Chopra (ed.) (2015), vol. 15, p. 260. This *Hindustan Times* article
     published in 1950 says that he did so in 1930. The earliest reference
     to 'Harijan Ashram' in the pages of the Times of India was in January
     1934. See 'Harijan Worker to Join Mr. Gandhi', *Times of India*, 2
     January 1934, p. 10.

19   Guha (2017).

20   Hutton (1933), p. 471.

21   *Indian Franchise Committee* (1932), vol. 1, p. 109.

22   Gait (1904), p. 163; Gait (1913), p. 296.

23 House of Commons (6 August 1918), available at: https://api.
    parliament.uk/historic-hansard/commons/1918/aug/06/mr-
    montagus-statement (last visited 26 March 2020).

24 *Report on Indian Constitutional Reforms* (1918), pp. 127, 189.

25 Ambedkar (1945), p. 1. Non-brahmin political parties emerged in
    Madras and Bombay in 1916 and 1917 respectively. Galanter (1984),
    p. 26. The non-Brahmin movement in Bombay dated back to 1870
    and eventually 'emerged triumphant' in the Congress party. Zelliot,
    p. 16.

26 Ambedkar (1945), pp. 5–6.

27 Included in these was the Southborough Franchise Committee (1919).
    Indian Franchise Committee (1932), vol. 1, p. 109.

28 Marten (1924), p. 225.

29 Ibid.

30 The nominees were: 10 in Madras, 4 in the Central Provinces, 2 in
    Bombay, 2 in Bihar, 1 in Bengal and 1 in the United Provinces. One
    member of the depressed classes was also nominated by the Governor
    General to the central legislative assembly. See speech of Earl Winterton
    in the House of Commons, 2 April 1928, available at: https://api.
    parliament.uk/historic-hansard/commons/1928/apr/02/depressed-
    classes-representation#S5CV0215P0_19280402_HOC_17 (last
    visited 26 March 2020).

31 House of Commons, 21 December 1925, available at: https://
    api.parliament.uk/historic-hansard/commons/1925/dec/21/
    depressed-classes-representation (last visited 26 March 2020). See
    further, Winterton's speech in the House of Commons on 23 April
    1928, available at: https://api.parliament.uk/historic-hansard/
    commons/1928/apr/23/depressed-classes#S5CV0216P0_19280423_
    HOC_12 (last visited 26 March 2020).

32 Hutton (1933), p. 471.

33 In the mid-19th century, British colonial officials did not encourage
    lower-caste children to attend English schools, in order to ensure that
    English education would spread further among the more numerous
    castes. Zelliot (1969), p. 47.

34 See Hutton (1933), p. 472.

35 Zelliot (1969), p. 84.

36   Ibid., p. 86.
37   Hutton (1933), p. 485.
38   Ibid., p. 473.
39   Ibid., p. 473.
40   Ibid., p. 472.
41   Ibid.
42   Ibid., p. 486. For more on the inter-caste rivalry among the Chambhar, Mahar and Mang castes in Bombay province, See Zelliot (1969), pp. 31–32.
43   Hutton (1933), p. 484.
44   Ibid. See further, Ambedkar (1945), p. 107; Zelliot (1969), p. 201. Zelliot points out that Gandhi did not fast or use satyagraha to help untouchable castes gain entry into temples.
45   Hutton (1933), p. 484.
46   Ibid.
47   See Ambedkar (1945), p. 184.
48   Hutton (1933), p. 484. See further, O'Malley (1934), p. 51. However, members of the depressed classes often worshipped deities that were not a part of the high-caste pantheon. For instance, Mahars and Mangs in Bombay worshipped ghosts and spirits like Mariai, Janai and Jokhai. O'Hanlon (1983), p. 215.
49   See Patel's speech at the Harijan Ashram (reported in the Bombay Chronicle, 25 September 1935); Chopra (ed.) (2015), vol. 5, p. 160; Ambedkar (1936), p. 7.
50   Patel's intervention in Kavitha (reported in the *Tribune*, 2 October 1935). Chopra (ed.) (2015), vol. 5, p. 166.
51   See Note by J.N. Mandal on Treatment of Scheduled Castes by Caste Hindus, 22 April 1947. Zaidi (ed.) (1993), vol. 1 (part 1), p. 584ff., at p. 586.
52   Ibid.
53   Ibid., p. 585.
54   Patel's speech at the Patidar Students Hostel at Vadodara (16 April 1947). Chopra (ed.) (2015), vol. 12, p. 49.
55   Hutton (1933), p. 472.
56   In Bombay province, Mahars were considered 'untouchable' because they handled dead cattle and 'ate the carrion beef of the carcasses'

which they handled. Zelliot (1969), p. 23. Zelliot's doctoral thesis sets out disturbing Marathi proverbs which shed light on how poorly members of the Mahar community were treated in Bombay. The caste name of Mahar 'literally stood as a synonym for Untouchable'. Zelliot (1969), pp. 24–26.

57 Hutton (1933), p. 473.

58 See Zelliot (1969), p. 6. By 1903, they had developed parallel temples and schools.

59 Hutton (1933), p. 473.

60 Ibid., p. 471.

61 Ibid., p. 485.

62 Ibid.

63 Ibid.

64 Ibid., p. 494.

65 Ibid.

66 Yeatts (1946), p. 98.

67 Ambedkar (1947), p. 77.

68 *Report of the Indian Statutory Commission* (1930), vol. 1, pp. 37–38.

69 *Indian Franchise Committee* (1932), vol. 1, p. 109.

70 *Indian Franchise Committee* (1932), vol. 2, pp. 125–26.

71 Available at: https://hansard.parliament.uk/lords/1935-03-13/ debates/ff3d75dd-5121-4335-805a-5ecfe55337f6/LordsChamber (last visited 26 March 2020). Even the Lothian committee used the definition of untouchability. Ambedkar (1947), p. 77.

72 For instance, in Bombay, 2 members of the depressed classes were nominated to the legislative council. *Memorandum Submitted by the Government of Bombay to the Indian Statutory Commission* (1930), p. 231.

73 For more on separate electorates, see Chandrachud (2020).

74 Munshi (2012), vol. 1, p. 24; 'Simon Commission', *Encyclopedia Britannica*, available at: https://www.britannica.com/topic/Simon-Commission (last visited 29 December 2018).

75 He was a member of the committee appointed by the Bombay Legislative Council to 'co-operate' with the Simon Commission. *Reports of the Committees Appointed by the Provincial Legislative Councils to Co-operate with the Indian Statutory Commission* (1930), p. 87.

76 *Reports of the Committees Appointed by the Provincial Legislative Councils to Co-operate with the Indian Statutory Commission* (1930), p. 151.

77 Ibid., p. 152.

78 Ibid.

79 Ibid., p. 153.

80 That is, filled through nomination with a pass examination (Ibid., p. 155).

81 Ibid.

82 Ibid., p. 153.

83 'Round Table Conference', *Encyclopedia Britannica*, available at: https://www.britannica.com/event/Round-Table-Conference (last visited 26 March 2020).

84 Ambedkar (1945), pp. 40–41.

85 The work at the conference was divided between nine committees. Ambedkar (1945), p. 41.

86 Ambedkar (1945), p. 47. In a report submitted to the Simon Commission, Ambedkar had asked for joint electorates with adult franchise. He had written: 'I hold communal electorates to be an evil and adult suffrage to be a good.'

87 See *Joint Committee on Indian Constitutional Reform* (1934), vol. 1, p. 69.

88 Ambedkar (1945), p. 48. See further, *Report of the Indian Statutory Commission* (1930), vol. 3, p. 105, 88.

89 Ibid., p. 51.

90 Cf. O'Malley (1931), pp. 205–27.

91 Desai (ed.) (1953), vol. 1, p. 52.

92 Ambedkar (1945), p. 74. Ambedkar did not sign the requisition.

93 Ibid., pp. 79, 81.

94 Ambedkar (1945), p. 82.

95 Ibid., p. 87.

96 Zelliot (1969), p. 187.

97 Ambedkar (1945), p. 103. Munshi said that it happened five days later (Munshi [2012], vol. 1, p. 38).

98 Clauses 1 and 3. Ambedkar (1947), p. 54.

99 Ambedkar (1945), p. 90.

100 Around 18 per cent of the seats allotted to the general electorate in the central legislature were to be reserved for the depressed classes.

Clause 4. Ambedkar (1947), p. 54. In other words, the depressed classes would not actually get 18 per cent of all seats, only 18 per cent of seats for which the general electorate (as opposed to special electorates) could vote.

101 Clause 6. Ambedkar (1947), p. 55.

102 Clause 2, Ibid., p. 54.

103 Cf., *Return Showing the Results of Elections in India, 1937* (1937), p. 28.

104 Clause 8. Ambedkar (1947), p. 55.

105 Clause 9. Ibid.

106 Ambedkar (1945), p. 94.

107 It only contested 14 reserved seats. Zelliot (1969), p. 249.

108 *Return Showing the Results of Elections in India, 1937* (1937), pp. 28–33; Zelliot (1969), pp. 249–50 (fn 5). The official return shows his party having won only 10 reserved seats, but Zelliot points out that one candidate was wrongly shown in it as being an Independent. His party was just referred to as 'Ambedkar's Party' in this document. His Scheduled Castes Federation was only formed in 1942. See Choudhary (ed.) (1984–95), vol. 6, p. 172. The party he founded in 1936 was called the 'Independent Labour Party'. Eventually, he took steps to establish the Republican Party, which was formed after his death. Zelliot (1969), pp. 243, 281.

109 See R.S. Shukla to Patel, 20 December 1945. Das (ed.) (1972), vol. 2, p. 340; Patel to Brijlal Biyani, 25 December 1945. Das (ed.) (1972), vol. 2, p. 344; Shukla to Patel, 17 April 1946. Das (ed.) (1972), vol. 2, p. 377.

110 Patel to Gangadharrao Deshpande, 9 January 1946. Das (ed.) (1972), vol. 2, p. 264.

111 *Joint Committee on Indian Constitutional Reform* (1934), vol. 1, p. 69.

112 *Proposals for Indian Constitutional Reform* (1933), p. 26; *Joint Committee on Indian Constitutional Reform* (1934), vol. 1, p. 70.

113 Ibid.

114 *Joint Committee on Indian Constitutional Reform* (1934), vol. 1, p. 70.

115 Bombay, Punjab, Central Provinces and Berar. Part III, Clause 8; Part VI, Clause 8; Part VIII, Clause 8; 6th Schedule, Government of India Act, 1935. These were the only provisions which expressly relaxed voting eligibility for Scheduled Caste voters.

116 See R.R. Diwakar's letter to Patel, 29 December 1945. Das (ed.) (1972), vol. 2, p. 261.

117 See Ambedkar's memorandum and draft articles on the rights of states and minorities (24 March 1947) (Rao (ed.) (2012), vol. 2, p. 84ff., at p. 108).

118 Ambedkar (1947), p. 57. Eventually, Ambedkar felt that his party would fare better if no seats were reserved for Scheduled Castes, as most reserved seats in a general electorate were going to the Congress party. Zelliot (1969), p. 279.

119 Zelliot (1969), p. 265.

120 Patel's letter to Dr N.B. Khare, leader of the Congress Assembly Party, Nagpur (10 July 1937). Chopra (ed.) (2015), vol. 7, p. 3.

121 See Choudhary (ed.) (1984–95), vol. 2, pp. 227–228. See further, Rajendra Prasad to Mahadev Desai, 21 July 1937. Choudhary (ed.) (1984–95), vol. 1, p. 61. Jaglal Choudhury was picked instead of Jagjivan Ram which 'caused some flutter'.

122 *Return Showing the Results of Elections in India, 1937* (1937). Even in independent India for a while, elections were held in plural-member constituencies with distributive voting (i.e., where a voter could not give more than one vote to one candidate). See Choudhary (ed.) (1984–95), vol. 12, p. 273; Patel's letter to Gopichand Bhargava, 20 December 1949. Das (ed.) (1972), vol. 9, p. 174ff., at p. 175. In November 1950, Nehru was 'entirely opposed to any two-member constituencies, except where a seat is reserved for the Scheduled Castes or Tribes'. Nehru's note to the Principal Private Secretary, 18 November 1950. Gopal (ed.) (1984–2015), Second Series, vol. 15 (part 2), p. 241.

123 Patel's speech in Bombay, reported in Bombay Chronicle (17 February 1937). Chopra (ed.) (2015), vol. 6, p. 175ff., at p. 176.

124 *Return Showing the Results of Elections in India, 1937* (1937). In the 1937 elections in Bombay province, they were held in only two constituencies. *Return Showing the Results of Elections in India, 1937* (1937), p. 28.

125 *Indian Franchise Committee* (1932), vol. 1, p. 108.

126 Ibid., p. 109.

127 Hutton (1933), p. 471.

128 Ibid., p. 504.

129 Ibid., p. 503.

130 Ibid.

131 Ibid., p. 507; *Report of the Indian Statutory Commission* (1930), vol. 1, p. 37.

132 Ibid., p. 505.

133 Ibid., pp. 505–06.

134 Ibid., p. 506.

135 Ibid., p. 507.

136 Ibid., p. 506.

137 *Indian Franchise Committee* (1932), vol. 1, p. 109.

138 Ibid., vol. 1, p. 135.

139 *Indian Round Table Conference* (1932), vol. 1, p. 532.

140 'Table of Seats', Fifth Schedule, Government of India Act, 1935.

141 13th Schedule, Government of India (Provincial Legislative Assemblies) Order, 1936, available at: https://archive.org/details/in.ernet.dli.2015.35682 (last visited 26 March 2020).

142 See Dhebar (1961), pp. 22–23; Guha (2007), p. 3307.

143 See Dhebar (1961), pp. 37–39.

144 See Sixth Schedule, Laws Local Extent Act, 1874, available at: http://legislative.gov.in/sites/default/files/legislative_references/1874.pdf (last visited 24 May 2020).

145 See Section 15(2), Government of India Act, 1919.

146 See Sections 91-92, Government of India Act, 1935. See further, Jayal (2013), pp. 234–235; Galanter (1984), p. 146.

147 See Articles 244–244A, Constitution of India.

148 Jayal (2013), p. 238; Galanter (1984), p. 147. This was under the fifth and sixth schedules to the Constitution.

149 See Nehru's speech at the opening session of the Conference on Scheduled Tribes and Scheduled Areas, New Delhi, 7 June 1952. Gopal (ed.) (1984–2015), Second Series, vol. 18, p. 370ff., at p. 373.

150 Ibid.

Chapter 2: The Other Backward Class of Colonial Bombay

1   Bidwell (ed.) (1870), p. 211.

2   Simcox (1877), p. 508. A 'backward class' in a school was also a group of students (i.e., 'class' as in 'classroom') that was not performing

well, compared to the 'advanced' classes. See, e.g., *The British Friend* (1859), p. 85.

3   Committee appointed to revise the Grant-in-aid Code to the Chief Secretary to the Government of Madras, 1 May 1885, p. 136ff., at p. 139 (pdf p. 114), in *Proceedings of the Government of India in the Home Department for the Month of July 1888: Education* (1888).

4   Cashman (1975), p. 38.

5   *Progress of Education in India, 1907–1912* (1914), vol. 1, pp. 255, 259.

6   There are hundreds of jatis in India but only four or five varnas. The jatis are grouped within each of the varnas. See Srinivas (1968), pp. 3–4.

7   This was unlike north India where the division was: Brahmin, Kshatriya, Vaishya, Shudra and Untouchable. Zelliot (1969), p. 12. See further Irschick (1969), pp. 5–9; Rao (2009), p. 42.

8   *Memorandum Submitted by the Government of Bombay to the Indian Statutory Commission* (1930), p. 44. The allied Maratha castes were Kunbis, Malis, Kolis, Bhandaris, Shimpis, Lohars, Kumbhars, Dhangars, Bhois, Baris, Lonaris, Bavins, Deolis or Shindes, Ahirs, Khatris, Parits, Gabits, Gavadas, Gavandis, Gavlis, Guraos, Nhavis, Kasais, Kasars, Koshtis, Salis, Sangars, Sutars, Telis, Agles, Agris and Wanjaris. Maureen Patterson referred to three primary castes in Maharashtra: Brahmins, Marathas and Mahars. Marathas constituted 25 per cent of the population (along with the Kunbis, 33 per cent), Mahars were 10 per cent, while Brahmins were 4 per cent of the population. Patterson (1954), p. 1065.

9   O'Hanlon (1983), pp. 19, 355.

10   O'Hanlon (1983), p. 178; Omvedt (1971), pp. 1969–1970. See further Srinivas (1968), p. 72; Patterson (1954), p. 1066. But see Omvedt (1971), pp. 1975–76.

11   O'Hanlon (1983), p. 20. See further Ghurye (1957), pp. 198–99. According to Ghurye (1957), British officials believed that high-caste officers in the army were responsible for the revolt and decided to use caste as part of their divide and rule policy thereafter. In 1910, instigated by the Muslim League, census commissioner G.A. Gait attempted to classify the depressed classes separately from Hindus.

Mendelsohn and Vicziany (2001), p. 28. But see 'Hindus and the Census' (1910).

12 See Omvedt (1973), p. 1422.

13 See, e.g., O'Hanlon (1983), pp. 185, 190.

14 Omvedt (1971), p. 1970.

15 O'Hanlon (1983), p. 21.

16 He belonged to the Mali caste, which was considered in the varna scheme to be a Shudra caste, but was as respectable as the Kunbi community. O'Hanlon (1983), p. 19.

17 O'Hanlon (1983), p. 198, 200–01.

18 Omvedt (1971), p. 1973.

19 O'Hanlon (1983), p. 191.

20 O'Hanlon (1983), pp. 300–02.

21 O'Hanlon (1983), p. 21, 316–317.

22 *Memorandum Submitted by the Government of Bombay to the Indian Statutory Commission* (1930), pp. 227–28.

23 O'Hanlon (1983), p. 26; Omvedt (1971), p. 1971. The 96 Maratha families were called 'assal' or true Maratha families. O'Hanlon (1983), p. 24 (fn 3).

24 Omvedt (1971), p. 1971. See further, O'Hanlon (1983), pp. 342–43.

25 O'Hanlon (1983), p. 342.

26 O'Hanlon (1983), pp. 362–63, 366.

27 Omvedt (1971), p. 1971.

28 The term 'Sanskritization' was used by M.N. Srinivas to describe a process by which a 'low' Hindu caste or group changed its customs, rituals, etc. in imitation of those of higher castes, and then claimed higher caste status. See Srinivas (1968), p. 6.

29 O'Hanlon (1983), p. 214.

30 O'Hanlon (1983), p. 343.

31 Omvedt (1971), p. 1978. After the 1923 elections, non-Brahmin legislators in the Bombay Legislative Council were referred to as the 'non-Brahman party'. They secured a ministership after the 1923 elections. *Memorandum Submitted by the Government of Bombay to the Indian Statutory Commission* (1930), p. 230. Non-brahmins in Bombay eventually moved to the Congress. Patterson (1954), p. 1066.

32 Copland (1973), p. 213.

33 Copland (1973), p. 213.

34 Shrimant Jayasingrao Abasaheb Ghatge, chief of Kagal. Copland (1973), pp. 215–16.

35 Rosenthal (1973), p. 905; Latthe (1924), vol. 1, p. 81.

36 Latthe (1924), vol. 1, p. 152.

37 Copland (1973), p. 214. For more on the Chitpavan Brahmins, see Cashman (1975), p. 18.

38 Rosenthal (1973), p. 905.

39 Latthe (1924), vol. 1, pp. 138–39, 141, 144, 147–48.

40 Copland (1973), pp. 216–17. *See further*, Cashman (1975), p. 115.

41 Rosenthal (1973), p. 906. The advisor was from the Chandraseniya Kayastha Prabhu (CKP) community. See further Cashman (1975), p. 115.

42 Cashman (1975), p. 116.

43 Cashman (1975), p. 116.

44 Copland (1973), p. 217; Rosenthal (1973), p. 906.

45 Latthe (1924), vol. 1, p. 188.

46 Latthe (1924), vol. 1, p. 188.

47 Latthe (1924), vol. 1, pp. 195, 197.

48 *Memorandum Submitted by the Government of Bombay to the Indian Statutory Commission* (1930), p. 228. During the Peshwa regime, Prabhus were ordered not to recite Vedic mantras but only Puranic ones. Fukazawa (1968), p. 42.

49 Latthe (1924), vol. 1, p. 193.

50 Latthe (1924), vol. 1, pp. 194, 198.

51 Cashman (1975), p. 117.

52 On this, see further Srinivas (1968), p. 9.

53 O'Hanlon (1983), pp. 28–48.

54 Cashman (1975), p. 117.

55 Setalvad (1946), p. 79.

56 Cashman (1975), p. 117.

57 Setalvad (1946), pp. 79-80.

58 Cashman (1975), p. 47.

59 Cashman (1975), p. 117.

60 Latthe (1924), vol. 1, p. 212.

61 Latthe (1924), vol. 1, p. 220. See further Pawar (2018), p. 19.

62 Latthe (1924), vol. 1, p. 221.

63 Cashman (1975), p. 116.

64 Copland (1973), p. 218.

65 Cashman (1975), p. 116.

66 Rosenthal (1973), p. 906.

67 Copland (1973), p. 221.

68 Zelliot (1969), pp. 91-92.

69 Zelliot (1969), pp. 91-92.

70 Rosenthal (1973), p. 906.

71 Officials like William Lee-Warner and Mountstuart Elphinstone. Cashman (1975), pp. 20, 23.

72 Cashman (1975), p. 37.

73 See Copland (1973), pp. 214–15; Rosenthal (1973), p. 906.

74 Copland (1973), p. 220.

75 Copland (1973), p. 215.

76 Omvedt (1974).

77 Cashman (1975), p. 118.

78 Cashman (1975), p. 118.

79 Cashman (1975), p. 118; O'Hanlon (1983), p. 27. Tilak gave Shivaji a high-caste twist by claiming that he was advised by a Brahmin adviser and that he was the defender of Hindu orthodoxy. Omvedt (1971), p. 1973.

80 Cashman (1975), p. 118 (fn 78).

81 Cashman (1975), p. 118 (fn 78).

82 Cashman (1975), p. 118.

83 See Maharashtra State Reservation (of seats for admission in educational institutions in the State and for appointments or posts in the public services under the State) for Educationally and Socially Backward Category (ESBC) Ordinance, 2014, available at: https://www.maharashtra.gov.in/Site/Upload/Acts%20Rules/English/esbc_13_11072014.pdf (last visited 4 May 2020). The 2015 Act is available here: http://14.139.60.153/bitstream/123456789/11110/1/Maharashtra_state_reservation_for_ESBC_Act_2014.pdf (last visited 25 May 2020).

84 Irschick (1969), p. 14.

85 Irschick (1969), pp. 48, 51.

86   Irschick (1969), p. 70.

87   Irschick (1969), p 92.

88   *Report of the Indian Statutory Commission* (1930), vol. 1, p. 139. See further Irschick (1969), pp. 162, 165.

89   *Report of the Indian Statutory Commission* (1930), vol. 1, p. 139. These were on the basis of the recommendations of the Joint Select Committee in 1919. See *Report from the Joint Select Committee on the Government of India Bill* (1919), p. 7. Under the Government of India Act, 1935, seven seats continued to be reserved for Marathas in the legislative assembly of Bombay. Clause 4(i), 5th Schedule, Government of India Act, 1935.

90   Further, they were self-liquidating in the sense that if a non-Brahmin or Maratha respectively was able to get elected without the reservation, the reserved seat would become a general seat. See Clause II, Schedule I, Madras Rules, and Clause IV, Schedule I, Bombay Rules, Electoral Rules for Provincial Legislative Councils. See *Rules under the Government of India Act* (1921), pp. 38, 52.

91   Irschick (1969), p. 178.

92   See *Return Showing the Results of Elections in India* (1921), p. iv.

93   Irschick (1969), pp. 236–37, 368–72. The Communal G.O.s sought to revive an order issued by the Madras government in 1851 which had tried to reduce the number of Brahmin revenue officials, but which had never really been implemented. Irschick (1969), pp. 219–20.

94   Dushkin (1974), pp. 86, 89.

95   Miller, a member of the Indian Civil Service, had been a judge of the Madras High Court between 1906 and 1914. He served as Chief Judge of Mysore for around eight years from 1914. See Reed (ed.) (1922), p. 841; 'Sir Leslie Miller' (1925).

96   Dushkin (1974), p. 89. The committee was formally called the 'Committee Appointed to Consider Steps Necessary for the Adequate Representation of Backward Communities in the Public Service'.

97   See Rao (1936), pp. 305–06.

98   Paragraph 6, Miller (1919).

99   Paragraph 6, Miller (1919).

100 Paragraph 6, Miller (1919).

101 Paragraph 3, Miller (1919).

102 Dushkin (1974), pp. 96–97.

103 See *B.S. Kesava Iyengar* v. *State of Mysore*, AIR 1956 Mys 20: (1955) SCC Online Kar 51 (paragraphs 17–18). See further Clause 2, Revised Rules of Recruitment Governing Subordinate Services of Government, order of the Mysore Government dated 3 July 1934, available at https://archive.org/details/TheMysoreVillageManualPartI (last visited 26 May 2020), p. 224 (of archive.org).

104 Dushkin (1974), p. 100.

105 'Depressed Classes' (1928).

106 Depressed Classes and Aboriginal Tribes Committee. Zelliot (1969), p. 163 (fn 46).

107 Zelliot (1969), p. 163; 'Depressed Classes' (1928).

108 National Archives of India, File No. 50/II/1934-Poll, Identifier: PR_000005002445, p. 20 of the file (internal p. 8) (available on the Abilekh Patal website). Sujit Choudhry was, therefore, wrong when he said that 'Other Backward Classes' was a 'term that was introduced into Indian political discourse by Prime Minister Nehru during the Constituent Assembly debates'. Choudhry (2015), p. 30.

109 National Archives of India, ibid.

110 Ibid.

111 Dracup (1933), p. 380.

112 National Archives of India, File No. 50/II/1934-Poll, Identifier: PR_000005002445, p. 21 of the file (internal, p. 9) (available on the Abilekh Patal website). The resolution of the Bombay government was dated 29 May 1933 (Resolution No. 9330).

113 *Annual Report on the Working of the Backward Class Department for the Year 1945–46* (1948) (paragraphs 6–8, 10).

114 Ibid., paragraph 11. Additionally, 10 per cent of the 'inferior servants' posts were reserved only for the depressed classes.

115 Ibid., paragraph 13. See further Letter from O.H.B. Starte to Secretary to Government, 21 September 1933, (first report of the Backward Class Officer, for the period 1931–1933) (on file with the author).

116 National Archives of India, File No. 50/II/1934-Poll, Identifier: PR_000005002445, p. 23 of the file (internal, p. 11) (available on the Abilekh Patal website). By 1936, the list had 49 Scheduled Classes, and 140 Other Backward Classes. *Annual Report on the Working of*

the Backward Class Department, 1935–36 (1937). By 1945–46, there were 49 Scheduled Classes, 29 Aboriginal and Hill Tribes, and 130 Other Backward Classes. Importantly, Marathas were not a part of the list of Other Backward Classes. *Annual Report on the Working of the Backward Class Department for the Year 1945–46* (1948).

117 See Siddiqui (1982), p. 244; *Annual Report on the Working of the Backward Class Department, 1935–36* (1937).

118 'Annual Report on the Working of the Backward Class Department for 1933–34', sent by D. Symington, Backward Class Officer, Bombay Presidency, Poona to Secretary to Government, General Department, Bombay, letter dated 1 October 1934. M.R. Jayakar Papers, National Archives of India, File No. 179, Identifier: PP_000000010187 (available on the Abhilekh Patal website), p. 266.

119 Clause 26, Schedule I, Part I, and Clause 19, Schedule V, Government of India Act, 1935.

120 House of Lords, 18 July 1946. Available at: https://api.parliament.uk/historic-hansard/lords/1946/jul/18/the-mission-to-india (last visited 26 March 2020).

121 Fifth Schedule, Government of India Act, 1935.

122 According to the Poona Pact, in the central legislature, 18 per cent of the seats allotted to the *general electorate* were supposed to be reserved for the depressed classes, not 18 per cent of the *total* seats. In other words, this did not include the seats for which voting would be by separate electorates. See Ambedkar (1947), p. 54; Hutton (1933), p. 494.

123 19 out of 250 seats (British India) in the Federal Assembly and 6 out of 150 seats (British India) in the Council of State were reserved for Scheduled Castes. First Schedule, Government of India Act, 1935.

124 19 out of 105 general seats (British India) in the Federal Assembly (18 per cent) and 151 out of 808 general seats in the provincial legislatures (18.6 per cent) were reserved for the Scheduled Castes. Though 6 out of 75 general seats (British India) were reserved for Scheduled Castes in the Council of State (8 per cent), in independent India there is no reservation for Scheduled Castes in the upper house of Parliament. First and Fifth Schedules, Government of India Act, 1935.

125 Government of India (Scheduled Castes) Order, 1936, available at: https://archive.org/details/GOIAct1935SCOrder/mode/2up (last visited 26 March 2020).

126 Article 298.

127 Resolution passed by the Government of India, Home Department, 4 July 1934. *Joint Committee on Indian Constitutional Reform* (1934), vol. 2, pp. 315–16.

128 See Kalelkar (1955), pp. 127–28.

129 Patel to Gopichand Bhargava, 2 September 1948. Das (ed.) (1972), vol. 6, p. 408.

130 Ibid.

Chapter 3: Ambedkar Produces a Formula

1 See Ambedkar (1945), p. 196; Ambedkar (1947), p. 77. See further H.J. Khandekar's Memorandum on Minorities (2 April 1947). Rao (ed.) (2012), vol. 2, p. 324; Memorandum by the Working Committee of the All-India Adi-Hindu Depressed Classes Association (15 April 1947). Rao (ed.) (2012), vol. 2, p. 381. Though the 1941 census said that there were around 48 million Scheduled Castes in India, these figures were considered to be inaccurate. See speech of V.I. Muniswamy Pillay. Constituent Assembly Debates, vol. 9, p. 646 (24 August 1949).

2 See speech of Winston Churchill in the House of Commons (18 July 1946), available at: https://api.parliament.uk/historic-hansard/commons/1946/jul/18/india-cabinet-mission (last visited 27 March 2020).

3 Later, the 73rd and 74th amendments to the Constitution introduced reservations of seats in panchayats and municipalities as well. On these amendments, see Bihari Lal Rada v. Anil Jain (Tinu), (2009) 4 SCC 1; K. Krishna Murthy v. Union of India, (2010) 7 SCC 202; Vikas Kishanrao Gawali v. State of Maharashtra, (2021) SCC Online SC 170. Further, various other facilities are given to the backward classes, e.g., scholarships, special hostels, preferential allotment of petrol pumps, etc. Sitapati (2016), p. 738.

4 Articles 16(4), 330, 332, 335. Rao (ed.) (2012), vol. 4, pp. 754, 869–71.

5   According to Marc Galanter, the proportion of Scheduled Castes and Scheduled Tribes in the Rajya Sabha and upper houses of state legislatures is consequently small. Scheduled Castes and Scheduled Tribes also usually lose elections in general constituencies. Galanter (1984), p. 48; Deshpande (2013), p. 272.

6   There is, however, a convention of having one or some members of the cabinet from backward classes. Galanter (1984), p. 48.

7   However, by convention, judges from backward classes may be elevated to the Supreme Court in supersession of some of their senior peers if the court lacks backward class judges. See Chandrachud (2014).

8   Article II, Section IV, Clause 2. Ambedkar's Memorandum and Draft Articles on the Rights of States and Minorities (24 March 1947), Rao (ed.) (2012), vol. 2, p. 93.

9   H.J. Khandekar's Memorandum on Minorities (2 April 1947). Rao (ed.) (2012), vol. 2, p. 325; Jagjivan Ram's Reply to the Questionnaire (3 April 1947). Rao (ed.) (2012), vol. 2, p. 333.

10   Memorandum (15 April 1947). Rao (ed.) (2012), vol. 2, p. 382. Khandekar asked for these reservations as well. Constituent Assembly Debates, vol. 9, p. 666 (24 August 1949).

11   Ambedkar was appointed Union Law Minister on 15 August 1947. See Munshi (2012), vol. 1, p. 184.

12   See speech of Chandrika Ram, Constituent Assembly Debates, vol. 9, p. 690 (24 August 1949).

13   See speech of S. Nagappa, Constituent Assembly Debates, ibid., p. 679 (25 August 1949).

14   Rao (ed.) (2012), vol. 2, p. 398.

15   Constituent Assembly Debates, vol. 5, p. 200 (27 August 1947).

16   Ambedkar (1945), p. 99.

17   Article III, Clause 5. Note and Draft Articles on Fundamental Rights (17 March 1947). Rao (ed.) (2012), vol. 2, p. 74. Munshi wrote that he, Alladi Krishnaswami Ayyar and N. Gopalaswamy Ayyangar were referred to as the 'Three Musketeers' in the Constituent Assembly. Munshi (2012), vol. 1, p. 115.

18   Clause 5, Report of the Subcommittee on Fundamental Rights (16 April 1947). Rao (ed.) (2012), vol. 2, p. 171.

19 Minutes of the Advisory Committee (22 April 1947). Ibid., p. 259. In the subcommittee on minorities, it was Sardar Ujjal Singh who first suggested that the equality of opportunity clause should not debar reservations for minorities in public services. Minutes of the Subcommittee on Minorities meeting dated 17 April 1947. Rao (ed.) (2012), vol. 2, p. 200. The interim report of the subcommittee on 19 April 1947 suggested that a proviso be prepared to the equality of opportunity clause. Rao (ed.) (2012), vol. 2, p. 208. A proviso to the equality of opportunity clause was then drafted by a committee consisting of C. Rajagopalachari, Ambedkar, K.M. Panikkar and K.M. Munshi. Rao (ed.) (2012), vol. 2, pp. 287, 290 (21–22 April 1947).

20 Hutton (1933), p. 276.

21 See Chandrachud (2015), p. 36. Further, as Sitapati points out, not merely were government salaries higher (at the lower end) than private salaries, but government jobs provided job security. Sitapati (2016), pp. 728–29.

22 In its report dated 8 August 1947 on minority rights, the Advisory Committee refused to guarantee representation in the services to minorities on the basis of their population. Rao (ed.) (2012), vol. 2, p. 416.

23 Patel to Baldev Singh, 16 September 1949. Das (ed.) (1972), vol. 8, p. 343.

24 See Chandrachud (2017), pp. 194–95.

25 Constituent Assembly Debates, vol. 7, p. 699 (30 November 1948).

26 Ibid., p. 701.

27 Ibid., pp. 701–02.

28 See speech of H.J. Khandekar in the Constituent Assembly. Ibid., p. 692.

29 Constituent Assembly Debates, vol. 7 (30 November 1948), p. 702.

30 Ibid.

31 Zelliot (1969), pp. 265, 267-268. Before partition, he was appointed to the Constituent Assembly by the Muslim League in Bengal.

32 Zelliot (1969), p. 271.

33 Zelliot (1969), p. 273. However, he was a member of the Rajya Sabha. Zelliot (1969), p. 274.

34 Rajya Sabha Debates, 2 September 1953, p. 874. This was during the debate on the Andhra State Bill, 1953.

35 Articles 330(2) and 332(3). This was originally recommended by the Advisory Committee in its report dated 8 August 1947. Rao (ed.) (2012), vol. 2, p. 418.

36 See Sardar Patel's letter to Prithvi Singh Azad, 29 November 1950. Das (ed.) (1972), vol. 9, p. 394. 'The electoral roll figures,' said Patel, 'are, therefore, irrelevant.'

37 On this, see Surendranath (2013).

38 See Clause 4, Schedule I, Scheduled Castes and Scheduled Tribes Orders (Amendment) Act, 1956.

39 See Tyagi's profile on the website of the Rajya Sabha, available at: https://rajyasabha.nic.in/rsnew/pre_member/1952_2003/t.pdf (last visited 27 May 2020).

40 Constituent Assembly Debates, vol. 9, p. 671 (24 August 1949).

41 Minutes of the Advisory Committee meeting, Rao (ed.) (2012), vol. 2, p. 258 (22 April 1947).

42 Ibid., p. 259.

43 Ibid., p. 258.

44 Ibid., p. 258.

45 The Advisory Committee recommended the sunset clause in its report dated 8 August 1947. Rao (ed.) (2012), vol. 2, p. 417.

46 Article 334.

47 Article II, Section IV, Part III, Clause 2. Ambedkar's Memorandum and Draft Articles on the Rights of States and Minorities (24 March 1947). Rao (ed.) (2012), vol. 2, pp. 95–6. His draft also required fresh elections to be held before the matter could be voted on in parliament.

48 For more on him, see Kundapura (2014).

49 Constituent Assembly Debates, vol. 7, p. 690 (30 November 1948).

50 Ibid., p. 691.

51 See 'Jaipal Singh devoted life to Adivasi welfare'. He remained the team captain until the quarterfinals. The team eventually won a gold medal. His first wife, Tara Majumdar, was the granddaughter of W.C. Bonnerjee, the first president of the Indian National Congress. See Parmar (2012), p. 501 (fn 64); 'The Return of the Adibasi'.

52 Constituent Assembly Debates, vol. 7, vol. 9, p. 653 (24 August 1949).

53 See further, speech of H.J. Khandekar, Constituent Assembly Debates, vol. 9, p. 666 (24 August 1949).

54 Constituent Assembly Debates, vol. 9, p. 677 (25 August 1949). See further, speech of V.I. Muniswamy Pillay. Ibid., p. 680.

55 Constituent Assembly Debates, vol. 9, p. 697 (24 August 1949).

56 Kunzru was later a member of the Rajya Sabha for two terms. See Biographical Sketches of Rajya Sabha Members, available at: https://rajyasabha.nic.in/rsnew/pre_member/1952_2003/k.pdf (last visited 23 March 2020).

57 Constituent Assembly Debates, vol. 7, p. 679 (30 November 1948). See further, suggestion from Atul Chandra Gupta. Rao (ed.) (2012), vol. 4, p. 32.

58 Constituent Assembly Debates, vol. 9, p. 697 (25 August 1949).

59 Article 16(4). According to Jayal (2013), the use of the word 'class' instead of 'caste' in the term 'Other Backward Classes' was a 'deliberate misnaming' which 'concealed the discomfort with using caste officially'. Jayal (2013), p. 246. However, as we have seen in the previous chapters, the word 'class' was used instead of caste since at least the 1880s—untouchable castes were called depressed 'classes', and 'backward classes' was a term which was in vogue since then. The use of the terminology 'backward class' in the Constitution was, therefore, probably more a consequence of path dependency.

60 Articles 330 and 332.

61 Article 340.

62 Article 46.

63 See, e.g., Constituent Assembly Debates (30 November 1948), vol. 7: speeches of Damodar Swarup Seth, p. 679; Pandit Hirday Nath Kunzru, p. 679; V.I. Muniswamy Pillay, p. 688; Mohamed Ismail Sahib, p. 692; Hukam Singh, p. 694.

64 In the Constituent Assembly, S. Nagappa said that while 12–15 per cent of the general population in India was literate, only 1–2 per cent of Harijans were literate. Constituent Assembly Debates, vol. 9, p. 678 (25 August 1949).

65 Constituent Assembly Debates, vol. 7, p. 699 (30 November 1948).

66 Comment of R.R. Diwakar and S.V. Krishnamoorthy Rao on the draft constitution. Rao (ed.) (2012), vol. 4, p. 31. B.N. Rau considered this to be 'perhaps unnecessary'. See further the comment of Upendranath Barman on the draft constitution. Rao (ed.) (2012), vol. 4, p. 31.

67   Comments of T.A. Ramalingam Chettiar and the Madras Legislative Council on the draft constitution. Rao (ed.) (2012), vol. 4, p. 31.

68   Constituent Assembly Debates, (30 November 1948), vol. 7, p. 682. See further, speech of Mohamed Ismail Sahib, p. 693.

69   Ibid., p. 685.

70   Ibid., p. 686.

71   Ibid., p. 686.

72   Ibid., p. 691. See further the speech of R.M. Nalavade, ibid.

73   Ibid., p. 692.

74   See Drafting Committee's note on the Draft Constitution of February 1948. Rao (ed.) (2012), vol. 3, p. 521. Harnam Singh's draft on fundamental rights (18 March 1947) used the phrase 'Backward Classes' to describe communities 'such as Scheduled Castes, the Aboriginal Tribes, the Mazhabis, Ramdasis and Kabirpanthis'. Rao (ed.) (2012), vol. 2, p. 82.

75   Constituent Assembly Debates, vol. 7, p. 697 (30 November 1948).

76   Ibid., p. 697.

77   See Statement of Objects and Reasons, Bombay Depressed Classes (Protection of Rights) Bill. National Archives of India, Legislative Department, 1933, File No. 271, p. 7 (available on the Abhilekh Patal website, Identifier: PR_000005002649). See further, Annual Report (for the year ending 31 March 1938) submitted by the Bombay Legislature Congress Party. Choudhary (ed.) (1984–95), vol. 2, p. 239 and p. 244.

78   J. Choudhry's note, 24 September 1938. Choudhary (ed.) (1984–95), vol. 2, p. 288.

79   Zelliot (1969), p. 163; 'Depressed Classes: Government Appoint Inquiry Committee'. This has been discussed in the previous chapter.

80   Constituent Assembly Debates, vol. 7, p. 702 (30 November 1948).

81   See Ambedkar's letter to Nehru, 28 April 1948. Das (ed.) (1972), vol. 6, p. 330 at p. 332.

82   Articles 341–342. This was brought about by the Constituent Assembly on 17 September 1949 through the insertion of Articles 300A and 300B into the Constitution. See Constituent Assembly Debates, vol. 9, p. 1636 (17 September 1949).

83 Ibid., p. 1637. The 10th and 11th schedules to the October 1947 draft of the Constitution contained a list of Scheduled Tribes and Scheduled Castes respectively. Rao (ed.) (2012), vol. 3, pp. 183, 187. In the February 1948 draft of the Constitution, the term 'Scheduled Castes' was defined to mean (in some states) those included in the Government of India (Scheduled Castes) Order, 1936 [Article 303(w)], while 'Scheduled Tribes' were those set out in Parts I to IX of the 8th Schedule [Article 303(x)]. Rao (ed.) (2012), vol. 3, p. 637.

84 See Munshi (2012), vol. 1, p. 208.

85 Constituent Assembly Debates, vol. 9, pp. 1638–39 (17 September 1949).

86 Clauses 4–5, Schedule I, Scheduled Castes and Scheduled Tribes Orders (Amendment) Act, 1956.

87 Misra was later a member of the Swatantra Party and a member of the Rajya Sabha. See profile on the website of the Rajya Sabha, available at: https://rajyasabha.nic.in/rsnew/pre_member/1952_2003/m.pdf (last visited 28 May 2020).

88 Constituent Assembly Debates, vol. 7, p. 673 (30 November 1948).

89 Ibid., p. 679.

90 Ibid. See further, speech of Brajeshwar Prasad. Constituent Assembly Debates, vol. 10, p. 237 (14 October 1949).

91 See profile on the website of the Lok Sabha, available at: http://loksabhaph.nic.in/writereaddata/biodata_1_12/591.htm (last visited 28 May 2020).

92 Minute of dissent to the report of the Subcommittee on Minorities, 27 July 1947. Rao (ed.) (2012), vol. 2, p. 402.

93 Constituent Assembly Debates, vol. 5, p. 272 (28 August 1947).

94 Ibid.

95 See Yengde (2019).

96 Patel to R.S. Shukla, 24 December 1945. Das (ed.) (1972), vol. 2, p. 342. Shukla called him 'an unscrupulous man'. Shukla to Patel, 20 December 1945. Das (ed.) (1972), vol. 2, p. 340. Patel felt that Jagjivan Ram would be 'much more useful and helpful than Khandekar.' Patel to Rajendra Prasad, letter dated 6 January 1949. Das (ed.) (1972), vol. 8, p. 254.

97 Constituent Assembly Debates, vol. 9, pp. 672–73 (24 August 1949).

98   Ibid., p. 673.

99   See comments of Govind Das and Thakurdas Bhargava. Rao (ed.) (2012), vol. 4, p. 354.

100   On 27 July 1947, it was proposed in the subcommittee on minorities that 'members of a minority community who have reserved seats should have the right to contest unreserved seats as well.' Rao (ed.) (2012), vol. 2, p. 398. This was accepted by the Advisory Committee in its report dated 8 August 1947. Rao (ed.) (2012), vol. 2, p. 412–13. See further, speech of Ambedkar, Constituent Assembly Debates, vol. 9, p. 658 (24 August 1949).

101   Constituent Assembly Debates, vol. 9, p. 666 (24 August 1949).

102   Ibid., p. 668.

103   Ibid.

104   Ibid., p. 669.

105   Constituent Assembly Debates, vol. 7, p. 691 (30 November 1948).

106   Ibid., p. 692.

107   Ibid., p. 697.

108   Ibid.; Constituent Assembly Debates, Vol. 5, p. 200 (27 August 1947).

109   Article 335.

110   Patel to Ambedkar, 6 May 1948. Das (ed.) (1972), vol. 6, p. 334.

111   See Chandrachud (2020), pp. 60–61.

112   Constituent Assembly Debates, Vol. 5, p. 227 (27 August 1947).

113   Report of the Subcommittee on Minorities (27 July 1947). Rao (ed.) (2012), vol. 2, p. 398. In 1946, Patel had sought Gandhi's advice on this question. See Patel's letters to Gandhi dated 22 July and 30 July 1946. Chopra (ed.) (2015), vol. 10, pp. 247–48, 253–54.

114   Munshi (2012), vol. 1, p. 202.

115   Ibid.

116   Hutton (1933), p. 486.

117   In Chapter 1, we also saw that in a report submitted to the Simon Commission, Ambedkar had taken the view that separate electorates were 'evil' and that adult suffrage ought to be adopted instead.

118   See letter from Rajendra Prasad to Nehru, 16 February 1948. Choudhary (ed.) (1984–95), vol. 8, p. 88. See further, Austin (2015), pp. 14–15.

119   See Munshi (2012), vol. 2, p. 182.

Chapter 4: Nehru Dislikes the Word 'Dalit'

1   As Marc Galanter pointed out, even the task of identifying Scheduled
    Castes and Scheduled Tribes was beset with difficulties. However, at
    least the criteria for identifying them were more precise than those for
    Other Backward Classes. Galanter (1984), pp. 128, 133.

2   State of Madras v. Srimathi Champakam Dorairajan, AIR 1951 SC
    226 (from SCC Online) (7 judges).

3   See ibid., paragraphs 2–3.

4   Not, as Austin called them, 'General Orders'. Austin (2003), p. 95.
    See Srimathi Champakam Dorairajan v. State of Madras, (1950) SCC
    Online Mad 197.

5   State of Madras v. Srimathi Champakam Dorairajan, AIR 1951 SC
    226 (from SCC Online), paragraph 4.

6   Ibid., paragraph 9.

7   Ibid., paragraph 13.

8   Ibid., paragraph 13.

9   Ibid., paragraph 12.

10 Ibid., paragraph 10.

11 B. Venkataramana v. State of Madras, AIR 1951 SC 229 (7 judges).

12 Ibid., paragraph 2.

13 Ibid., paragraph 4.

14 Ibid., paragraph 4.

15 See Gopal (ed.) (1984–2015) (Second Series), vol. 16 (part 1), p. 153.

16 Nehru's letter to Raja, 11 April 1951. Gopal (ed.) (1984–2015)
    (Second Series), vol. 16 (part 1), pp. 153–54.

17 'Madras Ministers Meet Mr. Nehru'.

18 According to Galanter, it also 'caused a political furore in South India'.
    Galanter (1984), p. 164.

19 See AIR 1951 SC 226 (SCC Online version) (paragraph 12).

20 Choudhary (ed.) (1984–95), vol. 15, pp. 497-498.

21 See Chandrachud (2017), pp. 72-97.

22 Parliamentary Debates, 16 May 1951, p. 8821. Pandit Thakur Das
    Bhargava, for instance, argued that if the amendment's intent was to
    preserve the Communal G.O. through the 'backdoor', then he was
    against it. Ibid., pp. 8893–94 (17 May 1951).

23   Ibid., p. 8822 (16 May 1951).

24   Ibid., p. 9005 (18 May 1951). Nehru also referred to the Supreme
     Court's judgment in the Communal G.O. case. Ibid., pp. 9615–16
     (29 May 1951). However, the Champakam Dorairajan judgment was
     really the target of the amendment, not the Venkataramana judgment.

25   Ibid., p. 9006 (18 May 1951).

26   Ibid., p. 9007.

27   As Sitapati points out, though Article 15(4) did not speak of reservations,
     'special provision' has been interpreted to mean reservations. Sitapati
     (2016), p. 733.

28   The word 'economically', though originally intended to be a part of
     the amendment, was dropped by the parliamentary select committee.
     See Austin (2003), p. 97.

29   See, e.g., Parliamentary Debates (1 June 1951): K.T. Shah (p. 9814),
     S.L. Saksena (p. 9819), Hukam Singh (p. 9814), Naziruddin Ahmad
     (p. 9829).

30   See profile on the website of the Lok Sabha, available at: http://
     loksabhaph.nic.in/writereaddata/biodata_1_12/596.htm (last visited
     31 May 2020).

31   Parliamentary Debates, p. 9817 (1 June 1951).

32   Ibid., p. 9041 (18 May 1951).

33   See, e.g., Pandit Thakur Das Bhargava (p. 8893) (17 May 1951);
     Syamnandan Sahaya (p. 8928) (17 May 1951).

34   See, e.g., K.T. Shah (p. 9640) (29 May 1951), Hukam Singh (p.
     9822-9823) (1 June 1951), S.P. Mookerjee (p. 9710) (30 May 1951)
     and (p. 9824-9825) (1 June 1951), Kamath (p. 9826) (1 June 1951).

35   Ibid., p. 9830 (1 June 1951).

36   Ibid., p. 9830 (1 June 1951).

37   Ibid., p. 9616 (29 May 1951).

38   He was an advocate from Mysore and later a member of the Lok Sabha.
     See profile on the Lok Sabha website, available at: http://loksabhaph.
     nic.in/writereaddata/biodata_1_12/1363.htm (last visited 31 May
     2020).

39   Parliamentary Debates, p. 8999 (17 May 1951). See further,
     Deshmukh (pp. 9775-9776) (31 May 1951).

40   Ibid., pp. 10103–07 (2 June 1951).

41 Prasad's letter to K.N. Katju, 23 January 1953. Choudhary (ed.) (1984–95), vol. 16, p. 17ff. at p. 19.

42 29 January 1953. Report of the Backward Classes Commission (30 March 1955). Choudhary (ed.) (1984–95), vol. 16, p. 497.

43 A disciple of Gandhi, Kalelkar had written a book entitled 'Stray Glimpses of Bapu' (1950). He was nominated to the Rajya Sabha for two terms. See profile on the website of the Rajya Sabha, available at: https://rajyasabha.nic.in/rsnew/pre_member/1952_2003/k.pdf (last visited 1 June 2020).

44 Gopal (ed.) (1984–2015) (Second Series), vol. 21, p. 83ff. at p. 84.

45 Kalelkar (1955), pp. xiii–xiv. See further, Jayal (2013), pp. 246–47; Galanter (1984), p. 171. The Kalelkar Commission's report was not discussed in parliament for ten years, and it was eventually rejected. Jayal (2013), p. 247; Galanter (1984), p. 177.

46 Report of the Backward Classes Commission (30 March 1955). Choudhary (ed.) (1984–95), vol. 16, pp. 503–04.

47 Ibid.

48 Ibid.

49 Ibid.

50 Ibid., p. 533.

51 Ibid., p. 539.

52 Ibid., p. 539.

53 Ibid., pp. 539–40.

54 Ibid., p. 511. See further, Srinivas (1968), p. 21.

55 Report of the Backward Classes Commission (30 March 1955), Choudhary (ed.) (1984–95), vol. 16, p. 511.

56 Ibid., p. 527.

57 Ibid., pp. 526–27.

58 Ibid., pp. 539–40.

59 Ibid., p. 536.

60 Ibid., p. 527.

61 Ibid., p. 540.

62 Kalelkar (1955), p. 155.

63 Prasad to Nehru, 25 September 1949. Gopal (ed.) (1984–2015) (Second Series), vol. 13, p. 129 (fn 2).

64 Nehru to Prasad, 27 September 1949. Ibid., pp. 129–30.

65 Prasad's note dated 28 April 1956. Choudhary (ed.) (1984–95), vol. 18, p. 243.

66 The Constitution (Scheduled Castes) Order, 1950 and Constitution (Scheduled Tribes) Order, 1950 applied to Part A and Part B states. The Constitution (Scheduled Castes) Part 'C' States Order, 1951 and the Constitution (Scheduled Tribes) Part 'C' States Order, 1951 applied to Part C states. See Lokur (1965), p. 1.

67 For instance, after the Kalelkar commission, the lists were modified by the Scheduled Castes and Scheduled Tribes Order (Amendment) Act, 1956, and Scheduled Castes and Scheduled Tribes Lists (Modification) Order, 1956. Ibid., p. 1.

68 See G.S. Rarewala's letter to Sardar Patel, 2 May 1950. Das (ed.) (1972), vol. 9, p. 429. The Home Ministry was in charge of Scheduled Castes and Scheduled Tribes. See Patel's letter to Nehru, 16 September 1950. Das (ed.) (1972), vol. 10, pp. 443–44. See further, letter dated 19 December 1949 issued by the Joint Secretary to the Government of India to the Chief Secretaries of the provinces, File No. F.28/49-C, available at: http://nationalarchives.nic.in/sites/default/files/new/1949_28_C.pdf (last visited 2 June 2020).

69 Appendix V, Lokur (1965), pp. 42–54.

70 Lokur (1965), p. 6.

71 Ibid., p. 7.

72 Ibid., p. 7.

73 See Dhebar (1961), p. 7.

74 Dhebar (1961), p. 7.

75 Dhebar (1961), p. 7.

76 Lokur (1965), p. 15.

77 Ibid., p. 16.

78 Ibid., p. 16.

79 Kalelkar (1955), p. 128.

80 However, there was Other Backward Class reservation in some states at that time. For example, in Bombay, 12.8 per cent of all Class I and Class II posts were reserved for Scheduled Castes, Scheduled Tribes and Other Backward Classes. Ibid., p. 131.

81 Choudhary (ed.) (1984–95), vol. 16, p. 500.

82 Ibid., p. 503.

83 Ibid., p. 528.

84 Nehru's remarks at the Chief Minister's Conference, 23 October 1955. Gopal (ed.) (1984–2015) (Second Series), vol. 30, p. 303.

85 Gopal (ed.) (1984–2015) (Second Series), vol. 40, p. 280.

86 2 April 1958. Gopal (ed.) (1984–2015) (Second Series), vol. 42, p. 270

87 Ibid.

88 Ibid.

89 Ibid., p. 271.

90 Nehru's speech at Abu Road, Rajasthan, 17 October 1958. Gopal (ed.) (1984–2015) (Second Series), vol. 44, p. 215.

91 Krishna would eventually become the Union Deputy Minister for Defence, Industrial Development and Internal Trade. See Rajya Sabha profile, available at: https://rajyasabha.nic.in/rsnew/pre_member/1952_2003/k.pdf (last visited 2 April 2020).

92 20 December 1958. Gopal (ed.) (1984–2015) (Second Series), vol. 45, p. 324.

93 Ibid., p. 325.

94 'Sardar Patel on Division of Provinces on Linguistic Basis', Hindustan Times, 2 March 1950. Chopra (ed.) (2015), vol. 15, p. 71ff., at p. 72.

95 See Prasad's note on a memorandum received on backward classes, 19 August 1959. Choudhary (ed.) (1984–95), vol. 19, p. 191 at p. 192. There was no Other Backward Class reservation in central government jobs until 1990.

96 Ibid.

97 Lokur (1965), p. 7.

98 Nehru to Jatti, 15 August 1959. Gopal (ed.) (1984–2015) (Second Series), vol. 51, pp. 342–43.

99 Ibid., p. 343.

100 Nehru's letter to Sonavane, 20 March 1960. Gopal (ed.) (1984–2015) (Second Series), vol. 58, p. 170.

101 See 'Memorial to Mahatma'.

102 Nehru's note to his principal private secretary, 26 November 1957. Gopal (ed.) (1984–2015) (Second Series), vol. 40, p. 279; Nehru's note dated 22 January 1958 to K. Ram, his principal private secretary. Gopal (ed.) (1984–2015) (Second Series), vol. 41, p. 330.

103 Nehru's note to K. Ram, his principal private secretary. Gopal (ed.) (1984–2015) (Second Series), vol. 41, p. 330.

104 Nehru's note to G. Mukharji, secretary, Delhi Development Authority, New Delhi, 21 March 1958. Gopal (ed.) (1984–2015) (Second Series), vol. 41, p. 333.

105 A.V. Thakkar to Rajendra Prasad, 26 July 1937. Choudhary (ed.) (1984–95), vol. 1, pp. 69–70.

106 See '82nd Birthday of "Thakkar Bapa"'.

107 A.V. Thakkar's letter to Prasad, 31 July 1937. Choudhary (ed.) (1984–95), vol. 1, p. 78.

108 Nehru's letter to the Chief Ministers, 2 September 1952. Gopal (ed.) (1984–2015) (Second Series), vol. 19, p. 484. Some of the provincial governments had abolished the criminal tribes system even earlier: e.g., Madras (1947), Bombay (1949).

109 Nehru to Jairamdas Doulatram, 4 April 1952. Gopal (ed.) (1984–2015) (Second Series), vol. 18, p. 361. See further, Nehru to Bisnuram Medhi, 4 April 1952. Gopal (ed.) (1984–2015) (Second Series), vol. 18, p. 363.

110 Nehru to Jairamdas Doulatram, ibid.

111 See Nehru's speech at the All India Tribal Affairs Conference in New Delhi, 4 December 1954. Gopal (ed.) (1984–2015) (Second Series), vol. 27, p. 428ff., at pp. 429–30.

112 Nehru's letter to Chief Ministers, 3 December 1950. Gopal (ed.) (1984–2015) (Second Series), vol. 15 (part 2), p. 607ff., at p. 613.

113 'Sikh Leader's Five-Point Demand'.

114 Nehru to Giani Kartar Singh, 14 October 1951. Gopal (ed.) (1984–2015) (Second Series), vol. 16 (part 2), pp. 534–35.

115 See proviso to paragraph 3, Constitution (Scheduled Castes) Order, 1950; Clause 1, Schedules I–II, Scheduled Castes and Scheduled Tribes Orders (Amendment) Act, 1956. See further, Chandrachud (2020), p. 215 (fn 149).

116 See G.S. Rarewala's letter to Sardar Patel, 2 May 1950, and the latter's reply, 13 May 1950. Das (ed.) (1972), vol. 9, pp. 429, 432.

117 Gopal (ed.) (1984–2015) (Second Series), vol. 38, p. 203 (footnote 3). Ambedkar had first announced in 1935 that he would 'not die a Hindu'. Zelliot (1969), p. 196. Dalit converts to Buddhism are often called 'neo-Buddhists'. Weisskopf (2004), p. 4345.

118 Gopal (ed.) (1984–2015) (Second Series), vol. 38, p. 203 (fn 4).

119 According to the 1961 census, around 80 per cent of the members of the Mahar caste, to which Ambedkar belonged, had converted to Buddhism. Zelliot (1969), p. 239.

120 See Constitution (Scheduled Castes) Orders (Amendment) Act, 1990.

121 Nehru's note to his principal private secretary, 26 July 1957. Gopal (ed.) (1984–2015) (Second Series), vol. 38, p. 205.

122 Nehru's note to his principal private secretary, 18 July 1957. Gopal (ed.) (1984–2015) (Second Series), vol. 38, p. 204.

123 See Audio Archive of the Center of South Asian Studies, Cambridge University, available at: https://www.s-asian.cam.ac.uk/archive/audio/collection/u-n-dhebar/ (last visited 2 April 2020); 'Removing A.-I.M.O. Conference Defects of Congress'.

124 Nehru to UN Dhebar, 12 May 1958. Gopal (ed.) (1984–2015) (Second Series), vol. 42, p. 275.

125 See 'Archbishop Thomas Pothacamury', available at: http://www.catholic-hierarchy.org/bishop/bpath.html (last visited 2 April 2020).

126 Nehru's letter to Thomas Pothacamury, 7 November 1958. Gopal (ed.) (1984–2015) (Second Series), vol. 45, p. 317ff., at p. 318.

127 Only the states of East Punjab, Madhya Bharat and PEPSU opined that conversion should not result in loss of Scheduled Caste status. The states of West Bengal, Madras, United Provinces, Bihar, Assam, CP and Berar, Orissa, Bombay, Mysore, Travancore-Cochin, Saurashtra, and Hyderabad thought otherwise. File No. F.28/49-C, p. 497, available in the Abhilekh Patal website (Identifier: PR_000005002722).

128 Note by B.G. Murdeshwar, 2 March 1950, File No. F.28/49-C, p. 31, available in the Abhilekh Patal website.

129 See Clause 1, Schedules I–II, Scheduled Castes and Scheduled Tribes Orders (Amendment) Act, 1956; Constitution (Scheduled Castes) Orders (Amendment) Act, 1990.

130 Note by B.G. Murdeshwar (relying on Majumdar's 'The Matrix of Indian Culture' and the 1931 census report), 2 March 1950, File No. F.28/49-C, p. 33, available on the Abhilekh Patal website.

131 See Rajendra Prasad's note dated 23 June 1950. Choudhary (ed.) (1984–95), vol. 12, p. 184.

132 Letter dated 19 December 1949, issued by the Government of India to the Chief Secretaries of the provinces, File No. F.28/49-C, pp. 67–68 (available on the Abhilekh Patal website).

133 3 February 1950, file noting, File No. F.28/49-C, pp. 14–16, available in the Abhilekh Patal website.

134 Letter dated 7 January 1950 from the Madhya Bharat government to the Government of India (available on the Abhilekh Patal website).

135 Letter dated 10 January 1950 from the Mysore government to the government of India (available on the Abhilekh Patal website).

136 Note by B.G. Murdeshwar, 2 March 1950, File No. F.28/49-C, p. 33, available in the Abhilekh Patal website.

137 Letter dated 7 January 1950 sent by the UP government to the central government, File No. F.28/49-C, p. 173ff., at p. 179, available in the Abhilekh Patal website.

138 Speech delivered by Patel to the farmers of Dhoika Tehsil in Chalora village (12 June 1927). Chopra (ed.) (2015), vol. 2, p. 13ff., at p. 15. See further, Patel's speech at the Uttar Pradesh Kisan Conference (28 April 1935). Chopra (ed.) (2015), vol. 5, p. 81ff., at p. 90.

139 Patel's letter to Ambedkar dated 8 November 1935 (published in Gujarat Samachar dated 12 November 1935). Chopra (ed.) (2015), vol. 5, p. 192ff., at p. 195.

Chapter 5: Enter Mandal and Sawhney

1 See *Mysore Backward Classes Committee* (1960), p. 1.

2 Muslims were also identified as backward, though they are not a caste. *Mysore Backward Classes Committee* (1961), p. 20.

3 *Mysore Backward Classes Committee* (1961), p. 13.

4 Ibid., pp. 15, 43–44.

5 Ibid., p. 43.

6 Ibid., pp. 22–23.

7 MR Balaji v. State of Mysore, AIR 1963 SC 649 (SCC Online version) (five judges) (paragraph 8).

8 Sitapati refers to this as the 'relevant' standard, as opposed to the 'sole' and 'dominant' standards laid down in the N.M. Thomas and Indra Sawhney cases respectively. Sitapati (2016), p. 723. Later, in

R. Chitralekha v. State of Mysore, AIR 1964 SC 1823 (SCC Online version) (paragraph 15), it was held that caste did not *have to be* a factor. It could be taken into account for deciding backwardness, but this was not mandatory.

9   MR Balaji v. State of Mysore, AIR 1963 SC 649 (SCC Online version) (paragraph 22).

10 Ibid., paragraph 23.

11 Ibid., paragraph 23.

12 Ibid., paragraph 24.

13 Ibid., paragraph 25. The court at this time did not have the benefit of empirical studies which now suggest that affirmative action policies which target communities based on caste also result in targeting economically worse off families. See Deshpande (2013), p. 279.

14 MR Balaji v. State of Mysore, AIR 1963 SC 649 (SCC Online version), paragraph 26.

15 Ibid., paragraph 28.

16 Ibid., paragraph 21.

17 Ibid., paragraph 20.

18 Ibid., paragraph 29.

19 Ibid., paragraph 29.

20 Ibid., paragraph 31.

21 Ibid., paragraph 32.

22 Ibid., paragraph 34. The court noted the fact that the University Education Commission had recommended that reservations should not exceed one-third of the total number of seats, and the central government had recommended 35 per cent. Ibid., paragraphs 32–33.

23 Ibid., paragraphs 34/37.

24 Ibid., paragraph 35.

25 T. Devadasan v. Union of India, AIR 1964 SC 179 (five judges) (from SCC Online).

26 In other words, 18 per cent of 50.

27 Ibid., paragraphs 15–16.

28 Ibid., paragraph 14.

29 Ibid., paragraph 16/18.

30 Ibid., paragraph 18.

31 Ibid., paragraph 17.

32 See Gadbois (2011), p. 78.

33 T. Devadasan v. Union of India, AIR 1964 SC 179 (five judges) (from SCC Online), paragraph 26.

34 Ibid., paragraph 30.

35 Ibid., paragraph 26.

36 Ibid., paragraph 33.

37 Ibid., paragraph 33.

38 See (1976) 2 SCC 310 (seven judges) (paragraph 49).

39 (1976) 2 SCC 310 (seven judges).

40 Ibid., paragraph 124.

41 Ibid., paragraph 124.

42 Ibid., paragraph 124.

43 Ibid., paragraph 124.

44 Akhil Bharatiya Soshit Karamchari Sangh v. Union of India, (1981) 1 SCC 246 (paragraph 102).

45 (1976) 2 SCC 310 (seven judges), paragraph 42 (A.N. Ray CJ); paragraph 101 (M.H. Beg J).

46 Ibid., paragraph 143 (Krishna Iyer J); paragraph 191 (Fazal Ali J).

47 Ibid., paragraph 78 (Mathew J); paragraph 136 (Krishna Iyer J); paragraph 184 (Fazal Ali J).

48 Ibid., paragraph 191.

49 K.S. Jayasree v. State of Kerala, (1976) 3 SCC 730.

50 See P. Rajendran v. State of Madras, AIR 1968 SC 1012 (SCC Online version) (paragraphs 7–8); Triloki Nath Tika v. State of J&K, AIR 1969 SC 1 (SCC Online version) (paragraph 4); State of Andhra Pradesh v. U.S.V. Balram, (1972) 1 SCC 660 (paragraph 94). But see K.S. Jayasree v. State of Kerala, (1976) 3 SCC 730 (paragraphs 13/21); State of UP v. Pradip Tandon, (1975) 1 SCC 267 (paragraph 15).

51 See Akhil Bharatiya Soshit Karamchari Sangh v. Union of India, (1981) 1 SCC 246 (paragraph 88).

52 State of MP v. Nivedita Jain, (1981) 4 SCC 296 (paragraph 27).

53 General category students, on the other hand, needed 50 per cent in the aggregate and 33 per cent in each subject.

54 State of MP v. Nivedita Jain, (1981) 4 SCC 296, paragraph 27.

55 Deshpande refers to this as the 'mismatch hypothesis', i.e., that affirmative action policies harm backward class students by putting

them in programmes for which they are not academically suited. She points out that empirical evidence shows no evidence of the mismatch hypothesis, i.e., that quotas harm beneficiaries. Deshpande (2013), pp. 279–80.

56 K.C. Vasanth Kumar v. State of Karnataka, (1985) Supp SCC 714 (paragraph 35).

57 Ibid., paragraph 36.

58 Ibid., paragraph 40. However, Reddy felt that there were other factors that determined backwardness: e.g., dress habits, worshipping local gods (like Sunkalamma, Gangamma, Polimeramma or Yellamma in Andhra Pradesh), celebrating non-traditional festivals, etc. Ibid., paragraph 78.

59 On this point, the judges seemed to be equally divided. Justice Desai (paragraph 26) and Justice A.P. Sen (paragraphs 82/84) felt that economic criteria alone ought to be employed for determining backwardness. However, Justice Venkataramiah felt that economic criteria alone could not be used to determine backwardness (paragraph 115). K.C. Vasanth Kumar v. State of Karnataka, (1985) Supp SCC 714.

60 K.C. Vasanth Kumar v. State of Karnataka, (1985) Supp SCC 714 (paragraph 79). The same applied to the 'Patels of Gujarat, the Kayasthas of Bengal, the Reddys and Kammas of Andhra Pradesh', though many of them were 'poor farmers and agricultural labourers'. This was despite the fact that, as M.N. Srinivas pointed out, peasants (Okkaligas) and shepherds (Kurubas) in some parts of India would not accept cooked food and water from Marka Brahmins; Brahmins in several parts of India are considered ritually low; landowning Jats in Punjab looked upon Brahmins as their servants; and Thakurs in Madhopur village in eastern UP refused cooked food from all Brahmins except their gurus. Srinivas (1968), pp. 7, 9, 13.

61 K.C. Vasanth Kumar v. State of Karnataka, (1985) Supp SCC 714, paragraph 79.

62 Ibid., paragraph 51.

63 Ibid., paragraph 51.

64 Ibid., paragraph 55.

65 Ibid., paragraph 57.

66   Ibid., paragraph 58.

67   Reddy's letter to George H. Gadbois, Jr. (1984). Chandrachud (2018),
      p. 185.

68   Mandal (1980), p. ix.

69   See profile on the website of the Lok Sabha, available at: http://
      loksabhaph.nic.in/writereaddata/biodata_1_12/1842.htm (last visited
      8 April 2020).

70   Mandal (1980), p. 61.

71   Ibid., p. 52, paragraphs 11.23–11.25.

72   The rate had to be 25 per cent and 10 per cent above the state average
      for females and males in rural areas respectively, and 10 per cent and 5
      per cent respectively in urban areas.

73   Ibid., p. 52.

74   Ibid., p. 64.

75   Mandal (1980) p. 58.

76   See Jayal (2013), p. 249.

77   The reservations would be given to those castes or communities that
      were identified as backward in both the Mandal Commission report
      and the Other Backward Class lists prepared by state governments.

78   Jayal (2013), p. 251.

79   Economically backward communities that were not Scheduled Castes,
      Scheduled Tribes or Other Backward Classes.

80   She was also referred to in the press as 'Indira' Sawhney. See, e.g.,
      'Economic Criteria Ignored by Mandal'.

81   A good way to read the court's decision is to read paragraph 555
      (Sawant J) along with paragraphs 860, 862 and 861(A), (B), (C) (B.P.
      Jeevan Reddy J with three others), which is obviously the majority view.

82   Indra Sawhney v. Union of India, (1992) Supp (3) SCC 217.

83   Ibid., paragraph 788 (B.P. Jeevan Reddy J and three others); paragraph
      131 (Pandian J).

84   Ibid., paragraph 782 (B.P. Jeevan Reddy J and three others); paragraph
      82 (Pandian J); paragraph 449 (Sawant J); paragraphs 271/277
      (Thommen J).

85   Ibid., paragraph 800 (B.P. Jeevan Reddy J and three others);
      paragraph 99 (Pandian J); paragraph 478 (Sawant J); paragraph 635(2)
      (b) (Sahai J).

86 Ibid., paragraph 447 (Sawant J); paragraph 788 (B.P. Jeevan Reddy J and three others).

87 Ibid., paragraph 771.

88 Ibid, paragraphs 552 (Sawant J); 859(3)(a) (B.P. Jeevan Reddy J and three others).

89 Ibid., paragraph 795 (B.P. Jeevan Reddy J and three others); paragraph 126 (Pandian J); paragraphs 446–47 (Sawant J).

90 Ibid., paragraph 787 (B.P. Jeevan Reddy J); paragraphs 116–17 (Pandian J). But see paragraph 433 (Sawant J).

91 Ibid., paragraphs 802/843 (B.P. Jeevan Reddy J and three others); Sawant J (paragraph 524). But see paragraph 210 (Pandian J). In fact, in Atyant Pichhara Barg Chhatra Sangh v. Jharkhand State Vaishya Federation, (2006) 6 SCC 718 (paragraph 21), the Supreme Court held that it was impermissible to club backward class and extremely backward class candidates together, as it amounts to treating unequals equally.

92 Indra Sawhney, ibid., paragraphs 799/845 (B.P. Jeevan Reddy J and three others); paragraph 239 (Pandian J); paragraphs 480-481 (Sawant J).

93 Ibid., paragraph 484.

94 The court found that Article 16(4) was exhaustive qua the backward classes: paragraph 743 (B.P. Jeevan Reddy J and three others); paragraph 243(1) (Pandian J); paragraphs 431–32, 492 (Sawant J). In other words, concessions given to backward classes are also given under Article 16(4), not 16(1). However, the judges agreed that reservations could be provided for classes apart from those specified under Article 16(4) as well: paragraph 744 (B.P. Jeevan Reddy J and three others); paragraph 168 (Pandian J); paragraphs 430–31, 513 (Sawant J).

95 Ibid., paragraph 741 (B.P. Jeevan Reddy J and three others); paragraph 168 (Pandian J); paragraphs 428/430 (Sawant J).

96 Ibid., paragraph 555 (Sawant J); paragraph 860(4) (B.P. Jeevan Reddy J and three others). On this exception, see Parents' Association v. Union of India, (2000) 2 SCC 657 (paragraph 33) (Andaman and Nicobar Islands); Union of India v. Rakesh Kumar, (2010) 4 SCC 50 (paragraph 44) (scheduled areas); K. Krishna Murthy v. Union of India, (2010) 7 SCC 202 (paragraph 66) (north-eastern states, fifth

schedule areas). Further, it has been held that a rule that posts for promotion only be filled from a feeder cadre does not violate the 50 per cent rule. Akhilesh Kumar Singh v. Ram Dawan, (2015) 16 SCC 619 (paragraph 12).

97 Indra Sawhney v. Union of India, (1992) Supp (3) SCC 217, paragraph 531 (Sawant J); paragraphs 807–10 (B.P. Jeevan Reddy J and three others).

98 Ibid., paragraph 814/817 (B.P. Jeevan Reddy J); paragraph 516 (Sawant J). They overruled Devadasan's case to the extent that it struck down the carry forward rule entirely, since it was possible to work out the carry forward rule without violating the 50 per cent cap on reservations in any given year. Ibid., paragraphs 817, 860(4) (B.P. Jeevan Reddy J), paragraph 555 (Sawant J).

99 Justice Kuldip Singh, on the other hand, said that an economic test must be used. Ibid., paragraph 385.

100 Ibid., paragraph 792. He also said that the creamy layer concept did not apply to the Scheduled Castes and Scheduled Tribes. See further, ibid., paragraph 860(5) (B.P. Jeevan Reddy J and three others); paragraph 555 (Sawant J). On the determination of the creamy layer, see further Ashoka Kumar Thakur v. State of Bihar, (1995) 5 SCC 403 (paragraphs 3, 10); Nair Service Society v. State of Kerala, (2007) 4 SCC 1. In Indra Sawhney v. Union of India (Indra Sawhney 2), (2000) 1 SCC 168 (paragraph 65), it was held that non-exclusion of the creamy layer would violate the basic structure of the Constitution. However, the creamy layer exclusion principle does not apply to political representation. K. Krishna Murthy v. Union of India, (2010) 7 SCC 202 (paragraph 56).

101 Indra Sawhney, ibid., paragraphs 520–21. See further Minor A. Peeriakaruppan v. State of T.N., (1971) 1 SCC 38 (paragraph 29).

102 Indra Sawhney, ibid., paragraphs 200, 225–26.

103 Ibid., paragraphs 796-797 (B.P. Jeevan Reddy J); paragraph 323(4) (Thommen J).

104 Justice B.P. Jeevan Reddy (and three others) also held that the creamy layer concept did not apply to Scheduled Castes and Scheduled Tribes. Ibid., paragraph 792. See further, paragraph 803 (B.P. Jeevan Reddy J and three others), holding that separate reservations can be applied to them.

105 Ibid., paragraphs 822, 827–28, 831, 860(8) (B.P. Jeevan Reddy and
      two others); paragraph 242 (Pandian J); paragraph 307 (Thommen J);
      paragraph 555 (Sawant J).

106 See General Manager, Southern Railway v. Rangachari, AIR 1962 SC
      36; State of Punjab v. Hira Lal, (1970) 3 SCC 567; Akhil Bharatiya
      Soshit Karamchari Sangh v. Union of India, (1981) 1 SCC 246;
      Comptroller and Auditor-General of India v. K.S. Jagannathan,
      (1986) 2 SCC 679.

107 Indra Sawhney v. Union of India, (1992) Supp (3) SCC 217, paragraph
      828, 860(8) (B.P. Jeevan Reddy J and two others); paragraph 555
      (Sawant J); paragraph 242 (Pandian J). See further, paragraph 307
      (Thommen J). However, Reddy J felt that certain relaxations/
      concessions in promotions were permissible (e.g., the relaxation in the
      N.M. Thomas case). Ibid., paragraph 831.

108 The judges also decided the following propositions: (1) Reservations can
      be provided by executive order: paragraphs 859(1)(a)–(b) (B.P. Jeevan
      Reddy J and three others); paragraph 170 (Pandian J); paragraph 526
      (Sawant J); paragraph 392 (Kuldip Singh J). (2) The court's power of
      judicial review in such cases was limited: paragraphs 737, 798, 842 (B.P.
      Jeevan Reddy J and three others); paragraph 174 (Pandian J); paragraphs
      529, 530, 537 (Sawant J). The court was unable to agree about what
      kinds of areas reservations should be excluded from: paragraphs 838–40
      (B.P. Jeevan Reddy J and three others); paragraph 508 (Sawant J).

109 General Manager, Southern Railway v. Rangachari, AIR 1962 SC 36.

110 See K.C. Vasanth Kumar v. State of Karnataka, (1985) Supp SCC 714
      [paragraph 2(1)–(2)].

Chapter 6: An Era of Constitutional Amendments

1   See, e.g., speech of P.H. Pandiyan, 9 May 2000, Lok Sabha Debates,
      p. 506; Salkhan Murmu, 9 May 2000, Lok Sabha Debates, p. 544;
      Mayawati, 22 August 2000, Lok Sabha Debates, p. 370; Dr. Raghuvansh
      Prasad Singh, 22 August 2000, Lok Sabha Debates, pp. 377–78.

2   According to Sujit Choudhry, the 50 per cent rule and creamy layer
      test were limits imposed by the Supreme Court to ensure that a 'spoils
      system' does not emerge in India, under which Other Backward

Class political coalitions assume power and distribute benefits disproportionately to themselves. Choudhry (2015), p. 40.

3   Sitapati argues that courts have rarely stood up to Parliament on questions of reservation. Sitapati (2016), pp. 728, 735.

4   See Statement of Objects and Reasons, Constitution (Seventy-Sixth Amendment) Act, 1994.

5   Ibid.

6   Palkhivala (1994).

7   See I.R. Coelho v. State of T.N., (2007) 2 SCC 1.

8   Lok Sabha Debates, 25 August 1994, pp. 490–505.

9   Voice (Consumer Care) Council v. State of T.N. (I), (1995) Supp (1) SCC 632; Voice (Consumer Care) Council v. State of T.N. (III), (1995) Supp (1) SCC 635; Voice (Consumer Care) Council v. State of T.N. (VI), (1995) Supp (1) SCC 640; Voice (Consumer Care) Council v. State of T.N., (1996) 11 SCC 740. See further Voice (Consumer Care) Council v. State of T.N. (II), (1995) Supp (1) SCC 633; Voice (Consumer Care) Council v. State of T.N. (IV), (1995) Supp (1) SCC 637; Voice (Consumer Care) Council v. State of T.N. (V), (1995) Supp (1) SCC 638.

10 The petitioner in that case submitted that the judgment of the Supreme Court in S.V. Joshi's case had rendered the matter infructuous. The SLP was therefore dismissed as infructuous. Voice (Consumer Care) Council v. State of Tamil Nadu, SLP (C) No. 13526 of 1993, order dated 6 July 2011.

11 S.V. Joshi v. State of Karnataka, (2012) 7 SCC 41.

12 Ibid., paragraph 4.

13 (2006) 8 SCC 212.

14 (2008) 6 SCC 1.

15 (2006) 8 SCC 212 (paragraph 48).

16 See ibid., paragraphs 82, 106–07.

17 Ibid., paragraph 110.

18 Dr. Jishri Patil v. Chief Minister of State of Maharashtra, (2019) SCC Online Bom 1107 (paragraph 253).

19 Ibid., paragraph 257.

20 Ibid., paragraph 275. However, 16 per cent reservation for the Maratha community was held to be excessive since the Commission appointed

by the State Government had recommended 12 to 13 per cent. Ibid., paragraph 296.

21   Shri Sanjeet Shukla v. State of Maharashtra, (2014) SCC Online Bom 1672 (Para 33, 67, 82).

22   Dr. Jaishri Laxmanrao Patil v. Chief Minister, (2021) SCC Online SC 362. See *further*, Dr. Jaishri Laxmanrao Patil v. Chief Minister, (2021) 2 SCC 785 (interim order).

23   Dr. Jaishri Laxmanrao Patil v. Chief Minister, (2021) SCC Online SC 362, paragraphs 150–52, 229–31, 237, 449(13) (per Bhushan and Nazeer JJ); paragraphs 454, 478 (per Rao J); paragraph 480 (per Gupta J); paragraph 188(1)–(3) (per Bhat J).

24   Dr. Jaishri Laxmanrao Patil v. Chief Minister, (2021) SCC Online SC 362, paragraphs 132–34 (per Bhushan and Nazeer JJ); paragraphs 454, 478 (per Rao J); paragraph 480 (per Gupta J); paragraph 188(1)–(3) (per Bhat J).

25   Dr. Jaishri Laxmanrao Patil v. Chief Minister, (2021) SCC Online SC 362, paragraphs 213, 217 (per Bhushan and Nazeer JJ); paragraphs 454, 478 (per Rao J); paragraph 480 (per Gupta J); paragraph 188(1)–(3) (per Bhat J).

26   Dr. Jaishri Laxmanrao Patil v. Chief Minister, (2021) SCC Online SC 362, paragraphs 242, 247 (per Bhushan and Nazeer JJ); paragraphs 454, 478 (per Rao J); paragraph 480 (per Gupta J); paragraph 188(1)–(3) (per Bhat J). The court also agreed that the majority view of the Supreme Court in Indra Sawhney's case was contained in paragraphs 809-810 of Justice B.P. Jeevan Reddy's judgment: paragraph 131 (per Bhushan and Nazeer JJ); paragraphs 454, 478 (per Rao J); paragraph 480 (per Gupta J); paragraph 188(1)-(3) (per Bhat J).

27   Dr. Jaishri Laxmanrao Patil v. Chief Minister, (2021) SCC Online SC 362, paragraphs 297, 300, 306–08 (per Bhushan and Nazeer JJ); paragraphs 454, 478 (per Rao J); paragraph 480 (per Gupta J); paragraph 188(1)-(3) (per Bhat J). The court held, however, that a previously forward community could be found backward on the basis of new data: paragraphs 315-316 (per Bhushan and Nazeer JJ); paragraphs 454, 478 (per Rao J); paragraph 480 (per Gupta J); paragraph 188(1)–(3) (per Bhat J).

28   Civil Appeal No. 3609 of 2002, judgment dated 22 April 2020 (5 judges).
29   Ibid., paragraph 104(e).
30   Ibid., paragraph 115.
31   Ibid., paragraphs 130, 133.
32   Ibid., paragraph 153. For a critique of this judgment, see, Sundar (2020).
33   R.K. Sabharwal v. State of Punjab, (1995) 2 SCC 745 (paragraphs 4, 5, 8 and 10). On the roster system, see further, Prakash (2019); Gupta (2019); Gupta and Thorat (2019). For an example of a model roster, see Annexure II, Office Memorandum dated 31 January 2019 issued by the Department of Personnel and Training, Government of India. To be sure, the 50 per cent rule still applies under the roster system. In essence, however, under the roster system, the 50 per cent rule applies to the strength of the cadre, not to the number of vacancies which arise in any given year.
34   See Post Graduate Institute of Medical Education & Research v. Faculty Association, (1998) 4 SCC 1 (paragraphs 34-35, 37) [impliedly overruling State of Punjab v. G.S. Gill, (1997) 6 SCC 129]; State of U.P. v. M.C. Chattopadhyaya, (2004) 12 SCC 333 (paragraph 6); State of UP v. Bharat Singh, (2011) 4 SCC 120 (paragraph 73); Akhilesh Kumar Singh v. Ram Dawan, (2015) 16 SCC 619 (paragraph 9). But see K. Krishna Murthy v. Union of India, (2010) 7 SCC 202 (paragraph 69).
35   Office Memorandum dated 2 July 1997 issued by the Department of Personnel and Training, Government of India; Office Memorandum dated 31 January 2019 issued by the Department of Personnel and Training, Government of India.
36   If two categories get past a natural number at the same time, then one of them is accommodated on the next seat or a previous seat. For instance, at the 20th position of the 200-point roster, both the Scheduled Caste and Economically Weaker Sections categories cross natural numbers. In this case, the 20th seat is earmarked for a Scheduled Caste person, while the 21st seat is for Economically Weaker Sections. When a category is accommodated on a previous seat, this is referred to as 'squeezing'. For instance, at the 98th and 99th points in the 200-point roster, Economically Weaker Sections and Scheduled

Castes are given seats respectively, though they only get past natural numbers at the 100th point on the roster. Squeezing is resorted to because three groups—Scheduled Caste, Other Backward Class and Economically Weaker Sections—all get past natural numbers at the 100th point.

37 At the 200th post, none of the numbers have any fractions.

38 Following this system ensures that Scheduled Caste, Scheduled Tribe, Other Backward Class and Economically Weaker Section categories get a near perfect distribution of 15 per cent, 7.5 per cent, 27 per cent and 10 per cent of the available seats. Out of 200 seats, each category gets the following number of seats: 30 (Scheduled Caste), 15 (Scheduled Tribe), 54 (Other Backward Class) and 20 (Economically Weaker Sections).

39 See further, Kale and Kumar (2019).

40 The reserved category teachers might be distributed unevenly through the different departments, e.g., some departments might have 5 reserved teachers (amounting to 100 per cent reservation in that department), while others might have none.

41 Vivekanand Tiwari v. Union of India, (2017) SCC Online All 2729 (paragraph 58). The Supreme Court dismissed the SLP. Vijay Prakash Bharati v. Union of India, (2019) 12 SCC 410.

42 See Gupta and Thorat (2019); Mann and Ram (2019).

43 Section 3(2), Central Educational Institutions (Reservation in Teachers' Cadre) Act, 2019.

44 In M. Nagaraj v. Union of India, (2006) 8 SCC 212 (paragraph 68), the Supreme Court held that the 81st amendment gave legislative assent to the Supreme Court's judgment in R.K. Sabharwal's case, (1995) 2 SCC 745.

45 In its Maratha reservations judgment, the Supreme Court found that the 81st amendment gave constitutional status to the 50 per cent rule. Dr. Jaishri Laxmanrao Patil v. Chief Minister, (2021) SCC Online SC 362, paragraph 209 (per Bhushan and Nazeer JJ); paragraphs 454, 478 (per Rao J); paragraph 480 (per Gupta J); paragraph 188(1)-(3) (per Bhat J).

46 Lok Sabha Debates, 10 May 2000, p. 390.

47 Prakash Ambedkar.

48   Speech dated 9 May 2000, Lok Sabha Debates, p. 539. See further, speech of Salkhan Murmu, 9 May 2000, Lok Sabha Debates, p. 544.

49   Ibid., p. 541.

50   R.K. Sabharwal v. State of Punjab, (1995) 2 SCC 745 (paragraph 4); M. Nagaraj v. Union of India, (2006) 8 SCC 212 (paragraph 60); Rajesh Kumar Daria v. Rajasthan Public Service Commission, (2007) 8 SCC 785 (paragraph 9). In Nagaraj's case, the Supreme Court held that if a substantial number of reserved category students obtain general seats, then this is a ground for the government to review reservations. See further, Pradeep Singh Dehal v. State of HP, (2019) 9 SCC 276 (paragraph 14), where it was held that separate interviews cannot be held for general and reserved category candidates, and every person should first be considered a general category candidate.

There is so far no definitive judgment of the Supreme Court on the question of whether a reserved category candidate who has obtained a relaxation (e.g., age relaxation) can opt for a general seat. Both Jitendra Kumar Singh v. State of UP, (2010) 3 SCC 119 (paragraph 72) (2 judges) and Deepa E.V. v. Union of India, (2017) 12 SCC 680 (paragraphs 10–11) (2 judges) involved the court interpreting rules enacted in different states, without really laying down any general proposition.

51   Interestingly, including MRCs in the reserved quota would not necessarily mean that the remaining seats are reserved for general candidates in a communal manner. Consider the following example. Let us say that there is a government department of 100 employees, in which the government has instituted a policy of 10 per cent reservation for Scheduled Castes. Let us say that 15 Scheduled Caste candidates get selected on their own merit and get jobs in the department. Counting 10 of the 15 Scheduled Castes as part of the reserved quota will not mean that the remaining 5 Scheduled Castes will not be able to take up jobs in the department. In other words, counting MRCs as part of the 10 per cent reserved quota will not mean that the balance 90 per cent seats are only reserved for open category candidates. The logic adopted by the Supreme Court in refusing to consider MRCs as part of the reserved quota is, therefore, flawed.

52 Ritesh R. Sah v. Dr. Y.L. Yamul, (1996) 3 SCC 253 (paragraph 13); Samta Aandolan Samiti v. Union of India, (2014) 14 SCC 745 (paragraphs 18, 19, 22); Tripurari Sharan v. Ranjit Kumar Yadav, (2018) 2 SCC 656 (paragraphs 5, 11–13, 16, 24); Dega Venkata Harsha Vardhan v. Akula, (2019) 12 SCC 735 (paragraphs 6–7, 22).

53 See Union of India v. Ramesh Ram, (2010) 7 SCC 234 (paragraph 42); Alok Kumar Pandit v. State of Assam, (2012) 13 SCC 516 (paragraphs 24.1-24.2).

54 Indra Sawhney v. Union of India, (1992) Supp (3) SCC 217, paragraph 812 (BP Jeevan Reddy J and three others), paragraphs 513–14 (Sawant J). Mahesh Gupta v. Yashwant Kumar Ahirwar, (2007) 8 SCC 621 (paragraph 13); Union of India v. National Federation of the Blind, (2013) 10 SCC 772 (paragraph 42). See *further*, NTR University of Health Sciences v. G Babu Rajendra Prasad, (2003) 5 SCC 350.

55 See Shiv Prasad v. Government of India, (2008) 10 SCC 382; A.P. Public Service Commission v. Baloji Badhavath, (2009) 5 SCC 1 (paragraph 45); K. Krishna Murthy v. Union of India, (2010) 7 SCC 202 (paragraph 64). The Women's Reservation Bill, which seeks to give 33 per cent reservations for women in the Lok Sabha, has not yet been passed as this book is being written. See 'Women's Reservation Bill'; Sitapati (2016), p. 726.

56 Rajesh Kumar Daria v. Rajasthan Public Service Commission, (2007) 8 SCC 785 (paragraph 8). See further, Anil Kumar Gupta v. State of UP, (1995) 5 SCC 173 (paragraph 17), where the Supreme Court said that horizontal reservations are better as 'compartmentalized' reservations, not 'overall' reservations, the latter being taken out of the general category alone.

57 Rajesh Kumar Daria v. Rajasthan Public Service Commission, (2007) 8 SCC 785 (paragraphs 9–10).

58 Strictly speaking, Parliament cannot overrule a judgment, though it can remove the basis of a judgment.

59 See speech of Sita Ram Kesari, Lok Sabha Debates, 31 May 1995, p. 221.

60 Ibid.

61 On 2 June 1995, Nitish Kumar said that '[a]lmost' all parties had agreed on providing reservations for Other Backward Classes in promotions. Lok Sabha Debates, 2 June 1995, p. 321.

62 Dr. Mumtaz Ansari, Janata Dal, 2 June 1995, Lok Sabha Debates, p. 332.

63 See, e.g., speech of Dr. G.L. Kanaujia, 31 May 1995, Lok Sabha Debates, p. 215; speech of Basudeb Acharya, 31 May 1995, Lok Sabha Debates, p. 216; Mohammad Ali Ashraf Fatmi, 31 May 1995, Lok Sabha Debates, p. 217.

64 Indra Sawhney v. Union of India, (1992) Supp (3) SCC 217, paragraph 860(8) (B.P. Jeevan Reddy J and two others), paragraph 555 (Sawant J), paragraph 242 (Pandian J). See further, speech of Sobhanadreeswara Rao Vadde, Lok Sabha Debates, 31 May 1995, p. 214.

65 See speech of Mukul Wasnik (Minister of State), Lok Sabha Debates, 31 May 1995, p. 219; Sita Ram Keasri, 1 June 1995, Lok Sabha Debates, p. 219; Dr. R. Mallu, 1 June 1995, Lok Sabha Debates, p. 219; 2 June 1995, Lok Sabha Debates, p. 315.

66 Speech of Nitish Kumar, Lok Sabha Debates, 2 June 1995, pp. 322–23.

67 See speech of Pravin Rashtrapal, 22 August 2000, Lok Sabha Debates, p. 392, citing a minister's response to a starred question and the 1991 census.

68 Lok Sabha Debates, 2 June 1995, p. 416.

69 2 June 1995, Lok Sabha Debates, p. 368.

70 2 June 1995, Lok Sabha Debates, pp. 368–69.

71 (1996) 6 SCC 580 (paragraphs 5 and 9).

72 22 August 2000, Lok Sabha Debates, p. 438. Thereafter, in Rohtas Bhankhar v. Union of India, (2014) 8 SCC 872, the Supreme Court held that S. Vinod Kumar's case was no longer good law.

73 (1995) 6 SCC 684.

74 Ibid., paragraph 25.

75 (1996) 2 SCC 715. Though the Supreme Court tried to revoke the rule in Jagdish Lal v. State of Haryana, (1997) 6 SCC 538 (3 judges), it was reiterated by a Constitution Bench in Ajit Singh (II) v. State of Punjab, (1999) 7 SCC 209 (5 judges).

76 The amendment was with retrospective effect from 17 June 1995, i.e., the date on which Article 16(4A) was inserted into the Constitution. See speech of Vasundhara Raje (mover of the bill), 28 November 2001, Lok Sabha Debates, p. 385.

77 28 November 2001, Lok Sabha Debates, pp. 471–72.

78 (2006) 8 SCC 212 (5 judges).

79 In paragraph 79, the court found that the catch-up rule and consequential seniority were elements of service jurisprudence and not a part of the basic structure of the Constitution.

80 That is, under Articles 16(4), 16(4A) or 16(4B). See further, Bir Singh v. Delhi Jal Board, (2018) 10 SCC 312 (5 judges) (paragraph 37).

81 (2006) 8 SCC 212 (paragraphs 86, 102, 107, 117, 123).

82 (2006) 8 SCC 212, paragraph 108.

83 See ibid., paragraphs 110, 120–23.

84 (2006) 8 SCC 212, paragraph 110.

85 Ibid., paragraphs 107, 123. The court also said that the carry-forward rule should be limited by a time-cap determined by the government. Ibid., paragraph 100. On these provisions being enabling provisions, see Dr. Gulshan Prakash v. State of Haryana, (2010) 1 SCC 477 (paragraphs 9, 11, 16); S. Panneer Selvam v. State of TN, (2015) 10 SCC 292 (paragraph 24); Chairman and Managing Director, Central Bank of India v. Central Bank of India SC/ST Employees Welfare Association, (2015) 12 SCC 308 (paragraph 26); Suresh Chand Gautam v. State of UP, (2016) 11 SCC 113 (paragraphs 44–45); Mukesh Kumar v. State of Uttarakhand, (2020) SCC Online SC 148 (paragraph 12).

86 See Bhatia (2019), pp. 105–07.

87 In 2012, a bill was introduced in the Rajya Sabha to undo the judgment, but it lapsed. Sitapati (2016), p. 736.

88 E.V. Chinnaiah v. State of AP, (2005) 1 SCC 394 (paragraphs 19, 26).

89 (2018) 10 SCC 396.

90 Ibid., paragraphs 23–24, 34.

91 Ibid., paragraphs 26–28, 30, 35.

92 See B.K. Pavitra v. Union of India, (2019) SCC Online SC 694 (paragraphs 116, 118, 119, 121-122, 127, 129–30, 132). The court also held that the creamy layer principle will not apply to consequential seniority. Ibid., paragraph 179.

Thereafter, a Constitution Bench of the Supreme Court in a recent judgment, Chebrolu Leela Prasad Rao v. State of AP, Civil Appeal No. 3609 of 2002, judgment dated 22 April 2020 (5 judges), held that the M. Nagaraj principles do not apply to paragraph 5, Schedule V of the

Constitution, concerning scheduled areas. In a cryptic paragraph, the court also seemed to suggest that the Nagaraj principles only apply in cases of promotions (paragraph 124). However, the court in Chebrolu did not consider the Constitution Bench decision in Bir Singh's case, where the contrary was held on this point. Bir Singh v. Delhi Jal Board, (2018) 10 SCC 312 (5 judges) (paragraph 37).

93 The principle of creamy layer exclusion also applies to reservations in educational institutions. See Ashoka Kumar Thakur v. Union of India, (2008) 6 SCC 1, paragraphs 173, 226 (Balakrishnan CJI), paragraphs 357, 358(7) (Pasayat J with another), paragraph 630 (Bhandari J), paragraph 665 (Raveendran J).

94 The cadre strength is the unit for the purpose of the 50 per cent rule and in order to determine whether a group is inadequately represented. Uttar Pradesh Power Corporation Ltd. v. Rajesh Kumar, (2012) 7 SCC 1 [paragraph 81(iv)]. As Anup Surendranath points out, this means that if the reservation is for the post of station master, the government must collect data to show that backward classes are inadequately represented in station master posts, not in the railways generally. Surendranath (2015). See further Vivekanand Tiwari v. Union of India, (2017) SCC Online All 2729 (paragraph 58). The Supreme Court dismissed the SLP. Vijay Prakash Bharati v. Union of India, (2019) 12 SCC 410.

95 After the 102nd amendment to the Constitution, it is now arguable that even socially and educationally backward classes identified by the central government under Article 342A of the Constitution are presumed to be backward and no quantifiable data concerning backwardness are required to be shown to the court to justify SEBC reservation. See Dr. Jaishri Laxmanrao Patil v. Chief Minister, (2021) SCC Online SC 362: paragraphs 476, 478 (per Rao J); paragraph 481 (per Gupta J); paragraph 188(5) (per Bhat J).

96 Indian Medical Association v. Union of India, (2011) 7 SCC 179 (paragraph 202).

97 See, e.g., 'Mandal-II will notch up a wide footprint', *Times of India*, 9 April 2006, p. 6; 'Mandal II: Think beyond reservations', *Indian Express*, Mumbai, 9 April 2006. Sitapati points out that Other Backward Class reservations were gradually introduced—by southern

states in the 1950s, by some northern states in the 1980s, and by the central government in 2005. Sitapati (2016), p. 728.

98 (2005) 6 SCC 537 (paragraphs 124, 125, 128-130). Later, in MP Rajya Sahakari Bank Maryadit v. State of MP, (2007) 12 SCC 529 (paragraph 12), the Supreme Court would hold that reservations were not permissible in cooperative societies in which the government held less than 51 per cent share capital.

99 21 December 2005, Lok Sabha Debates, p. 494.

100 Ibid., pp. 453, 565.

101 Ibid., p. 641.

102 Ibid., p. 463.

103 See speech of Dharmendra Pradhan, ibid., p. 497.

104 Ibid., p. 499.

105 Ibid., p. 564.

106 See, e.g., speech of Ram Vilas Paswan, 25 August 1994, Lok Sabha Debates, p. 412; Nitish Kumar, 25 August 1994, Lok Sabha Debates, p. 418; G.M.C. Balayogi, Lok Sabha Debates, 2 June 1995, p. 350; Sukdeo Paswan, 9 May 2000, Lok Sabha Debates, 534; A. Krishnaswamy, 9 May 2000, Lok Sabha Debates, 537; Mayawati, 22 August 2000, Lok Sabha Debates, p. 370; Bal Krishna Chauhan, 28 November 2001, Lok Sabha Debates, p. 403.

107 See Pragya Singh, 'Reservation Shadowlines', *Indian Express*, 8 April 2006; 'Quotas will divide India: Ratan Tata', *Mumbai Mirror*, 9 April 2006.

108 See Sitapati (2016), p. 731.

109 'Reservations—Over Arjun', *Indian Express*, 10 April 2006.

110 Varghese K. George, 'On pvt sector quotas, Group of Ministers tells Cabinet: It's sensitive, you decide', *Sunday Express*, 9 April 2006.

111 See Ashoka Kumar Thakur v. Union of India, (2008) 6 SCC 1 (5 judges); Indian Medical Association v. Union of India, (2011) 7 SCC 179 (2 judges); Pramati Educational and Cultural Trust v. Union of India, (2014) 8 SCC 1 (5 judges) (paragraph 38).

112 Ashoka Kumar Thakur v. Union of India, (2008) 6 SCC 1 (5 judges), paragraphs 173, 226 (Balakrishnan CJI), paragraphs 357, 358(7) (Pasayat J with another), paragraph 630 (Bhandari J), paragraphs 650, 665 (Raveendran J).

113 (1994) 4 SCC 401 (3 judges).

114 Ibid., paragraph 6.

115 Ibid., paragraph 9.

116 Ibid. In the Lok Sabha, Prakash Ambedkar once argued that India's education system only tests 'mugging power', not intelligence. Lok Sabha Debates, 9 May 2000, p. 560.

117 Post Graduate Institute of Medical Education and Research, Chandigarh v. K.L. Narasimhan, (1997) 6 SCC 283 (3 judges).

118 Ibid., paragraph 25.

119 Ibid.

120 (1999) 7 SCC 120 (5 judges).

121 Ibid., paragraphs 2–5. See further, P.V. Indiresan (2) v. Union of India, (2011) 8 SCC 441 (paragraph 53).

122 Dr. Preeti Srivastava, ibid., paragraph 30. This was especially so because even for the MBBS course, the minimum qualifying marks were 45 per cent (general) and 35 per cent (reserved). Ibid., paragraph 30. It was for an expert body like the Medical Council of India to decide, said the court, how much relaxation should be permitted in the minimum qualifying marks, for reserved category students. Ibid., paragraph 29.

123 Ibid., paragraph 13.

124 Ibid., paragraph 22.

125 Ibid.

126 Ibid.

127 Ibid., paragraph 10.

128 Ibid., paragraph 26.

129 Ibid., paragraph 23. See further Faculty Association of All India Institute of Medical Sciences v. Union of India, (2013) 11 SCC 246.

130 Dr. Preeti Srivastava, ibid., paragraph 22.

131 Ibid., paragraphs 31 and 37.

132 Ibid., paragraph 32. See further paragraph 48.

133 Elements of Article 335 of the Constitution, said the court, must be applied to postgraduate medical admissions as well. Ibid., paragraph 25.

134 Indian Medical Association v. Union of India, (2011) 7 SCC 179 (paragraphs 57, 69).

135 Ibid., paragraphs 202–03.
136 See, e.g., speech of Rupchand Murmu, 2 June 1995, Lok Sabha Debates, p. 305; Baju Ban Riyan, 22 August 2000, Lok Sabha Debates, p. 366; Buta Singh, 28 November 2001, Lok Sabha Debates, p. 389; Dr. Chinta Mohan, 21 December 2005, Lok Sabha Debates, p. 466.
137 Desai (1953), p. 52.
138 Nappi (1995).
139 Indian Medical Association v. Union of India, (2011) 7 SCC 179, paragraph 219.
140 Ibid., paragraph 221.
141 Ibid., paragraph 222.
142 Ibid., paragraph 223.
143 (1997) 5 SCC 201.
144 Ibid., paragraph 23.
145 Ibid., paragraph 23.
146 Ibid., paragraph 38.
147 Ibid., paragraph 3.
148 (2019) SCC Online SC 694.
149 Ibid., paragraph 156.
150 Ibid., paragraphs 157, 163–64. The court relied on Marc Galanter's work on this question.
151 Ibid., paragraphs 161–62. The court also added that since all candidates in Karnataka had to satisfy the requirement of seniority cum merit, efficiency in services was assured. Paragraph 166.
152 The amendment came into force on 14 January 2019.
153 See paragraph 2, Office Memorandum dated 13 September 2017 issued by the Department of Personnel and Training, Government of India.
154 See paragraph 4, Office Memorandum dated 31 January 2019, Department of Personnel and Training, Government of India.
155 Reddy et al. (2019), p. 12.
156 The criteria for backwardness are different under Articles 15(4)/16(4) and Articles 243D/243T of the Constitution. See K. Krishna Murthy v. Union of India, (2010) 7 SCC 202 (paragraph 63).
157 K.C. Vasanth Kumar v. State of Karnataka, (1985) Supp SCC 714 (paragraph 79). The same applied to the 'Patels of Gujarat, the

Kayasthas of Bengal, the Reddys and Kammas of Andhra Pradesh', though many of them were 'poor farmers and agricultural labourers'.

158 M. Nagaraj v. Union of India, (2006) 8 SCC 212 (paragraph 110; also see paragraph 48).

159 See, e.g., speech of Mohan Rawale, 2 June 1995, Lok Sabha Debates, p. 368.

160 Surendranath (2019). The same argument applies for horizontal reservations as well. No quantifiable data are required, for instance, to provide reservations to women.

161 Reddy et al. (2019), p. 13.

162 State-Wise Percentage of Population Below Poverty Line by Social Groups, 2004–2005, website of the Ministry of Social Justice and Empowerment.

Chapter 7: Marriage, Conversion, Migration

1 Chatturbhuj Vithaldas Jasani v. Moreshwar Parashram, AIR 1954 SC 236 (3 judges) (SCC Online version) (paragraph 50); C.M. Arumugam v. S. Rajgopal, (1976) 1 SCC 863 (3 judges) (paragraphs 10, 12). For a discussion of the Jasani case, see, Galanter (2018), p. 105. That case involved a man from the Mahar Scheduled Caste who had adopted the Mahanubhava sect. For more on this sect, see Zelliot (1969), p. 28.

2 Ibid. According to Zelliot, when members of the Mahar caste in Maharashtra converted to Christianity or Islam, they were released from their caste only if they were educated and 'did not follow a stigmatized occupation'. Zelliot (1969), p. 200.

3 Kailash Sonkar v. Maya Devi, (1984) 2 SCC 91 (3 judges) (paragraph 28). In Jasani's case and Arumugam's case, ibid., however, this third requirement was considered not to be relevant.

4 S. Anbalagan v. B. Devarajan, (1984) 2 SCC 112 (3 judges) (paragraph 13). The judgment of the Supreme Court in S. Rajagopal v. C.M. Armugam, AIR 1969 SC 101 (SCC Online version) (paragraph 16) (2 judges), is therefore no longer correct when it held that conversion from Hinduism to Christianity ipso facto results in loss of caste as Christianity does not recognize caste. But see, C.M. Arumugam v. S. Rajgopal, (1976) 1 SCC 863 (3 judges) (paragraph 10).

5   Ganpat v. Returning Officer, (1975) 1 SCC 589 (2 judges) (paragraph 11).

6   Punjabrao v. Dr. D.P. Meshram, AIR 1965 SC 1179 (SCC Online version) (5 judges) (paragraph 13). In this case, the fact that the Respondent's daughters had married Buddhists, that their wedding cards bore the image of Buddha instead of a Hindu family deity, and that the Respondent had converted a Shiva temple into a Buddha temple was taken into account as well. Paragraphs 6, 9–11.

7   Mohd. Sadique v. Darbara Singh Guru, (2016) 11 SCC 617 (paragraph 52).

8   Mohd. Sadique v. Darbara Singh Guru, (2016) 11 SCC 617 (paragraphs 51–52).

9   State of Kerala v. Chandramohanan, (2004) 3 SCC 429 (3 judges).

10 Ibid., paragraph 16.

11 Ibid., paragraph 16.

12 Ibid., paragraph 20.

13 Kailash Sonkar v. Maya Devi, (1984) 2 SCC 91 (3 judges) (paragraph 31). Further, a child who reconverts to Hinduism must have 'sufficient maturity to understand the religious significance and the social consequences of his decision to reconvert to the Hindu religion.' Kodikunnil Suresh v. N.S. Saji Kumar, (2011) 6 SCC 430 (paragraph 34).

14 Kailash Sonkar v. Maya Devi, (1984) 2 SCC 91 (3 judges) (paragraphs 29–31, 34); C.M. Arumugam v. S. Rajgopal, (1976) 1 SCC 863 (3 judges) (paragraph 16, 17, 19) (if any ceremonies are required to be performed for reconversion, then those must be performed); S. Anbalagan v. B. Devarajan, (1984) 2 SCC 112 (3 judges) (paragraph 13) (no particular ceremony is required for reconversion, unless the caste requires it); K.P. Manu v. Chairman, Scrutiny Committee, (2015) 4 SCC 1 (2 judges) (paragraphs 38, 47-50); Principal, Guntur Medical College v. Mohan Rao, (1976) 3 SCC 411 (5 judges) (paragraph 7). In K.P. Manu's case, (ibid.), S. Swvigaradoss v. Zonal Manager, (1996) 3 SCC 100 (2 judges) (paragraph 8) was held to be decided per incuriam on this point for not noticing several earlier authorities.

    A bench of 3 judges in Sonkar's case (ibid.) suggested that the opinion of the old caste might not be all that relevant, but did not consider the Constitution Bench judgment in Mohan Rao's case (ibid.). The court in Sonkar (ibid.) was also wrong to suggest, as it did in paragraph 33 of its judgment, that merely being elected in a reserved constituency is proof of acceptance of a reconvert by the members of the old caste. After all, a reserved constituency might have a majority of forward caste voters. According to Marc Galanter, the population of Scheduled Castes in reserved constituencies is usually 20 per cent, though the population of Scheduled Tribes in constituencies reserved for them is ordinarily higher. Galanter (1984), pp. 46–47.

In some judgments, the Supreme Court has held that a person does not really lose her caste upon conversion, but her caste is 'eclipsed'. S. Anbalagan v. B. Devarajan, (1984) 2 SCC 112 (3 judges) (paragraph 13); Kailash Sonkar v. Maya Devi, (1984) 2 SCC 91 (3 judges) (paragraph 34). However, in C.M. Arumugam v. S. Rajgopal, (1976) 1 SCC 863 (3 judges) (paragraph 10), the Supreme Court had held that the general rule was that conversion results in expulsion from caste. See further S. Rajagopal v. C.M. Armugam, AIR 1969 SC 101 (SCC Online version) (2 judges) (paragraph 16).

15 Kailash Sonkar v. Maya Devi, (1984) 2 SCC 91 (3 judges) (paragraph 34).

16 M. Chandra v. M. Thangamuthu, (2010) 9 SCC 712 (2 judges) (paragraphs 34, 42). But see S. Rajagopal v. C.M. Armugam, AIR 1969 SC 101 (SCC Online version) (2 judges) (paragraphs 14, 22), where it was held that a public declaration is sufficient for reconversion to Hinduism, though in that case the Appellant's conduct also showed reconversion to Hinduism. The Supreme Court in M. Chandra's case did not consider its earlier judgment in S. Rajagopal, AIR 1969 SC 101.

17 Valsamma Paul v. Cochin University, (1996) 3 SCC 545 (2 judges) (paragraphs 34, 36); Sobha Hymavathi Devi v. Setti Gangadhara Swamy, (2005) 2 SCC 244 (3 judges) (paragraph 10); Meera Kanwaria v. Sunita, (2006) 1 SCC 344 (2 judges) (paragraph 24). N.E. Horo v. Smt. Jahanara Jaipal Singh, (1972) 1 SCC 771, overruled. This applies to reservation under Art. 15(4), 16(4), 330 and 332 [Hymavathi (paragraph 10); Kanwaria (paragraph 32)].

18 Valsamma Paul's case (paragraph 36), ibid.

19   K.P. Manu v. Chairman, Scrutiny Committee, (2015) 4 SCC 1 (2 judges) (paragraph 45).

20   Rameshbhai Dabhai Naika v. State of Gujarat, (2012) 3 SCC 400 (2 judges) (paragraphs 48, 54, 55). See further Anjan Kumar v. Union of India, (2006) 3 SCC 257 (2 judges) (paragraph 14).

21   If he were found belong to a Scheduled Caste, then the more stringent provisions of the Scheduled Castes and Scheduled Tribes (Prevention of Atrocities) Act, 1989, would apply apart from the Indian Penal Code.

22   Roopanwal (2016), pp. 33-36.

23   See MCD v. Veena, (2001) 6 SCC 571 (2 judges) (paragraph 6).

24   Bir Singh v. Delhi Jal Board, (2018) 10 SCC 312 (5 judges) (paragraphs 34, 38, 69); Subhash Chandra v. Delhi Subordinate Services Selection Board, (2009) 15 SCC 458 (2 judges) (paragraph 29).

25   For union territories, see: Director, Transport Department v. Abhinav Dipakbhai Patel, (2019) 6 SCC 434 (2 judges) (paragraph 15); Puducherry SC People Welfare Association v. UT of Pondicherry, (2014) 9 SCC 236 (3 judges) (paragraphs 11, 13).

26   But see State of Maharashtra v. Kumari Tanuja, (1999) 2 SCC 462 (2 judges) (paragraph 8).

27   Marri Chandra Shekhar Rao v. Dean, (1990) 3 SCC 130 (5 judges) (paragraphs 6, 10, 13, 14, 23). In such cases, the Scheduled Caste migrant is not to be automatically considered an Other Backward Class member in State B, without a study. Subhash Chandra v. Delhi Subordinate Services Selection Board, (2009) 15 SCC 458 (2 judges) (paragraph 76).

28   Action Committee on issue of Caste Certificate to Scheduled Castes and Scheduled Tribes in the State of Maharashtra v. Union of India, (1994) 5 SCC 244 (5 judges) (paragraph 16).

29   See further letter dated 2 May 1975 issued by the Government of India, Ministry of Home Affairs, to the Chief Secretaries of all State Governments and Union Territory Administration, clause 2 (enclosure). Available at: http://socialjustice.nic.in/writereaddata/UploadFile/guide-certificate636017830879050722.pdf (last visited 27 April 2020).

30   Marri Chandra Shekhar Rao v. Dean, (1990) 3 SCC 130 (5 judges) (paragraphs 10, 13, 14).

31   Action Committee on issue of Caste Certificate to Scheduled Castes and Scheduled Tribes in the State of Maharashtra v. Union of India, (1994) 5 SCC 244 (5 judges) (paragraph 16).

32   Kishorilal Hans v. Raja Ram Singh, (1972) 3 SCC 1 (2 judges) (paragraph 12).

33   The court's power to judicially review the lists is very limited. See Shree Surat Valsad Jilla K.M.G. Parishad v. Union of India, (2007) 5 SCC 360 (paragraphs 9-11).

34   See further B. Basavalingappa v. D. Munichinnappa, AIR 1965 SC 1269 (5 judges) (paragraph 6).

35   State of Maharashtra v. Milind, (2001) 1 SCC 4 (5 judges) (paragraphs 12, 13, 15, 28).

36   Madhuri Patil v. Additional Commissioner, (1994) 6 SCC 241 (2 judges).

37   Nityanand Sharma v. State of Bihar, (1996) 3 SCC 576 (3 judges).

38   Bharati Balkrishna Dhongade v. State of Maharashtra, (2012) 1 SCC 566 (paragraphs 14–15).

39   Palghat Jilla Thandan v. State of Kerala, (1994) 1 SCC 359 (3 judges) (paragraphs 15-18). See further, State of Maharashtra v. Milind, (2001) 1 SCC 4 (5 judges) (paragraphs 28, 36) (overruling Dina Vithoba Naronwara v. Narain Singh, 38 ELR 212); State of Maharashtra v. Mana Adim Jamat Mandal, (2006) 4 SCC 98 (2 judges) (paragraph 20) (holding that Dadaji alias Dina v. Sukhdeobabu, (1980) 1 SCC 621 was impliedly overruled in the Milind case).

40   Heikham Surchandra Singh v. Representative of 'Lois' Kakching, (1997) 2 SCC 523 (2 judges) (paragraphs 12, 16); State of Maharashtra v. Ravi Prakash Babulalsing Parmar, (2007) 1 SCC 80 (2 judges) (despite considering the Milind case) (paragraphs 24, 34, 36).

41   E.V. Chinnaiah v. State of AP, (2005) 1 SCC 394 (5 judges) (paragraphs 13, 19, 26).

42   State of Punjab v. Davinder Singh, (2020) 8 SCC 1 (paragraph 58).

43   B. Basavalingappa v. D. Munichinnappa, AIR 1965 SC 1269 (5 judges) (paragraphs 6-10).

44   State of Orissa v. Dasarathi Meher, (2018) 18 SCC 176 (2 judges) (paragraphs 20, 27, 29).

45 State of Maharashtra v. Keshao Vishwanath Sonone, Civil Appeal No. 4096 of 2020, judgment dated 18 December 2020 (paragraphs 45–46, 62, 64, 80–81).

46 Madhuri Patil v. Additional Commissioner, (1994) 6 SCC 241 (2 judges).

47 Shalini v. New English High School Association, (2013) 16 SCC 526 (2 judges) (paragraph 7.1); Additional General Manager, Human Resource, BHEL v. Suresh Ramkrishna Burde, (2007) 5 SCC 336 (2 judges) (paragraph 13).

48 See Yogesh Ramchandra Naikwadi v. State of Maharashtra, (2008) 5 SCC 652 (2 judges) (paragraph 7); Sandeep Subhash Parate v. State of Maharashtra, (2006) 7 SCC 501 (2 judges) (paragraph 15); Kavita Solunke v. State of Maharashtra, (2012) 8 SCC 430 (2 judges) (paragraph 22); Shalini v. New English High School Association, (2013) 16 SCC 526 (2 judges) (paragraph 7.3); Arun v. State of Maharashtra, (2014) SCC Online Bom 4595 (full bench) (paragraph 47).

49 Sandeep Subhash Parate v. State of Maharashtra, (2006) 7 SCC 501 (2 judges) (paragraph 15); Yogesh Ramchandra Naikwadi v. State of Maharashtra, (2008) 5 SCC 652 (2 judges) (paragraph 9); Additional General Manager, Human Resource, BHEL v. Suresh Ramkrishna Burde, (2007) 5 SCC 336 (2 judges) (paragraph 13); R. Vishwanatha Pillai v. State of Kerala, (2004) 2 SCC 105 (3 judges) (paragraph 28).

50 See Bank of India v. Avinash D. Mandivikar, (2005) 7 SCC 690 (2 judges) (paragraphs 6, 10); LIC of India v. Sushil, (2006) 2 SCC 471 (2 judges) (paragraphs 6, 10); Union of India v. Dattatray, (2008) 4 SCC 612 (3 judges) (paragraph 5).

51 See State of Maharashtra v. Om Raj, (2007) 14 SCC 488 (2 judges) (paragraph 5).

52 Food Corporation of India v. Jagdish Balaram Bahira, (2017) 8 SCC 670 (3 judges) (paragraphs 2, 48, 52, 54, 55, 56).

53 Ibid., paragraph 56. Though the Supreme Court alone has the power, under Article 142 of the Constitution, to allow a candidate to continue, this power should not be exercised in such cases, said the court.

54 Madhuri Patil v. Additional Commissioner, (1994) 6 SCC 241, paragraph 13; Dayaram v. Sudhir Batham, (2012) 1 SCC 333 (3 judges) (paragraph 44).

55   Anand v. Committee for Scrutiny and Verification of Tribe Claims, (2012) 1 SCC 113 (2 judges) (paragraph 22).

56   See Madhuri Patil v. Additional Commissioner, (1994) 6 SCC 241 (2 judges) (paragraph 5).

57   Anand v. Committee for Scrutiny and Verification of Tribe Claims, (2012) 1 SCC 113 (2 judges) (paragraphs 21–22).

58   See Galanter (1984), p. 318.

59   Sitapati writes that this is colloquially called 'quota within quotas'. He says that this, aside from 'list revisions' and the 'creamy layer' test (which applies to individuals and not groups) are the three solutions which have been thought of to ensure that some castes do not corner all the benefits of reservations. Sitapati (2016), p. 725.

60   See Galanter (1984), pp. 107–08, 547; Jaffrelot and Rizvi (2020); Weisskopf (2004), pp. 4341–42. According to Zelliot (1969), in Maharashtra, the Chambhar caste was considered superior to the Mahar caste which, in turn, was thought of as superior to the Mang caste, though all were Scheduled Castes. Zelliot (1969), pp. 18, 31–32. Further, the Mahar caste is six times the size of the Chambhar caste and five times the size of the Mang caste. Zelliot (1969), p. 134.

61   See Surendranath (2013), pp. 2–3.

Conclusion

1   17 November 1949, Constituent Assembly Debates.

2   Weisskopf (2001), pp. 4719–20; Menand (2020).

3   Weisskopf (2001), p. 4720. Relying on Justice Powell's opinion in Regents of the University of California v. Allan Bakke, 438 U.S. 265 (1978).

4   Bhagwat (2009), p. 102 [relying on City of Richmond v. J.A. Croson Co., 488 U.S. 469 (1989) and Adarand Constructors v. Pena, 515 U.S. 200 (1995)]. Bhagwat argues that the Supreme Court applied strict scrutiny in a deferential manner in the case of Grutter v. Bollinger, 539 U.S. 306 (2003). According to Menand, most of the affirmative action cases that came after Bakke's case (including the Fisher cases) were 're-litigations' of the same principle, since most affirmative action cases are decided by narrow majorities.

5   Menand (2020).

6   Cottrol and Davis (2013). These authors explain the meaning of the 'Jim Crow' system in the early 20th century—a system of racial segregation in buses, park benches, water fountains, schools, etc. The suppression of black voting rights was also a part of this system. See Menand (2020).

7   2011 census data. Further, Scheduled Caste students have a lower enrollment rate in higher educational institutions than the rest of the population. The gross enrolment rate in higher educational institutions is 11.6 per cent in the total population, and 8.3 per cent in the Scheduled Caste population. Gross Enrollment Ratio (GER) Among Total Population and Scheduled Caste Population, website of the Ministry of Social Justice and Empowerment.

8   'Estimated employment in the public and private sectors', Statistical Year Book India, 2016, available at: http://www.mospi.gov.in/ statistical-year-book-india/2016/201 (last visited 11 May 2020); 2011 census data.

9   *Handbook on Social Welfare Statistics* (2018), p. 277.

10   Coffey and Spears (2018), p. 91.

11   State-Wise Percentage of Population Below Poverty Line by Social Groups, 2004–2005, website of the Ministry of Social Justice and Empowerment.

12   The total drop-out rate of India's population is 61.5 per cent (Classes I-X) while that of the Scheduled Caste population is 70.5 per cent (Classes I–X). Sex-wise Drop-Out Rates Among Total Population and S.C. Population, website of the Ministry of Social Justice and Empowerment.

13   From 16.63 per cent (Scheduled Caste) and 5.29 per cent (Other Backward Class) in 2004, the representation of these groups in central government services went up to 17.55 per cent (Scheduled Caste) and 18.24 per cent (Other Backward Class) in 2014. *Handbook on Social Welfare Statistics* (2018), p. 379.

14   See 'Classification of Central Government Posts', website of the Ministry of Personnel, Public Grievances and Pensions.

15   Weisskopf (2004), p. 4346.

16   *Handbook on Social Welfare Statistics* (2018), p. 381.

17   *Handbook on Social Welfare Statistics* (2018), p. 381.

18   See Weisskopf (2004).

19   *All India Survey on Higher Education, 2018–19* (2019), p. 18.

20   See further Weisskopf (2004), p. 4339.

21   *All India Survey on Higher Education, 2018–19* (2019), (pdf) pp. 95–98.

22   See Thakur and Babu (2017), p. 16; Weisskopf (2004), pp. 4342, 4344.

23   Sitapati (2016), p. 723.

24   On this term, see Galanter (1984), pp. 189–90.

25   (1992) Supp (3) SCC 217 [paragraph 860(2)] (per B.P. Jeevan Reddy J and three others); paragraph 555 (Sawant J).

26   (2008) 6 SCC 1.

27   M.R. Balaji v. State of Mysore, AIR 1963 SC 649.

28   SV Joshi v. State of Karnataka, (2012) 7 SCC 41.

29   Dr. Preeti Srivastava v. State of MP, (1999) 7 SCC 120 (paragraph 25).

30   Weisskopf criticizes the 'creamy layer' principle more generally because it excludes precisely those segments of the backward classes that would be most likely to successfully graduate from higher educational institutions. Weisskopf (2006), p. 719.

31   'Speedy Justice', *Times of India*, 25 February 1978, p. 6; 'Current Topics', *Times of India*, 12 April 1978, p. 8.

32   This would be under Articles 243D(6) and 243T(6) of the Constitution.

33   K. Krishna Murthy v. Union of India, (2010) 7 SCC 202 (paragraphs 56–57).

34   List revision and de-scheduling may not be helpful in such cases because the 'less backward' Scheduled Caste or Scheduled Tribe community might still be backward compared to the forward communities and might still require reservations.

35   The following paragraphs in a modified form first appeared in Chandrachud (2020b).

36   AIR 1963 SC 649.

37   Justice B.P. Jeevan Reddy- paragraphs 802, 843; Justice P.B. Sawant – paragraph 524.

38   (2005) 1 SCC 394.

39   (2020) 8 SCC 1.

40   (2006) 8 SCC 212.

41   (2018) 10 SCC 396.

42 Dr. Jishri Patil v. Chief Minister of State of Maharashtra, (2019) SCC Online Bom 1107 (paragraph 110).

43 Dr. Jaishri Laxmanrao Patil v. Chief Minister, (2021) SCC Online SC 362: paragraphs 476, 478 (per Rao J); paragraph 481 (per Gupta J); paragraph 188(5) (per Bhat J).

44 See Singh (1994).

45 See Surendranath (2013); Bhatia (2019).

46 National Legal Services Authority v. Union of India, (2014) 5 SCC 438 (paragraph 135.3).

47 Interestingly, in a recent case, the Supreme Court has held that in 'compartmentalized' horizontal reservations (as against 'overall' horizontal reservations), Scheduled Caste, Scheduled Tribe and Other Backward Class candidates can compete for general category horizontally reserved seats. Thus, for instance, in a department containing 50 general seats, if 10 general seats are reserved for women, even a Scheduled Caste, Scheduled Tribe or Other Backward Class woman who does not make it into the unreserved general category seats on her own merit can compete for those horizontally reserved 10 general seats on the basis of her merit. Saurav Yadav v. State of Uttar Pradesh, Miscellaneous Application No. 2641 of 2019, judgment dated 18 December 2020 (paragraphs 27, 29, 33): (2020) SCC Online SC 1034 (paragraphs 24, 25, 28, 41, 45–47).

48 Union of India v. National Federation of the Blind, (2013) 10 SCC 772 (paragraphs 41-42).

49 See, Anant Madaan v. State of Haryana, (1995) 2 SCC 135 (paragraph 9); Dr. Kriti Lakhina v. State of Karnataka, (2018) 17 SCC 453 (paragraph 11); Dr. Pradeep Jain v. Union of India, (1984) 3 SCC 654 (paragraph 21). The Karnataka High Court was of the view that domicile reservation is a form of horizontal reservation. See, Master Balachandar Krishnan v. State of Karnataka, Writ Petition No. 8788 of 2020, judgment dated 29 September 2020 (paragraph 130).

50 See further Weisskopf (2006), p. 717; Galanter (2018), p. 188.

51 National Legal Services Authority v. Union of India, (2014) 5 SCC 438.

52 Section 2(d), read with Section 12.

53   Friedersdorf (2015).

54   See Menand (2020).

55   Khaitan (2015). Khaitan advocates an affirmative action programme designed on the basis of neutral criteria that bear a strong correlation with low-caste groups.

56   Weisskopf (2004), pp. 4344–45.

57   Justice Powell in the Bakke case is usually credited with the 'diversity' justification for affirmative action. Interestingly, the petitioner in that case, Allan Bakke, was admitted into the medical school that he had applied to. He then worked as a doctor at Mayo Clinic, where he treated Justice Powell. See Menand (2020).

58   In Bakke's case, Justice Powell rejected the argument that the beneficiaries of affirmative action would serve their own communities. See Menand (2020).

Bibliography

All India Survey on Higher Education, 2018–19. 2019. Ministry of Human Resource Development, New Delhi.

Ambedkar, B.R. 1936. *Annihilation of Caste.* New Delhi: Ambedkar School of Thoughts, 3rd edition. Available on archive.org.

———. 1945. *What Congress and Gandhi Have Done to the Untouchables.* Bombay: Thacker & Co. Available at https://archive.org/details/dli. csl.7774/page/n3/mode/2up.

———. 1947. *States and Minorities: What Are Their Rights and How to Secure Them in the Constitution of Free India.* Bombay: Thacker & Co. Available at: https://archive.org/details/in.ernet.dli.2015.206568.

———. 1955. *Thoughts on Linguistic States.* Available at http://drambedkar. co.in/wp-content/uploads/books/category2/9thoughts-on-linguistic-states.pdf (last visited 2 May 2020).

Annual Report on the Working of the Backward Class Department for the Year 1945–46. 1948. Poona: Yeravda Prison Press. Available at https:// dspace.gipe.ac.in/xmlui/bitstream/handle/10973/39929/GIPE-037523.pdf?sequence=3&isAllowed=y (last visited 29 April 2020).

Annual Report on the Working of the Backward Class Department, 1935–36. 1937. Bombay: Government Central Press.

Austin, Granville. 2003. *Working a Democratic Constitution: A History of the Indian Experience,* reprint edition. New Delhi: Oxford University Press.

———. 2015. *The Indian Constitution: Cornerstone of a Nation*, reprint edition. New Delhi: Oxford University Press.

Bhagwat, Ashutosh. 2009. 'Affirmative Action and Benign Discrimination'. In Vikram David Amar and Mark V. Tushnet (eds.), *Global Perspectives on Constitutional Law*. New York: Oxford University Press.

Bhatia, Gautam. 2019. *The Transformative Constitution: A Radical Biography in Nine Acts.* Noida: Harper Collins.

Bidwell, W.H. (ed.). 1870. *The Eclectic Magazine of Foreign Literature, Science, and Art.* New York: E.R. Pelton. Available at https://babel.hathitrust.org/cgi/pt?id=coo.31924066196985&view=1up&seq=227 (last visited 15 May 2020).

Brown, F.H. 23 September 2004. 'Sir William Lee-Warner'. *Oxford Dictionary of National Biography* (online).

Cashman, Richard I. 1975. *The Myth of the Lokamanya: Tilak and Mass Politics in Maharashtra.* Berkeley: University of California Press. Available on archive.org.

Chandrachud, Abhinav. 2014. *The Informal Constitution: Unwritten Criteria in Selecting Judges for the Supreme Court of India.* New Delhi: Oxford University Press.

———. 2015. *An Independent, Colonial Judiciary: A History of the Bombay High Court During the British Raj, 1862–1947.* New Delhi: Oxford University Press.

———. 2017. *Republic of Rhetoric: Free Speech and the Constitution of India.* Gurgaon: Penguin Viking.

———. 2018. *Supreme Whispers: Conversations with Judges of the Supreme Court of India, 1980–1989.* Gurgaon: Penguin Viking.

———. 2020. *Republic of Religion: The Rise and Fall of Colonial Secularism in India.* Gurgaon: Penguin Random House.

———. 2020b. 'Guest Post: Sub-Classification in Reservations – II'. *Indian Constitutional Law and Philosophy Blog*, 4 September.

Channing, William E. 1837. *An Address on Temperance.* Boston: Weeks, Jordan & Company. Available at: https://babel.hathitrust.org/cgi/pt?id=hvd.32044088979737&view=1up&seq=5 (last visited 26 March 2020).

Chopra, P.N. (ed.). 2015. *The Collected Works of Sardar Vallabhbhai Patel.* New Delhi: Konark Publishers Pvt. Ltd.

Choudhary, Valmiki (ed.). 1984–95. *Dr. Rajendra Prasad: Correspondence and Select Documents*. Ahmedabad: Allied Publishers Pvt. Ltd.

Choudhry, Sujit. 2015. 'How to Do Constitutional Law and Politics in South Asia'. In Mark Tushnet and Madhav Khosla (eds.), *Unstable Constitutionalism: Law and Politics in South Asia*. New York: Cambridge University Press.

Coffey, Diane and Spears, Dean. 2018. 'Child Height in India: Facts and Interpretations from the NFHS-4, 2015–16'. *Economic and Political Weekly*, pp. 87–94.

Coffey, Diane, et al. 2018. 'Explicit Prejudice: Evidence from a New Survey'. *Economic and Political Weekly*, pp. 46–54.

Constituent Assembly Debates: Official Report. 1985. New Delhi: Lok Sabha Secretariat.

Copland, Ian. 1973. 'The Maharaja of Kolhapur and the Non-Brahmin Movement 1902–10'. *Modern Asian Studies*, pp. 209–25.

Cordner, John. 1868. *Twenty-Five Sermons: A Memorial of Twenty-Five Years' Ministry*. Montreal: John Lovell. Available at: https://babel.hathitrust.org/cgi/pt?id=nnc1.cr60033479&view=1up&seq=7 (last visited 26 March 2020).

Cottrol, Robert J and Davis, Megan. 2013. 'Affirmative Action'. In Mark Tushnet et al. (eds.), *Routledge Handbook of Constitutional Law*. Oxon: Routledge.

Das, Durga (ed.). 1972. *Sardar Patel's Correspondence: 1945–50*. Ahmedabad: Navajivan Publishing House.

Desai, Valji Govindji (ed.). 1953. *The Diary of Mahadev Desai*, vol. 1. Ahmedabad: Navajivan Publishing House. Available at: https://www.gandhiheritageportal.org/fundamental-workdetail/the-diary-of-mahadev-desai-vol-I#page/12/mode/2up (last visited 1 May 2020).

Deshpande, Ashwini. 2013. 'Social Justice through Affirmative Action in India: An Assessment'. In Jeannette Wicks-Lim and Robert Pollin (eds.), *Capitalism on Trial: Explorations in the Tradition of Thomas E. Weisskopf*. Cheltenham: Edward Edgar Publishing Ltd.

Deshpande, Ashwini and Newman, Katherine. 2007. 'Where the Path Leads: The Role of Caste in Post-University Employment Expectations'. *Economic and Political Weekly*, pp. 4133–40.

Dhavan, Rajeev. 2019. 'Reservation For Economically Weaker Can't Stand Up in Court'. *Economic Times*, 9 January. Available at: https://economictimes.indiatimes.com/news/politics-and-nation/view-reservation-for-economically-weaker-cant-stand-up-in-court/articleshow/67447383.cms?from=mdr (last visited 20 May 2020).

Dhebar, U.N. 1961. *Report of the Scheduled Areas and Scheduled Tribes Commission* (1960–61), vol. 1. Delhi: Manager of Publications. Available at: http://cslrepository.nvli.in/handle/123456789/17 (last visited 23 May 2020).

Dictionary of Canadian Biography. 1997. Toronto: University of Toronto Press. Available on Google Books.

Dracup, A.H. 1933. *Census of India 1931: Bombay Presidency (General Report)*. Available at: https://archive.org/details/in.ernet.dli.2015.56028 (last visited 28 March 2020).

Dushkin, Lelah. 1974. *The Nonbrahman Movement in Princely Mysore*. Doctoral Dissertation, submitted to the University of Pennsylvania.

Eddy, Sherwood. 1895. *The Supreme Decision of the Christian Student*. Chicago: Student Volunteer Movement for Foreign Missions. Available at: https://babel.hathitrust.org/cgi/pt?id=nnc1.50071613&view=1up&seq=7 (last visited 26 March 2020).

Friedersdorf, Conor. 2015. 'Does Affirmative Action Create Mismatches between Students and Universities?'. *The Atlantic*, 15 December. Available at: https://www.theatlantic.com/politics/archive/2015/12/the-needlessly-polarized-mismatch-theory-debate/420321/ (last visited 18 May 2020).

Fukazawa, Hiroshi. 1968. 'State and Caste System (Jati) in the Eighteenth Century Maratha Kingdom'. *Hitotsubashi Journal of Economics*, pp. 32–44. Available at: https://hermes-ir.lib.hit-u.ac.jp/rs/bitstream/10086/8053/24/HJeco0090100320.pdf (last visited 7 May 2020).

Gadbois, Jr, George H. 2011. *Judges of the Supreme Court of India: 1950–1989*. New Delhi: Oxford University Press.

Gait, E.A. 1904. *General Report of the Census of India, 1901*. London: His Majesty's Stationery Office. Available at: https://archive.org/details/pts_eastindiacensusg_3720-1115/page/n1/mode/2up (last visited 26 March 2020).

————. 1913. *Census of India, 1911*, vol. 1, Part I. Calcutta: Superintendent Government Printing. Available at: https://archive.org/details/censusofindiav1pt1indi/page/n8/mode/2up (last visited 26 March 2020).

Galanter, Marc. 1984. *Competing Equalities: Law and the Backward Classes in India*. Berkeley: University of California Press.

————. 1978. 'Who Are the Other Backward Classes? An Introduction to a Constitutional Puzzle'. *Economic and Political Weekly*, pp. 1812–28.

————. 2018. *Law and Society in Modern India*, reprint edition. New Delhi: Oxford University Press.

Ghurye, G.S. 1957. *Caste and Class in India*. Bombay: Book Depot. Available at: https://archive.org/details/CasteAndClassInIndia (last visited 24 May 2020).

Gopal, S. (ed.). 1972–82. *Selected Works of Jawaharlal Nehru (First Series)*. Various publishers.

Gopal, S. et al. (ed.). 1984–2015. *Selected Works of Jawaharlal Nehru: Second Series*. New Delhi: Jawaharlal Nehru Memorial Fund.

Guha, Ramachandra. 2007. 'Adivasis, Naxalites and Indian Democracy'. *Economic and Political Weekly*, pp. 3305–12.

————. 2017. 'The Rise and Fall of the Term "Harijan". *The Telegraph*, 10 June. Available at: http://ramachandraguha.in/archives/the-rise-and-fall-of-the-term-harijan-the-telegraph.html (last visited 26 March 2020).

Gupta, Anish and Thorat, Amit. 2019. 'Why Are the Reserved Categories Objecting to the 13-Point Roster?'. *Economic and Political Weekly*, pp. 12–16.

Gupta, Anish. 2019. 'Explained: The 13-Point, 200-Point Quota Roster Conundrum'. *Indian Express*, 12 March. Available at https://indianexpress.com/article/explained/upsc-civil-services-examination-13-point-200-point-quota-roster-conundrum-5621525/ (last visited 30 April 2020).

Handbook on Social Welfare Statistics. September 2018. Government of India, Ministry of Social Justice and Empowerment. Available at: http://socialjustice.nic.in/writereaddata/UploadFile/HANDBOOKSocialWelfareStatistice2018.pdf (last visited 11 May 2020).

Hutton, J.H. 1933. *Census of India, 1931*, vol. 1. Delhi: Manager of Publications. Available at: https://archive.org/details/bk867/mode/2up (last visited 21 May 2020).

India Today. 2020. 'Women's Reservation Bill: All You Need to Know about the Bill which Will Bring 33 Percent Reservation for Women in Lok Sabha', 7 March. Available at: https://www.indiatoday.in/education-today/gk-current-affairs/story/women-s-reservation-bill-all-you-need-to-know-about-the-bill-which-is-yet-to-be-passed-in-lok-sabha-1653451-2020-03-07 (last visited 29 April 2020).

Indian Franchise Committee, vol. 2. 1932. Calcutta: Government of India Central Publication Branch. Available at https://archive.org/details/in.ernet.dli.2015.8189/mode/2up (last visited 26 March 2020).

Indian Franchise Committee: Report of the Indian Franchise Committee, vol. 1. 1932. Calcutta: Government of India Central Publication Branch. Available at: https://archive.org/details/dli.csl.740/mode/2up (last visited 26 March 2020).

Indian Round Table Conference: Second Session (Proceedings of Federal Structure Committee and Minorities Committee), vol. 1. 1932. Calcutta: Government of India Central Publication Branch. Available at: https://archive.org/details/in.ernet.dli.2015.55074/page/n539/mode/2up/search/tribes (last visited 26 March 2020).

Irschick, Eugene F. 1969. *Politics and Social Conflict in South India: The Non-Brahman Movement and Tamil Separatism, 1916–1929.* Bombay: Oxford University Press. Available at: https://archive.org/details/PoliticsAndSocialConflictInSouthIndia/page/n1/mode/2up (last visited 2 May 2020).

Jaffrelot, Christophe. 2012. 'The Caste Based Mosaic of Indian Politics'. *Mainstream.* Available at: https://www.india-seminar.com/2012/633/633_christophe_jaffrelot.htm (last visited 1 May 2020).

Jaffrelot, Christophe and Rizvi, Haider Abbas. 2020. 'How Lockdown May Rewire Class-Caste Issues for Indian Politics'. *Indian Express*, 21 April. Available at: https://indianexpress.com/article/opinion/how-lockdown-may-rewire-class-caste-issues-for-indian-politics-6372027/ (last visited 29 April 2020).

Jayal, Niraja Gopal. 2013. *Citizenship and Its Discontents: An Indian History.* Cambridge: Harvard University Press.

Jodhka, Surinder S. and Newman, Katherine. 2007. 'In the Name of Globalisation: Meritocracy, Productivity and the Hidden Language of Caste'. *Economic and Political Weekly*, pp. 4125–32.

Joint Committee on Indian Constitutional Reform, vol. 1. 1934. New Delhi: Government of India Press. Available at: https://archive.org/details/in.ernet.dli.2015.63427/page/n1/mode/2up (last visited 26 March 2020).

Joint Committee on Indian Constitutional Reform, vol. 2. 1934. London: H.M. Stationery Office. Available at: https://archive.org/details/in.ernet.dli.2015.207018 (last visited 26 May 2020).

Kale, Rao Saheb, and Kumar, Arvind. 2019. 'Reservation in Higher Educational Institutions in Danger' (translated from Hindi). *The Print*, 3 March. Available at: https://hindi.theprint.in/opinion/post-based-roster-being-dangerous-for-reservation-in-higher-educational-institutions/47829/ (last visited 14 May 2020).

Kalelkar, Kaka. 1955. *Report of the Backward Classes Commission*, vol. 1. Simla: Government of India Press. Available at: https://archive.org/details/dli.csl.681/page/n189/mode/2up (last visited 1 April 2020).

Karve, D.G. and Ambekar, D.V. (eds.). 1967. *Speeches and Writings of Gopal Krishna Gokhale.* Poona: Asia Publishing House. Available at: https://archive.org/details/speecheswritings00unse/page/198/mode/2up/search/%22work+enough%22 (last visited 26 March 2020).

Khaitan, Tarunabh. 2015. 'A Better Design for Social Justice'. *Indian Express*, 8 September. Available at: https://indianexpress.com/article/opinion/columns/a-better-design-for-social-justice/ (last visited 18 May 2020).

Kundapura, Vishwa. 2014. 'A Belated Centenary for Kolar Hero T. Chennaiah'. *The Hindu*, 11 November. Available at: https://www.thehindu.com/news/national/karnataka/a-belated-centenary-for-kolar-hero-chennaiah/article6586613.ece (last visited 27 May 2020).

Latthe, A.B. 1924. *Memoirs of His Highness Shri Shahu Chhatrapati Maharaja of Kolhapur,* vol. 1. Bombay: Times Press. Available at: https://archive.org/details/in.ernet.dli.2015.207078/page/n327/mode/2up (last visited 15 May 2020).

Lokur, B.N. 1965. *The Report of the Advisory Committee on the Revision of the Lists of Scheduled Castes and Scheduled Tribes.* Available at: https://

tribal.nic.in/writereaddata/AnnualReport/LokurCommitteeReport.
pdf (last visited 8 May 2020).

Mandal, B.P. 31 December 1980. *Report of the Backward Classes Commission (Mandal Commission Report)*. Available at: https://archive.org/details/dli.csl.2170/mode/2up.

Mann, Gayatri and Ram, Anya Bharat. 2019. 'Explainer: The Central Educational Institutions (Reservation in Teachers' Cadre) Bill, 2019'. PRS Legislative Research, 3 July. Available at: https://www.prsindia.org/theprsblog/relaxation-labour-laws-across-states (last visited 14 May 2020).

Marten, J.T. 1924. *Census of India, 1921*, vol. 1, Part I. Calcutta: Superintendent Government Printing. Available at: https://archive.org/details/in.ernet.dli.2015.62769/page/n1/mode/2up (last visited 26 March 2020).

Memorandum Submitted by the Government of Bombay to the Indian Statutory Commission. 1930. London: H.M. Stationery Office. Available at: https://babel.hathitrust.org/cgi/pt?id=mdp.39015027587594&view=1up&seq=7 (last visited 6 May 2020).

Menand, Louis. 2020. 'The Changing Meaning of Affirmative Action'. *The New Yorker*, 13 January. Available at: https://www.newyorker.com/magazine/2020/01/20/have-we-outgrown-the-need-for-affirmative-action (last visited 12 May 2020).

Mendelsohn, Oliver, and Vicziany, Marika. 2001. *The Untouchables: Subordination, Poverty and the State in Modern India*. Cambridge: Cambridge University Press.

Miller, Leslie C. 1919. *Report of the Committee Appointed to Consider Steps Necessary for the Adequate Representation of Communities in the Public Service*. Available at: https://roundtableindia.co.in/index.php?option=com_content&view=article&id=8894:miller-committee-report-1919&catid=115:dalitbahujan-renaissance&Itemid=127 (last visited 2 May 2020).

Moorhead, Max Wood (ed.). 1894. *The Student Missionary Enterprise*. Boston: T.O. Metcalfe & Co.,). Available at: https://babel.hathitrust.org/cgi/pt?id=wu.89065733818&view=1up&seq=12 (last visited 26 March 2020).

Munshi, K.M. 2012. *Indian Constitutional Documents: Pilgrimage to Freedom*. Mumbai: Bharatiya Vidya Bhavan.

Mysore Backward Classes Committee: Final Report. 1961. Bangalore: Government Press.

Mysore Backward Classes Committee: Interim Report. 1960. Bangalore: Government Press.

Nappi, Carla S. 1995. 'Former Indian Premier Speaks'. *The Harvard Crimson*, 30 September. Available at: https://www.thecrimson.com/article/1995/9/30/former-indian-premier-speaks-pdeep-concern/ (last visited 30 April 2020).

O'Hanlon, Rosalind. 1983. *Low Caste Protest and the Creation of a Political Identity: Mahatma Jotirao Phule and the Origins of Non-Brahman Ideology in Maharashtra, 1855–1890.* PhD Thesis, SOAS.

O'Malley, L.S.S. 1931. *The Indian Civil Service, 1601–1930.* London: John Murray. Available at: https://archive.org/details/pli.kerala.rare.30211 (last visited 23 May 2020).

———. 1934. *India's Social Heritage.* Oxford: Clarendon Press. Available at: https://archive.org/details/dli.csl.3724/page/n1/mode/2up (last visited 22 May 2020).

Omvedt, Gail. 1971. 'Jotirao Phule and the Ideology of Social Revolution in India'. *Economic and Political Weekly*, pp. 1969–80.

———. 1973. 'Development of the Maharashtrian Class Structure, 1818 to 1931'. *Economic and Political Weekly*, pp. 1417–32.

———. 1974. 'Non-Brahmans and Nationalists in Poona'. *Economic and Political Weekly*, pp. 201–16.

Parliamentary Debates of India.

Palkhivala, Nani A. 1994. 'Fraud on the Constitution: Crumbling of the Fundamental Law'. *Times of India*, 16 September, p. 12.

Panagariya, Arvind and Mukim, Megha. December 2013. 'A Comprehensive Analysis of Poverty in India'. World Bank Policy Research Working Paper 6714. Available at: http://documents.worldbank.org/curated/en/389241468283507057/text/WPS6714.txt (last visited 2 May 2020).

Parmar, Pooja. 2012. 'Undoing Historical Wrongs: Law and Indigeneity in India'. *Osgoode Hall Law Journal*, pp. 491–525. Available on SSRN.

Patterson, Maureen L.P. 1954. 'Caste and Political Leadership in Maharashtra: A Review and Current Appraisal'. *Economic and Political Weekly*, pp. 1065–67.

Pawar, Dr. Jaysingrao. 2018. *Rajarshi Shahu Chatrapatinche Jahirname va Hukumname.* Pune: Mehta Publishing House. Available on Google Books.

Peters, John C. 1866. *A Treatise on the Origin, Nature, Prevention, and Treatment of Asiatic Cholera.* New York: D. Van Nostrand. Available at: https://babel.hathitrust.org/cgi/pt?id=loc.ark:/13960/t2d80gj4q&view=1up&seq=7 (last visited 26 March 2020).

Prakash, Abhinav. 2019. 'Wiping the Board Clean', *DailyO*, 8 July. Available at: https://www.dailyo.in/politics/central-educational-institutions-bill-2019-narendra-modi-academia-caste/story/1/31339.html.

Proceedings of the Government of India in the Home Department for the Month of July 1888: Education. 1888. Calcutta: Superintendent of Government Printing. Available on the Abhilekh Patal website; identifier: PR_000003021764.

Progress of Education in India, 1907–1912, vol. 1. 1914. Sixth Quinquennial Review. London: H.M. Stationery Office. Available at: https://archive.org/details/in.ernet.dli.2015.128521/mode/2up (last visited 28 April 2020.

Proposals for Indian Constitutional Reform. 1933. London: H.M. Stationery Office. Available at: https://archive.org/details/in.ernet.dli.2015.34604/page/n1/mode/2up (last visited 26 March 2020).

Rao, Anupama. 2009. *The Caste Question: Dalits and the Politics of Modern India.* Berkeley: University of California Press.

Rao, B. Shiva (ed.). 2012. *The Framing of India's Constitution: Select Documents*, reprint. New Delhi: Universal Law Publishing Co. Pvt. Ltd.

Rao, M. Shama. 1936. *Modern Mysore.* Bangalore: Higginbothams. Available at: https://archive.org/details/modernmysore035292mbp (last visited 26 May 2020).

Reddy, Bheemeshwar A., et al. 2019. 'New Reservation Policy: Is It Empirically Justifiable?'. *Economic and Political Weekly*, pp. 12–14.

Reed, Sir Stanley (ed.). 1922? *The Indian Yearbook 1922.* Bombay: Bennett, Coleman & Co., Ltd.

Report from the Joint Select Committee on the Government of India Bill. 1919. London: H.M. Stationery Office. Available at: https://archive.org/details/dli.csl.954/mode/2up/search/Madras (last visited 2 May 2020).

Report of the Indian Statutory Commission, vol. 1. 1930. London: H.M. Stationery Office (Simon Commission). Available at: https://babel. hathitrust.org/cgi/pt?id=mdp.39015027588329;view=1up;seq=164 (last visited 26 March 2020).

Report of the Indian Statutory Commission, vol. 3. 1930. Calcutta: Government of India Central Publication Branch (Simon Commission). Available at: https://archive.org/details/dli.csl.761/mode/2up (last visited 1 May 2020).

Report on Indian Constitutional Reforms. 1918. London: H.M. Stationery Office. Available at: https://babel.hathitrust.org/cgi/pt?id=ucl. b3456852&view=1up&seq=1 (last visited 26 March 2020).

Reports of the Committees appointed by the Provincial Legislative Councils to Co-operate with the Indian Statutory Commission. 1930. London: H.M. Stationery Office. Available at: https://babel.hathitrust.org/cgi/ pt?id=mdp.39015027588550&view=1up&seq=5 (last visited 6 May 2020).

Return Showing the Results of Elections in India, 1937. 1937. New Delhi: Government of India Press. Available at: https://archive.org/details/ in.ernet.dli.2015.209574 (last visited 1 May 2020).

Return Showing the Results of Elections in India. 1921. London: H.M. Stationery Office. Available at: https://babel.hathitrust.org/cgi/ pt?id=ucl.ee0000260158&view=1up&seq=3 (last visited 2 May 2020).

Roopanwal, Justice A.K. 2016. *Report by the Commission of Inquiry Regarding the Death of Shri Chakravarti R. Vemula, a Research Scholar at the University of Hyderabad*. Available at: https:// mhrd.gov.in/sites/upload_files/mhrd/files/document-reports/ JusticeAshokKumarRoopanwalReport.pdf (last visited 3 May 2020).

Rosenthal, Donald B. 1973. 'From Reformist Princes to "Co-operative Kings"'. *Economic and Political Weekly*, pp. 903–10.

Rules under the Government of India Act. 1921. London: H.M. Stationery Office. Available at: https://babel.hathitrust.org/cgi/ pt?id=mdp.35112105133187&view=1up&seq=5 (last visited 2 May 2020).

Sagar. 2020. 'Uttarakhand Scraps Reservations in Promotions, Emboldened by Biases of Apex Court, BJP and Congress'. *Caravan*, 28 March.

Available   at: https://caravanmagazine.in/law/uttarakhand-scraps-
reservations-in-promotions-supreme-court-bjp-congress (last visited
29 April 2020).

Setalvad, Chimanlal H. 1946. *Recollections & Reflections: An Autobiography*.
Bombay: Padma Publications Ltd. Available at: https://archive.org/
details/in.ernet.dli.2015.52194 (last visited 4 May 2020).

Shrikant, L.M. 1953. *Report of the Commissioner for Scheduled Castes and
Scheduled Tribes* (3rd report). Available on the Central Secretariat
Website.

Siddiqui, Iqtidar Husain. 1982. 'The Afghans and Their Emergence in
India as Ruling Elite During the Delhi Sultanate Period'. *Central
Asiatic Journal*, pp. 241–61.

Simcox, G.A. 1877. 'Old and Young—Cities and Men'. *Fraser's Magazine*,
pp. 507–18.

Singh, M.P. 1994. 'Are Articles 15(4) and 16(4) Fundamental Right?', 3
SCC (Jour) 33.

Sitapati, Vinay. 2016. 'Reservations'. In Sujit Choudhry et al., *The Oxford
Handbook of the Indian Constitution*. Oxford: Oxford University
Press.

Srinivas, M.N. 1968. *Social Change in Modern India*. Berkeley: University
of California Press.

Stanton, Henry B. 1849. *Sketches of Reforms and Reformers of Great Britain
and Ireland*. New York: John Wiley. Available at: https://babel.
hathitrust.org/cgi/pt?id=mdp.39015049827986&view=1up&seq=14.

Subramanian, Ajantha. 2019. *The Caste of Merit: Engineering Education in
India*. Cambridge: Harvard University Press.

Sundar, Nandini. 2020. 'Why India Needs Scheduled Tribes to Educate
Its Future Judges'. *The Wire*, 28 April. Available at: https://thewire.
in/rights/why-india-needs-scheduled-tribes-to-educate-future-judges
(last visited 1 May 2020).

Surendranath, Anup. 2013. *Judicial Discourse on India's Affirmative Action
Policies: The Challenge and Potential of Sub-Classification*. DPhil
Thesis, Oxford University.

———. 2015. 'Possibilities and Limitations'. *Frontline*, 15 May.

———. 2019. 'The Ambiguity of Reservations for the Poor'. *The Hindu*,
22 January.

Thakur, Manish and Babu, Rajesh R. 2017. 'IIMs and Reservations'. *Economic and Political Weekly*, pp. 15–16.

The British Friend: A Monthly Journal, Chiefly Devoted to the Interests of the Society of Friends. 1859. Glasgow: William and Robert Smeal. Available at: https://babel.hathitrust.org/cgi/pt?id=hvd. ah6icb&view=1up&seq=115 (last visited 10 May 2020).

'The Return of the Adibasi: The Multiple Worlds of Jaipal Singh Munda' (announcement). N.d. *South Asian Studies, Oxford School of Global and Area Studies.* Available at: https://www.southasia.ox.ac.uk/event/the-return-of-the-adibasi-the-multiple-worlds-of-jaipal-singh-munda (last visited 27 May 2020).

Thoburn, Bishop. 1894. *Light in the East.* Evanston: Thomas Craven. Available at: https://babel.hathitrust.org/cgi/pt?id=ien.35556001604 875&view=1up&seq=5 (last visited 26 March 2020).

Thorat, Sukhadeo and Attewell, Paul. 2007. 'The Legacy of Social Exclusion: A Correspondence Study of Job Discrimination in India'. *Economic and Political Weekly*, pp. 4141–45.

Thorat, Sukhadeo, et al. 2015. 'Urban Rental Housing Market: Caste and Religion Matters in Access'. *Economic and Political Weekly*, pp. 47–53.

Times of India, The. 1910. 'Hindus and the Census', 12 December, p. 10.

———. 1925. 'Sir Leslie Miller: Death at Delhi', 19 February, p. 10.

———. 1949. 'Kisans Clash with Intruders: Demonstration in Lucknow', 26 November, p. 9.

———. 1951. 'Madras Ministers Meet Mr. Nehru'. 28 April, p. 7.

———. 1951. 'Sikh Leader's Five-Point Demand: Refusal to Be Congress Nominee', 15 October, p. 7.

———. 1952. 'Memorial to Mahatma', *Times of India*, 7 March, p. 1.

———. 1958. 'Removing A.-I.M.O. Conference Defects of Congress', 5 May, p. 1.

———. 1970. 'Jaipal Singh Devoted Life to Adivasi Welfare'. *Times of India*, 21 March, p. 4.

———. 1991. 'Economic Criteria Ignored by Mandal'. *Times of India*, 25 January, p. 22.

———. 4 December 1950. '82nd Birthday of 'Thakkar Bapa', p. 5.

———. 7 November 1928. 'Depressed Classes: Government Appoint Inquiry Committee', p. 12.

Yeatts, M.W.M. *Census of India, 1941* (Delhi: Manager of Publications, 1946), vol. 1, part 1: https://archive.org/details/in.ernet. dli.2015.85472/page/n103/mode/2up (last visited 26 March 2020)

Weisskopf, Thomas E. 2001. 'Consequences of Affirmative Action in US Higher Education: A Review of Recent Empirical Studies'. *Economic and Political Weekly*, pp. 4719–34.

————. 2004. 'Impact of Reservation on Admissions to Higher Education in India'. *Economic and Political Weekly*, pp. 4339–49.

————. 2006. 'Is Positive Discrimination a Good Way to Aid Disadvantaged Ethnic Communities?'. *Economic and Political Weekly*, pp. 717–26.

Yengde, Suraj. 2019. *Caste Matters*. Gurgaon: Penguin Viking.

Zaidi, Z.H. (ed.). *Jinnah Papers*. Islamabad: National Archives of Pakistan, 1993.

Zelliot, Eleanor Mae. 1969. *Dr. Ambedkar and the Mahar Movement*. University of Pennsylvania, PhD dissertation.

Index

aboriginals 1, 3, 17, 21, 29
affirmative action policies 131,
    135–36, 156
All-India Adi-Hindu Depressed
    Classes Association 34
Ambedkar, B.R. 5, 9–15, 18,
    20, 25, 29, 36, 38, 41–44,
    48–50, 58, 60, 87, 89–91, 93,
    140–41; barred from studying
    Sanskrit 6; conversion to
    Buddhism 70; for 'educational
    merit' 11; on efficient vs good
    government 11; memorandum
    to the minorities committee
    12; on separate seat 6; speech
    on reservation 33–34, 39, 146;
    vision of 40, 74; on 'welfare of
    large classes of people' 11
amendment to the Constitution 53,
    57, 92, 95, 97, 104–05, 148;
    76th 93; 77th 107–9, 110–11;

81st 103; 82nd 110–12; 85th
    111; 93rd 115; 102nd 147;
    103rd 120
Anti-Aryanism 20–23
Aryan race theory 21

backward class(es) 19–21,
    25–27, 29–31, 36–40,
    42–44, 47–49, 56–63,
    66–70, 83–96, 108, 118–22,
    136–40, 142–43, 145–48,
    150–53; in government jobs
    39, 50–51, 57, 65, 113,
    141; representation of 109;
    reservation for 85; students 20,
    30, 81, 104–07, 116, 138–39
Backward Classes Commission 60
backward communities 1–4, 29, 33,
    36, 39–40, 94, 112, 117, 136,
    141, 144, 151, 156; economic
    86–87, 89; label for 3

Harijans 3, 13, 43, 46, 48, 54, 56,
  66, 71, 80, 90, 118; high-caste
  Hindus' oath against 8
high-caste Hindus 7, 12, 22, 83,
  143; against education to
  depressed class 8; in Punjab 8
Hinduism 9, 71, 73, 122, 124–25
Hindu Scheduled Castes 70–71
horizontal reservations 106–07,
  150–52
Hutton, J.H. 3, 49; census of 6–10

Independent Labour Party 15
Indian Administrative Service (IAS)
  67
Indian Civil Service 13, 29
Indian Franchise Committee 9, 17
Indian National Congress 4, 10,
  12–15, 28, 38, 67–68, 70–71,
  85, 108–09, 114; Harijan
  candidate 16; resolution by 5
Indra Sawhney case 86–87, 89–90,
  93, 107, 110, 112, 115, 120,
  140, 146, 149; Supreme Court
  judgement in 92, 95–96, 103,
  108–09
injustice to individuals 79
Islam 9, 62, 71–73, 122

Jarnail Singh v. *Lachhmi Narain
  Gupta* 91, 112, 148
Jeevan Reddy, B.P. (J) 110, 115
Justice Party, Communal G.O.s of
  27–28

Kalelkar, Kaka 53, 60, 65

Kalelkar Commission 60–63, 65,
  83
Khandekar, H.J. 34, 42, 45–46,
  49, 154
Krishna Iyer, (J) 79–80, 90
Kumar, Nitish 109

legislative councils 4, 10, 12, 14
Lokur committee 64, 67

Macdonald, Ramsay 13–14
Mahratta 23–26
Mandal, Bindhyeshwari Prasad 83
Mandal Commission 83–86, 89,
  91, 107, 113, 120, 139, 141,
  149
Mandal II 113–15
Marathas 21–27, 43, 62, 95; case
  for reservations of 148–9;
  labelling of 22
merit 24–25, 44–47, 66, 82, 90,
  104–07, 115, 117–19, 142,
  151–55
'meritorious reserved candidates'
  (MRCs) 104–07
migration 62, 122–23, 125,
  126–27, 132; and interlocking
  reservations 104–07
Miller, Leslie, Sir 28
Miller Committee 28–29, 153
minority communities 40, 48
minority of seats 34, 36–39, 74,
  89–90, 141, 150
M. Nagaraj v. *Union of India* 49,
  94, 111–12, 120, 148, 152
Montagu, Edwin 4–5, 10, 15, 27